ART, THEORY, REVOLUTION

ART, THEORY, REVOLUTION

THE TURN TO GENERALITY IN CONTEMPORARY LITERATURE

Mitchum Huehls

THE OHIO STATE UNIVERSITY PRESS

COLUMBUS

Library of Congress Cataloging-in-Publication Data
Names: Huehls, Mitchum, 1976– author.
Title: Art, theory, revolution : the turn to generality in contemporary literature / Mitchum Huehls.
Description: Columbus : The Ohio State University Press, [2022] | Includes bibliographical references and index. | Summary: "Examines works by Sheila Heti, Chris Kraus, Salvador Plascencia, Percival Everett, Jonathan Foer, and Rachel Kushner to rethink the politics of form in twenty-first-century US fiction"—Provided by publisher.
Identifiers: LCCN 2022018752 | ISBN 9780814215241 (cloth) | ISBN 0814215246 (cloth) | ISBN 9780814282366 (ebook) | ISBN 0814282369 (ebook)
Subjects: LCSH: Heti, Sheila, 1976—Criticism and interpretation. | Kraus, Chris—Criticism and interpretation. | Plascencia, Salvador, 1976—Criticism and interpretation. | Everett, Percival—Criticism and interpretation. | Foer, Jonathan Safran, 1977—Criticism and interpretation. | Kushner, Rachel—Criticism and interpretation. | American fiction—21st century—History and criticism. | Literary form—History—21st century. | Art and literature. | Politics and literature.
Classification: LCC PS374.A76 H84 2022 | DDC 813/.609—dc23/eng/20220623
LC record available at https://lccn.loc.gov/2022018752
Other identifiers: ISBN 9780814258460 (paper) | ISBN 0814258468 (paper)

Cover design by Larry Nozik
Text composition by Stuart Rodriguez
Type set in Minion Pro

In memory of my mom

CONTENTS

Acknowledgments   ix

INTRODUCTION   The End of Everything, or the Political Vacillations
                    of Form   1

CHAPTER 1   Art, Life Writing, and the Generic   34

CHAPTER 2   Theory, Metafiction, and Constructivism   73

CHAPTER 3   Revolution, Historical Fiction, and Gesture   109

CODA   Mark Bradford and the Generality of Abstraction   153

Works Cited   163

Index   175

ACKNOWLEDGMENTS

The ideas and arguments in this book were shaped by dozens of conversations I've had with friends and colleagues over the past several years. Thanks in particular go to Jason Baskin, Steven Beletto, Kim Calder, Michael Clune, Peter Conroy, Jason Gladstone, Matthew Hart, Andrew Hoberek, Michael Lemahieu, Matthias Nilges, Rachel Greenwald Smith, Dave Van Etten, Benjamin Widiss, and Matthew Wilkins.

Thank you to the UCLA English Department for supplemental funding. Thank you to *Contemporary Literature,* where a version of chapter 2 was originally published as "The Post-Theory Theory Novel," vol. 56, no. 2, 2015. Thank you to the anonymous readers of my manuscript who made my arguments better. Thank you to Ana Jimenez-Moreno and the rest of The Ohio State University Press team for their diligent and exacting work.

Thank you to Mark Bradford and Hauser & Wirth for permission to use images of Bradford's *Pickett's Charge.* All images © Mark Bradford and courtesy Hauser & Wirth.

Most of all, thanks to Marissa for her endless patience, love, encouragement, faith, fight, and strength.

The End of Everything, or the Political Vacillations of Form

> The last few years have been marked by an inverted
> millenarianism in which premonitions of the future, catastrophic
> or redemptive, have been replaced by senses of the end of this
> or that (the end of ideology, art, or social class; the "crisis" of
> Leninism, social democracy, or the welfare state, etc., etc.).
>
> —Fredric Jameson, *Postmodernism*

This book is about three big ideas—art, theory, and revolution—that have persisted in contemporary fiction despite having been supposedly killed off by postmodernism. Why, if the late twentieth century witnessed the "end" or "death" of art, theory, and revolution,[1] do those themes remain so prominent in twenty-first-century literature? Did literary authors not get the memo? Or might contemporary literature's treatment of art, theory, and revolution reveal new ways to think about those big ideas after their apparent ends? That's what I argue: art, theory, and revolution didn't die, but the forms they took throughout the twentieth century—along with the political claims made on behalf of those forms—have little purchase on the twenty-first. Instead, a close investigation of a cross section of contemporary US fiction reveals new approaches to art, theory, and revolution that deploy forms of generality in an effort to rethink—and in many cases, to attenuate—the politics typically linked to those three big ideas.

Historically, art, theory, and revolution have acquired distinct political valences through homological thinking, specifically through homologies that

---

1. Examples abound, but an initial survey might include Arthur Danto's *After the End of Art*; Donald Kuspit's *The End of Art*; David Joselit's *After Art*; Chris Campanioni's *Death of Art*; Terry Eagleton's *After Theory*; Nicholas Birns's *Theory after Theory*; Jane Elliott and Derek Attridge's *Theory after "Theory"*; Frida Ghitis's *The End of Revolution*; Alasdair Roberts's *The End of Protest*; and Micah White's *The End of Protest*.

scholars and critics identify between the conceptual forms of art, theory, and revolution on the one hand, and political forms on the other. Throughout the book, I will refer to the correlation that results from such homological thinking as the form-politics homology, a concept that I treat expansively: for me, homologous thinking includes but isn't limited to structural or formal isomorphism. In addition, I will also use the concept to describe any relation of perceived entailment—necessary or potential—between conceptual and political forms. Rhetorically, scholars and critics articulate those relations of perceived isomorphism or entailment in any number of ways. Form might be said to mirror, model, echo, adhere to the same logic as, prefigure, point toward, give shape to, make possible, open onto, or even necessitate and require a specific political mode or ideology. For example, Walter Benn Michaels deploys the form-politics homology when he ascribes an anticapitalist politics to aesthetic autonomy, or when he suggests that memoir is a quintessentially neoliberal literary form. Caroline Levine uses it to derive a progressive model of labor from the rhythm and rhyme of Christina Rossetti's "Goblin Market." Slavoj Žižek relies on it to argue that the horizontal immanence of Deleuze and Guattari's work looks too much like global capitalism to ground an effectively resistant politics. Fredric Jameson depends on it to proffer the speculative forms of science fiction as the only space available for utopian thought today. In fact, artists, theorists, critics, and scholars—myself included—use the form-politics homology all the time to give their concepts just a little bit more heft and significance in and for the world, to extend conceptual form into the political sphere.

In this book, the *form* side of the form-politics homology designates the conceptual forms of art, theory, and revolution, not their specific material forms. Conceptual forms are the structures of thought that shape a given field's self-understanding; they are the abstract theoretical ideas that have dominated the respective discourses of art, theory, and revolution for decades and sometimes centuries. For example, in the first chapter, I don't focus on the formal qualities of specific art objects but instead on art's formal autonomy and heteronomy, two conceptual forms that have governed Western aesthetic theory since at least the eighteenth century. (Broadly speaking, aesthetic autonomy names an art object's separation from the world, and aesthetic heteronomy names its engagement with it.) Similarly, the second chapter isn't particularly interested in the form of specific theories but instead highlights the mandated reflexivity of theoretical thought itself. There I will situate theory's demand that thought think its own conditions of possibility, that knowing must always be self-aware, as the dominant conceptual form of a wide swath of poststructurally oriented theory from the second half of the twentieth century. Finally, rather than investigating the form of actual historical revolutions, the third chapter explores the tension between immanent and transcendent theories of revolution. Those two conceptual forms—immanence and transcendence—are at the core of a longstanding theoretical debate within revolutionary discourse about whether revolutions should develop organically, out of the everyday lives of their participants (that's the immanence position), or if they require hierarchies and top-down leadership (that's the transcendence position).

I treat the politics side of the form-politics homology with similar abstraction. Instead of discussing specific political debates, policy questions, or ideological antagonisms, *politics* in this book designates broader concepts like freedom, equality, justice, inclusion, liberation, democracy, and their opposites. Putting the two sides of the form-politics homology together, we will see, for example, arguments about the democratizing potential of participatory art's aesthetic heteronomy, claims championing the political radicalism implicit in the reflexivity of antifoundationalist theory, and thinking that links literary fiction's narrative point of view with the possible production of revolutionary consciousness. However, in each instance we will also find a vacillation in the form-politics homology that renders the relationship between politics and the conceptual forms of art, theory, and revolution ambiguous and undecidable. For every argument about the anticapitalist logic of autonomous art and the neoliberal politics of heteronomous art, for example, we will find arguments about the status-quo complicity of autonomous art and the radically collectivizing power of heteronomous art. The same goes for the reflexivity of theoretical inquiry: sometimes its antifoundational unmooring is deemed politically radical and liberating while at other times it's read as politically irresponsible navel gazing, an abdication of the political altogether. And in conceptual debates about revolution, some champion the radically democratizing power of immanent protest and view transcendent forces like the party as dangerously hierarchical, while others contend that politically successful revolutions require transcendent figures and worry that more immanent forms merely reproduce the homogenized logic of capital. All of these contradictory correlations between form and politics exemplify what I will describe throughout as the *vacillation* of the form-politics homology.

To be sure, this vacillation is not a new phenomenon. Ever since Plato saw danger and Aristotle potential in the representational arts, form's political valence has been up for grabs. According to Fredric Jameson, however, capital's increasingly totalized grasp on forms of social, cultural, and political value at the end of the twentieth century has intensified the vacillation of the form-politics homology, rupturing any meaningful relation between its two terms. Jameson registers this intensification in a 2008 afterword he appends to an essay, "Ideological Analysis: A Handbook," originally written in 1981 and then updated again in 1990. There he observes that earlier forms of ideological analysis, which "were predicated on the presupposition that a space existed outside the system," "a place or point from which something else could be thought, from which negativity could be projected," no longer obtain because all possible externalities have now been completely "incorporated into the system" (*Valences* 357).[2] As a consequence, Jameson concludes, "we are no longer in the position of evaluating whether a given thought system or aesthetic form is progressive or reactionary" (358). In other words, the vacillating relationship between form and politics has become permanently undecidable.

Delineating the historical development of the form-politics homology and its vacillations is beyond the scope of this project, which is why I don't necessarily endorse Jameson's sense that the vacillation is worse now than it used to be. Regardless, his historical, qualitative assessment doesn't have to be true for his description of our contemporary moment to be accurate. Accordingly, my project shares Jameson's sense that "we are no longer in the position of evaluating whether a given thought system or aesthetic form is progressive or reactionary." Indeed, as we will see in detail over the ensuing chapters, the inability to confidently link art, theory, and revolution to leftist politics—that is, the permanent vacillation and ultimate undecidability of the form-politics homology—was directly responsible for the sense that art, theory, and revolution had all come to an end in the waning decades of the twentieth century. If a heteronomous art practice like relational aesthetics reads as both radically democratic and neoliberally complicit, if the same act of theoretical deconstruction is deemed both epistemologically liberating and nihilistically apolitical, if an immanent theory of revolution looks like both an attack on capital and a symptom of it, then the form-politics homology would appear to be broken and the fields of art, theory, and revolution politically impotent. Thus, we have what Jameson describes in the epigraph above as an "inverted millenarianism" declaring the end of everything (*Postmodernism* 1), or what Stuart Sim calls the "endism" of late twentieth-century intellectual culture (12).

Of course, the stakes of this vacillation extend beyond the conceptual discourses of art, theory, and revolution. For critics and scholars, it's a way to talk about the exhausted ends of these discursive domains, but for artists,

---

2. Also see Jeffrey Nealon's discussion of *Valences* in *Post-Postmodernism*, pages 20–24. Echoing Jameson, Nealon suggests that "the ethos of liberation that surrounds cultural postmodernism (the transgressions of hybridity, the individual ethics of self-fashioning, Dionysiac celebrations of multiplicity, endlessly making it new) can't simply be walled off from the substantially more sinister work that these very same notions index within the economic realm—they're the watchwords of neoliberal capitalism as well" (23).

theorists, and revolutionaries, it impinges much more directly on their work. Because, if the audience engaging their work is no longer able to determine if "a given thought system or aesthetic form is progressive or reactionary," then the work's legibility and potential political impact is deeply compromised. It has less meaning, less purchase on the world. We might imagine that this indeterminacy has yielded political apathy, but the past two decades suggest to me that it has instead resulted in a topsy-turvy world in which the political valence of creative and intellectual work is radically fungible. The political significance of such work doesn't wane; it's just entirely unmoored and up for grabs. Left becomes right and right becomes left. Capitalists speak like anticapitalists; anticapitalists speak like capitalists. Democracy is killing us, but also the only thing that will save us. It's why we have fiction like Ben Lerner's *10:04*, a novel that explicitly thematizes its own inability to know whether its constitutive forms are reactionary, progressive, or something else entirely. That self-interrogation plays out aesthetically, in the novel's narrative point of view and address, but it also comprises the bulk of its content, as the entire plot of *10:04* could be read as an extended account of one man's struggle to parse the vacillations of the form-politics homologies that define his quotidian existence. What does it mean that the narrator lets an Occupy protestor use his shower but isn't on the frontlines himself; that he volunteers at his local co-op, but that his local co-op is in Park Slope; or that he masturbates to Asian anal porn, but only to produce the seed that he's generously agreed to donate to his best friend so she can have a baby? The stakes of the form-politics homology's persistent vacillation, in other words, extend to the very possibility of meaning itself—to the meaning and value of our art, our ideas, and even our daily actions and interactions with each other and the world. It forces us to ask whether or not and how we can determine the valences and values of twenty-first-century life.

As *10:04* demonstrates, contemporary authors aren't running away from these questions. Thus, my book asks why, *despite* the apparent ends of art, theory, and revolution, *despite* the permanent vacillation and undecidability of the form-politics homology, do we continue to see the worlds of art, theory, and revolution play such a prominent role in contemporary fiction? I have in mind here contemporary art novels such as Chris Kraus's *I Love Dick* (1997), *Aliens and Anorexia* (2000), and *Torpor* (2006), Don DeLillo's *The Body Artist* (2001) and *Point Omega* (2010), Zadie Smith's *On Beauty* (2005), Sheila Heti's *How Should a Person Be?* (2010), Ben Lerner's *Leaving Atocha Station* (2011) and *10:04* (2014), Teju Cole's *Open City* (2012), Claire Messud's *The Woman Upstairs* (2013), Tao Lin's *Taipei* (2013), Donna Tartt's *The Goldfinch* (2013), Ali Smith's *How to Be Both* (2014), Siri Hustvedt's *The Blazing World* (2014),

Percival Everett's *So Much Blue* (2017), and Ottessa Moshfegh's *My Year of Rest and Relaxation* (2018); contemporary theory novels such as Percival Everett's *Glyph* (1999), *Erasure* (2001), *I Am Not Sidney Poitier* (2009), and *Percival Everett by Virgil Russell* (2013), Ben Marcus's *Notable American Women* (2002) and *The Flame Alphabet* (2012), Salvador Plascencia's *People of Paper* (2005), Nicole Kraus's *The History of Love* (2005), Jonathan Safran Foer's *Tree of Codes* (2010), Sam Lipsyte's *The Ask* (2010), Jeffrey Eugenides's *The Marriage Plot* (2011), Elif Batuman's *The Idiot* (2017), and Ben Lerner's *The Topeka School* (2019); and contemporary novels about revolution and revolt such as Susan Choi's *American Woman* (2003) and *A Person of Interest* (2008), Christopher Sorrentino's *Trance* (2005), Dana Spiotta's *Eat the Document* (2006), Hari Kunzru's *My Revolutions* (2007), Peter Carey's *His Illegal Self* (2008), Rachel Kushner's *Telex from Cuba* (2008) and *The Flamethrowers* (2013), Jonathan Lethem's *Dissident Gardens* (2013), Viet Nguyen's *The Sympathizer* (2015), and Cory Doctorow's *Walkaway* (2017).[3]

Some of these authors double down on the form-politics homology and attempt to rearticulate a reliably meaningful connection between its two terms. Other contemporary authors, however, seem to have accepted and internalized the disconnect between politics on the one hand and aesthetic, theoretical, and revolutionary forms on the other. And yet, despite starting from the assumption that there is no meaningful or necessary relationship between their conceptual forms and politics, these authors do not retreat from the fields of art, theory, and revolution altogether. Some of them, including authors like Jeffrey Eugenides, Jonathan Lethem, and Dana Spiotta, whose work I'll discuss at length later, diagnose and think through the implications of the disarticulated relationship between form and politics. The authors I'll be most interested in, however, are those who don't just diagnose the vacilla-tion as a particularly pressing problem, but who also pursue and develop new ways to think about the production of value and the political valence of form.

This is where the concept of generality comes in. As the ensuing readings will demonstrate, a smaller cross section of authors, writing after the end of everything, has turned to the singular-general relationship, rather than the form-politics relationship, as a way to reconceive the political value of aes-thetic, theoretical, and revolutionary forms. I will have much more to say about this singular-general relationship and its distinct mode of value produc-tion later. For now, though, I will simply note that my readings of Sheila Heti's and Chris Kraus's art novels will discuss how and why they replace forms of

---

3. An obviously partial and incomplete list, I intend the assembled texts to indicate that the oft-proclaimed deaths of art, theory, and revolution did little to mitigate authorial interest in those topics and perhaps even provoked an increased attention to them. It's also worth not-ing that these three prominent themes overlap a great deal in many of these books.

aesthetic autonomy and heteronomy with generic forms of being. My treatment of theory novels from Salvador Plascencia, Percival Everett, Ben Marcus, and Jonathan Safran Foer will demonstrate how they substitute deconstructive forms of theoretical self-reflexivity that make universal claims with constructive forms of historically contingent thought that make general claims. And my reading of Rachel Kushner's *The Flamethrowers* will explore that novel's preference for gestural forms of political engagement over more immanent and/or transcendent forms of revolution. These various forms of generality that I identify in my literary archive—the generic, the constructive, and the gestural—emerge as new ways to produce value outside the form-politics homology and its undecidable vacillations.

But this is just half the story *Art, Theory, Revolution* tells. That's because, the process by which contemporary authors explore new conceptual forms for art, theory, and revolution, and develop their thinking about forms of generality, is a distinctly *literary* project. Advancing new takes on art, theory, and revolution, in other words, goes hand in hand with innovating new literary forms. For example, the texts interested in aesthetic autonomy and heteronomy (Sheila Heti's *How Should a Person Be?* and Chris Kraus's novels) also intervene in literary-formal debates about life writing. Those focusing on theory's self-reflexivity (experimental work from Salvador Plascencia, Ben Marcus, Percival Everett, and Jonathan Safran Foer) also reshape our critical understanding of metafiction. And those fictions wrestling with the immanence and transcendence of revolution (Jonathan Lethem's *Dissident Gardens,* Dana Spiotta's *Eat the Document,* and Rachel Kushner's *Telex from Cuba* and *The Flamethrowers*) also grapple with the limitations of the contemporary historical novel.[4]

Complementing this book's theoretical thesis about forms of generality and their reconfiguration of politics, then, is a literary thesis about these same authors' reworking of specific literary forms—life writing, metafiction, and the historical novel—that have historically been granted distinct political value, also through the power of homological thinking. As with aesthetic autonomy and heteronomy, theoretical self-reflexivity, and revolutionary immanence and transcendence, these literary forms also acquired specific, but also vacillating, political valences throughout the twentieth century. Life writing, for example, has been correlated with progressive feminist politics and the pur-

---

4. Some might quarrel with my characterization of life writing, metafiction, and historical fiction as literary *forms.* Might it not make more sense to think of them as genres? Perhaps, but as with my thinking about the conceptual forms of art, theory, and revolution, I'm using form here quite broadly to designate literature's general how-ness as opposed to its what-ness. Or, form for me is synonymous with modality. At the same time, the readings of my primary texts will highlight formal features like narrative point of view, syntax, emplotment, reference, and modes of representation.

suit of justice for victims of human rights violations, but also with the reified subjectivities of neoliberal entrepreneurialism. Metafiction has been described as both politically radical and narcissistically detached from the sociopolitical sphere. And the historical novel, sometimes viewed as one possible means of achieving a collective, material-historical consciousness, has also been characterized as a postmodern simulacrum signifying nothing.

In response to these vacillations, the authors discussed here, working from a *disarticulated* form-politics relationship, originate forms of literary generality, the value of which does not depend on a homological connection to politics. In their respective efforts to rethink life writing's female subject outside the aesthetic discourse of autonomy and heteronomy, for example, Sheila Heti and Chris Kraus explore the formal possibilities of genre and case study. Plascencia, Marcus, Everett, and Foer—all of whom refuse theory's demand that thought reflexively interrogate its conditions of possibility—offer a new approach to metafiction, which, rather than using theoretical reflexivity to deconstruct worlds, builds them out of literalized theoretical concepts. I name this new form of constructivist metafiction *theoretical literalism*. And Rachel Kushner's *The Flamethrowers,* which turns to the logic of gesture to circumvent immanent and transcendent forms of revolution, also deploys a gestural realism that addresses the perceived impossibility of writing historical fiction today.[5] Consequently, many of the novels discussed here offer not only new conceptual forms of generality that art, theory, and revolution might pursue after their respective deaths, but also new literary forms for authors interested in rethinking literary value in nonhomological ways. Genre, case study, theoretical literalism, and gestural realism are contemporary forms of literary generality that resuscitate life writing, metafiction, and historical fiction after their respective claims to political value are rendered impotent by the vacillations of the form-politics homology.

The stakes of the overall investigation are thus twofold. First, independent of the literary field, the domains of art, theory, and revolution face a set of conceptual impasses that have eroded their political purchase on the world, prompting the sense that they have each come to an end. Despite their apparent ends, however, each of those big ideas persists in contemporary fiction. Given its rich formal complexity, I wager that literature's treatment of those themes will advance our understanding of art, theory, and revolution beyond the conceptual impasses and vacillating formal politics that killed them off at the end of the twentieth century. Methodologically, then, I'm treating literature as a laboratory, a research and development department that produces and test runs new conceptual takes on art, theory, and revolution that might

---

5. See Fredric Jameson's "Historical Novel Today."

renew those ideas for the twenty-first century. Second, in addition to advancing our conceptualization of art, theory, and revolution via literature, I'm also using literature's engagement with the conceptual impasses in those domains to learn something about contemporary literature itself. Because the novels do their conceptual work through specific formal innovations, we can also discover how authors today cope with the vacillating political valences of contemporary literary forms. In turn, understanding the developments in life writing, metafiction, and the historical novel that authors deploy in response to that vacillation will help us identify key differences between contemporary novels and their late twentieth-century, postmodern predecessors.

Throughout *Art, Theory, Revolution,* I will argue that the primary conceptual shift that occurs in response to the vacillation of the form-politics homology, and one way to differentiate contemporary novels from their postmodern predecessors, entails a turn to forms of generality. The generic, the constructive, and the gestural are conceptual forms of generality that respond to conceptual impasses in the fields of art, theory, and revolution. Genre, case study, theoretical literalism, and gestural realism are literary forms of generality that respond to the vacillations of the form-politics homology in the literary realm. For reasons I'll discuss at length later, these various forms of generality recommend themselves to a historical moment struggling to think about the political significance of form. Because their value stems from a logic of generality, they are uniquely invulnerable to homologous thinking, offering instead a more context-dependent way to conceive form's value and significance. Although these forms of generality refuse correlation with any particular politics, it would be incorrect to view them as apolitical. Better, perhaps, to describe them as not not political, while remaining open to and modest about the politics they might engender.[6] As we'll see, generality's forms are not inherently, or homologously, political, but they don't necessarily preclude politics either.

Now, it might have occurred to you that I'm attributing a lot of intentional agency to these authors, which is why I want to be clear about how I'm conceiving contemporary authorship and the relationship these contemporary authors have to the philosophical concepts and ideas that I'm suggesting their works engage. First, I do not mean to imply that Sheila Heti sat down to write

---

6. Lauren Berlant's notion of the "juxtapolitical" is akin but not identical to the politics of generality I'll be discussing. For Berlant, the "juxtapolitical" describes a cultural politics that "thrives in proximity to the political, occasionally crossing over in political alliance, even more occasionally doing some politics, but most often not, acting as a critical chorus that sees the expression of emotional response and conceptual recalibration as achievement enough" (*Female Complaint, x*). Generality's politics share the juxtapolitical's ambivalence about politics conventionally conceived, but the turn to generality will also prove more antihumanist than Berlant's approach.

a meditation on aesthetic autonomy and heteronomy and ended up with *How Should a Person Be?*, or that Rachel Kushner's *Flamethrowers* is the end result of her deliberate attempt to rethink the relationship between revolutionary immanence and transcendence. I would argue, however, that ideas about aesthetic autonomy and heteronomy, concerns about theoretical self-reflexivity, and immanent and transcendent modes of revolutionary activity all make their way into contemporary fiction about art, theory, and revolution because those are the dominant philosophical and conceptual frameworks that structure contemporary thinking about those themes. Just because these authors don't use precise philosophical language, in other words, doesn't mean that their texts aren't rich with philosophical thought. In turn, it's not surprising that the presence of these philosophical concepts in an author's work might prompt or require new approaches to literary form. Again, I don't mean to suggest that Chris Kraus, for example, decided to write fiction as case study because she had already decided that it was the best way to supersede the impasse between aesthetic autonomy and heteronomy. I do think, however, that while writing novels about art and aesthetics, Kraus was challenged to identify a literary form that could accommodate the distinct and innovative way that her novels were working to conceive aesthetics. This prompted her to explore case study as a form that would allow for those accommodations, resulting in a text that implicitly engages a broader critical conversation about literary forms of life writing.

This vision of contemporary authorship echoes Ben Lerner's emphasis on the unreal "virtuality" of the contemporary novel. Conceiving the novel today "as a fundamentally *curatorial* form," Lerner values the novel's speculative virtuality because it allows the novel to function as "a genre that assimilates and arranges and dramatizes encounters with other genres" ("Actual World"). Lerner is thinking in particular about the novel's relationship to poetry, criticism, and art, and I would add philosophy, theory, and politics to the list. Many contemporary authors working today, in other words, are what Alexandra Kingston-Reese describes as "novelist-critics" (22). They are writers who are also readers, authors who "illuminate the act of writing, frame and reframe their artistic processes, and examine their own aesthetic, formal, critical, theoretical, and sociopolitical investments" (23).[7] Given the influence

---

7. Kingston-Reese's conception of contemporary authorship draws on comments Amy Elias makes in "Postmodern, Postwar, Contemporary: A Dialogue on the Field." Compellingly, Kingston-Reese also argues that scholarly analyses of the "critical fiction" that novelist-critics produce requires a more generous, postcritical methodology that includes a heightened attentiveness to interviews and essays in which authors explicitly discuss their critical, theoretical, and political commitments.

of the program era, the economic precarity that drives many contemporary authors into the stabilizing embrace of the university, and the contemporary media environment's demand for constant self-promotion and advertisement, it's not surprising that today's novelists are as fluent in the language of criticism and theory as they are in the language of literature. This is true of every author I discuss in *Art, Theory, Revolution*. Many of them are ensconced at universities; many are authors of art and literary criticism; many are essayists who comfortably treat complicated concepts and ideas in argumentative, nonfictional prose; many are well-read in art, critical, and political theory; many have explicitly discussed and theorized the way they would like their work to be read; and many openly share their thinking about contemporary theorists and their theories.

Finally, the likes of Ben Lerner and Tom McCarthy notwithstanding, it's also worth noting that the contemporary novelist-critic comfortable with this abstract, conceptual approach to art, literature, and politics is no longer an exclusively white, male subject. Despite a longstanding Western intellectual tradition that associates white men with universal, abstract ideas and women and people of color with particular, specific experiences ("poet-men, presenters of ideas, and actress-women, presenters of themselves," Chris Kraus writes in *I Love Dick* [177]), female authors play a central role in *Art, Theory, Revolution*, and African American artists like Percival Everett and Mark Bradford will demonstrate their commitment to conceptual abstraction as well. In fact, at least among contemporary authors writing literary fiction, it's hard to think of novelists who *aren't* doing the conceptual/theoretical work of novelist-critics, regardless of their identification: Viet Nguyen, Namwali Serpell, Raven Leilani, Ling Ma, Ocean Vuong, Colson Whitehead, Chris Abani, Ayad Akhtar, and Karen Yamashita all come to mind, with Zadie Smith perhaps functioning as the paradigmatic type.

The Antinomous Forms of Art, Theory, and Revolution

Although there are many different ways one might conceptualize art, theory, and revolution, I will focus on a few conceptual forms that have dominated theoretical discourse in each domain, in some cases for centuries. Given this focus, much of the theoretical and philosophical work I draw on in *Art, Theory, Revolution* is dominated by white men. Crucially, though, that means that when we find contemporary novelist-critics engaging and moving beyond those historically dominant conceptual forms, we should appreciate that they are also intervening in and critiquing that longstanding patriarchal discourse.

Along the way, we will also see theorists like Lauren Berlant, Carrie Noland, and Juana Rodriguez complementing the interventions and critiques that I will be developing out of my primary literary texts.

To fully appreciate the value of those literary interventions, however, we first need a fuller understanding of the dominant conceptual forms that define the theoretical discourses on art, theory, and revolution. Each of the following chapters will unpack those defining concepts at much greater length, so for now I only want to highlight their shared antinomous structure—that is, the way each discourse organizes itself around a pair of mutually exclusive concepts conducive to homological thinking. In practice, of course, these concepts need not remain antinomous and mutually exclusive. We can imagine, for example, describing a work of art as autonomous in some ways and heteronomous in others. My investigation, however, is conceptual and theoretical, and at that level, these terms are, by definition, antinomous and mutually exclusive.

Ever since Kant's *Critique of Judgment,* for example, aesthetic discourse has been dominated by the antinomy between autonomy and heteronomy.[8] Autonomous art, like an Anthony Caro sculpture or an Ad Reinhardt painting, severs itself from the external world and adheres to its own laws. Heteronomous art, like a Marina Abramović performance or Picasso's *Guernica,* accedes to laws that are external to it, potentially implicating itself in the sociopolitical sphere. By definition, then, autonomous and heteronomous art are mutually exclusive aesthetic forms. In Kant's *Critique of Judgment,* for example, judgment can only be aesthetic judgment when purged of all externally motivated interest. The moment such heteronomous interest intrudes, aesthetic autonomy disappears.

In the world of theory, which here refers narrowly to a particular version of poststructuralism popularized in US English departments after 1970 and eventually institutionalized as the linguistic turn in literary and cultural studies, we find an antinomy between first- and second-order thought. First-order thought is empirical and experiential while second-order thought, hewing to theory's mandate that thought must think its own conditions of possibility, is reflexive and recursive. Again, these are mutually exclusive conceptual forms.

---

8. *Aesthetic and Artistic Autonomy,* edited by Owen Hulatt, offers a good overview. Key touchstones in the philosophical history of the autonomy-heteronomy antinomy are Immanuel Kant's *The Critique of Judgment,* G. F. W. Hegel's *Aesthetics,* Friedrich Schiller's *On the Aesthetic Educations of Man,* Theodor Adorno's *Aesthetic Theory,* Clement Greenberg's "Modernist Painting," Jacques Rancière's *The Politics of Aesthetics,* Walter Benn Michaels's *The Beauty of a Social Problem,* and Nicholas Brown's, *Autonomy.*

Once Derrida introduces *différance* into Western epistemology, there's no going back. Thinking one way precludes thinking the other.

Finally, when it comes to revolutionary discourse, we find the antinomy of immanence and transcendence.[9] Immanence names a form of pure inherence that never stands outside itself, as in the Zapatistas' motto *Preguntando caminamos* (Asking, we walk), which captures the lived and embodied nature of their immanent revolution. A transcendental approach, like the party-organized Bolshevik revolution, stands outside the flow of being, positing a goal or end for which the revolution then fights. Once again, at the conceptual level, these are mutually exclusive forms that shape a great deal of twentieth-century thought about revolutionary possibility.

The mutually exclusive nature of these conceptual forms lends itself to the form-politics homology. Once practitioners, critics, or scholars grant one of these terms a specific political value, then it naturally follows that the countervailing term would accrue the opposing political value. Sometimes, as with Kant, it's a simple distinction between politics and its absence, with autonomous art remaining apolitical and the political heteronomies of the social sphere having no access to the aesthetic at all. But if aesthetic autonomy is awarded more than just an apolitical valence, as when Walter Benn Michaels connects it to a leftist class politics, then the opposing term, in this case *aesthetic heteronomy,* automatically accrues the opposing politics, which is why Michaels consistently reads heteronomous art as complicit with the neoliberal status quo. Similarly, if reflexively turning thought against itself seems navel-gazingly quiescent, then speaking the first-order truths of lived experience becomes empowering.[10] But for those who find thought based in empirical experience to be naïve and simpleminded, then a more sophisticated form of second-order, reflexive thought would seem to get us closer to the truth of things. And if you believe that true revolution must be immanently lived and embodied, then strong leaders with utopian visions will register as antidemocratic and quasifascist. But if you think that utopian futures must be articulated before they can be achieved, then radically horizontal revolutionary activity like Occupy will seem like just so much counterrevolutionary dithering. In short, the mutual exclusivity of the defining conceptual forms of art, theory, and revolution transfers onto claims about the political significance of those forms, but not in any stable or reliable way.

---

9. For a broad examination of revolution's historical conceptual forms, see Jack Censer's *Debating Modern Revolution.* Also see Gilles Deleuze and Felix Guattari's *What Is Philosophy?:* "We need to distinguish between authoritarian utopias, or utopias of transcendence, and immanent, revolutionary, libertarian utopias" (100).

10. This was Barbara Christian's argument, for example, in "The Race for Theory."

Which is why, as I've already discussed above, those political homologies vacillate even as the conceptual mutual exclusivity of the terms remains consistent. At various points in the discursive histories of art, theory, and revolution, different conceptual forms have been politically privileged over others. Sometimes aesthetic autonomy was granted more political potency than aesthetic heteronomy, but at other times the reverse was true. Thinkers disagreed about which forms entailed which politics, but most twentieth-century artists and critics were confident that distinct political valences could be ascribed to specific conceptual forms.[11] Max Horkheimer and Theodor Adorno disagreed, for example, with Walter Benjamin about the politics entailed by mechanically reproduced art, but they never doubted that mechanically reproduced art

---

11. Of course, the idea that literary forms necessarily entail a politics is not universally held and has been the object of much methodological debate for the past several decades. For many, in fact, form is inherently apolitical, a matter of aesthetic distinction severed from the concerns and controversies of daily life. This idea goes back to Kant's late eighteenth-century emphasis on the disinterestedness of aesthetic beauty, a formal aestheticism removed from worldly interest that has endured as a prominent vein of humanistic inquiry ever since. For that tradition, ascribing political significance to aesthetic form entirely misunderstands the "purpose" of art, corrupting its timeless truths along the way. It's against those timeless truths, this metaphysical aestheticism, that Fredric Jameson levels his famous *cri de coeur*, "Always historicize!" in the opening pages of *The Political Unconscious* (9). Thereafter, for at least the next two decades, history would become the critical antidote to formalism, the guarantor of culture's political significance and worldly engagement. This mantle is taken up most forcefully by the new historicists of the 1980s and 1990s, who view cultural artifacts as ideologically saturated instantiations of the sociopolitical realities from which they emerge. In response to the overreaches of such overtly political criticism, however, the late 1990s and early aughts witness the rise of New Formalism, a catch-all camp of formalist sympathizers whom Marjorie Levinson divides into "normative" and "activist" factions ("What Is New Formalism?," 559). While the normative group resuscitates the literary values—beauty, pleasure, aesthetics—that they think the historicists ignore, the activists work to reconcile what they view as a tendentious divide between formalism and politics. For the activist new formalists, literary form follows from and speaks directly to the social, political, and historical conditions of its time. Although it's not always explicit, this homologous relationship between culture and society draws on a certain line of Marxist thought—stretching from Lukács through Adorno and Raymond Williams to Jameson—that understands aesthetic form as the efflux of a given historical moment's material conditions of production. Or as Jameson writes early in his career in *Marxism and Form*, "the essential characteristic of literary raw material or latent content is precisely that it never really is initially formless . . . but is rather already meaningful from the outset, being neither more nor less than the very components of our concrete social life" (402–3). Or, put more succinctly, aesthetic form "is itself ultimately dependent for its existence on the structures of the social raw materials themselves" (403).

Levinson's "What Is New Formalism?" puts the *PMLA*'s imprimatur on work that begins in the 1990s with George Levine's *Aesthetics and Ideology*. A special issue of *Modern Language Quarterly*, edited by Susan Wolfson, consolidates the movement in 2000. That special issue, with some additional essays, was republished in 2006 as *Reading for Form*, a collection coedited by Wolfson and Marshall Brown. Fredric Bogel's *New Formalist Criticism* offers a comprehensive, retrospective overview.

entailed a certain politics.[12] Linda Hutcheon and Fredric Jameson disagreed about the political implications of Charles Moore's Piazza d'Italia, but they were both quite certain that it had definite political implications.[13]

More recently, two important attempts to move past the historical vacillations of the form-politics homology have emerged. The first is Fredric Jameson's *Valences of the Dialectic,* and the second is Caroline Levine's *Forms.* In the former, Jameson champions the power of the dialectic, which enjoins us "to think the negative and the positive together at one and the same time, in the unity of a single thought" (421). Instead of vacillating, we need to be synthesizing. This "strategy of changing the valences" (428) requires us "to declare positive things which are clearly negative in our own world, to affirm that dystopia is in reality Utopia if examined more closely, to isolate specific features in our empirical present so as to read them as components of a different system" (434). The dialectic, Jameson suggests, offers a glimpse of this "different system" (424). It helps us think beyond mutually exclusive binaries without reducing one to the other, and it allows us to develop "new and more complex concept[s]" otherwise unavailable to conventional thought (429). I worry, however, that "changing the valences" might just be another vacillation of the valences rather than a true dialectical unity of positive and negative that results in an entirely new concept. Put differently, the many vacillations of the form-politics homology that I detail throughout the book might also be viewed as instances of failed dialectical synthesis. When the same form can be viewed as progressive, then reactionary, and then progressive again, value seems more circular than dialectical. In addition, it's worth noting that Jameson balances his passionate advocacy for dialectical thinking with a much grimmer vision of a dialectic pushed to the brink and offering only the most fleeting of glimpses—"like a diseased eyeball in which disturbing flashes of light are perceived"—of Utopia (612). Although I heartily agree with Jameson's diagnosis, then, I see contemporary literature pursuing a different, nondialectical path.[14]

---

12. See Max Horkheimer and Theodor Adorno's "The Culture Industry" alongside Walter Benjamin's "The Work of Art in the Age of Mechanical Reproduction." Also see Marianne DeKoven's "The Politics of Modernist Form" for an overview of modernism's aesthetically motivated politics, in addition to DeKoven's own take on the politics that follow from the dialectical contradictions of modernist aesthetics.

13. Compare Linda Hutcheon's "The Politics of Postmodernism," page 194, and Jameson's *Postmodernism,* page 100.

14. In *The Order of Forms,* Anna Kornbluh pursues a dialectical approach that views aesthetics as a powerful mediator of the social order. Kingston-Reese's *Contemporary Novelists* also emphasizes the aesthetic mediation of contemporary life, but in affective rather than dialectical ways.

Caroline Levine's *Forms* takes a different tack to the vacillations of the form-politics homology. Rather than dialectically synthesizing its antinomous forms and values, she collapses the form-politics relation in on itself, effectively turning homology into tautology. In her effort to conceive form as more than just a homologous indexing of the social and political spheres, Levine conflates form and politics: "Politics involves activities of ordering, patterning, and shaping. And if the political is a matter of imposing and enforcing boundaries, temporal patterns, and hierarchies on experience, then there is no politics without form" (3). In other words, because both form and politics are about configuring and ordering, form *is* politics, and vice versa. This flattened conflation allows Levine to lead with her politics, "to imagine how forms might be used to progressive ends and which new, more just forms should take the place of those that dominate and oppress us now" ("Forms" 79). She makes similar claims in the preface to *Forms*, where she affirms that "formalism offers a promising way forward" for those "who care passionately about unjust arrangements of power" (xiii). But Levine's methods here, along with the idea that there's such a thing as a "more just form," are perfectly backward, searching for the thing she already knows she wants.[15]

Rather than conflating or dialectically synthesizing the form-politics homology, the authors discussed throughout *Art, Theory, Revolution* follow a different path when they engage various forms of generality to conceive form's value anew. The exasperating vacillations of the form-politics homology may have prompted many writing at the turn of the millennium to declare the ends of art, theory, and revolution, but an important cross section of contemporary fiction has been hard at work birthing new forms that reconceive the significance of those fields. By the time *Art, Theory, Revolution* is finished, we will have thoroughly explored a set of *general* forms that offer a different, nonhomologous way to think about the significance and implications of aesthetic, theoretical, and revolutionary forms. At the same time, we'll see older literary forms (life writing, metafiction, and the historical novel), which have also been homologously linked to specific political valences, mutate into new literary forms (case study, theoretical literalism, and gestural realism) marked by the conspicuous absence of any clear political valence. Along the way, I will

---

15. Jonathan Kramnick and Anahid Nersessian offer a similar critique (along with their own tidy theory of form pegged to the specificity of disciplinary inquiry) in "Form and Explanation": "As being a formalist and promoting social change appear, for Levine, to be the same thing, one need only add a personal approval or disapproval to the recognition of a form in order to arrive at a political conclusion" (659). Also see Levine's "*Critical Response I*" to Kramnick and Nersessian, who in turn respond to Levine's response in their "*Critical Response V.*" In 2017, Carrie Noland's "On Caroline Levine's *Forms,*" a roundtable of responses to the influential monograph, was published in *PMLA*.

consider whether this mutation represents an abdication of politics altogether or an attempt to rethink what counts as politics in the first place. For now, I want briefly to trace the vacillations of these literary forms over the course of the twentieth century so we can fully appreciate the departures we'll see from them in the twenty-first.

Life Writing, Metafiction, and the Historical Novel

As with the defining conceptual forms of art, theory, and revolution, the history of literary form is rife with homological thinking. When scholars are called on to justify their work, when the political relevance of literature is challenged, the politics of form frequently saves the day. Each chapter in *Art, Theory, Revolution* will more thoroughly consider the political valences of a specific literary form—life writing, metafiction, and the historical novel—so for now I'll just provide a brief overview.

First, life writing—a literary form that exploded with the memoir boom at the beginning of the twenty-first century and just might come to define it.[16] Of course, nonfictional life writing has been around at least since Augustine's *Confessions* (397–400), and it emerges in full force for the first time at the turn of the nineteenth century in the wake of Jean Jacques Rousseau's *Confessions* (1782) and Benjamin Franklin's *Autobiography* (1793).[17] Back then, autobiography was primarily understood pedagogically, as a delightful means of instruction—life coaching for the broader reading public.[18] Here we also see an early

---

16. I am intentionally using the vague term "life writing" as a catch-all for any form of self-narration. *Art, Theory, Revolution* will not be particularly concerned with distinguishing between autobiography, memoir, creative nonfiction, etc. See Julie Rak's *Boom!* and the opening chapter of Ben Yagoda's *Memoir* for two accounts of the memoir explosion. Also see Nancy Miller's "The Entangled Self" where she speculates that "autobiography may emerge as a master form in the twenty-first century" (545).

17. Franklin's *Autobiography* wasn't described as such until the 1840s and was initially titled *Memoirs of the Private Life of Benjamin Franklin, Written by Himself*. This helps us see that, generally speaking, "autobiography" and "memoirs" are synonyms naming the chronicle of an entire life—usually a life of some sociopolitical import—while a "memoir" typically recounts a more circumscribed set of events in the life of an individual without any particular social prominence. Many scholars, however, see this as a distinction without much of a difference to the extent that both raise the literary problem of self-narration.

18. For example, Samuel Johnson explains in *The Rambler #60*: "Those parallel circumstances and kindred images to which we readily conform our minds, are, above all other writings, to be found in narratives of the lives of particular persons; and therefore no species of writing seems more worthy of cultivation than biography, since none can be more delightful or more useful, none can more certainly enchain the heart by irresistible interest, or more widely diffuse instruction to every diversity of condition" (127).

politicization of the form, as the individual lives treated autobiographically model a nascent liberalism that imbues each person with "a unified, unique selfhood which is also the expression of a universal human nature" (Anderson 5). The Romantic individualism that grows out of this liberal humanism tends to be conservative, reinforcing the status quo of bourgeois subjectivity, but in other circumstances it proves more politically radical. For example, when African Americans, women, and other marginalized populations adopt the autobiographical form, claiming that same liberal humanist subjectivity for themselves, autobiography's consolidation of the self proves much more incendiary. Nineteenth-century slave narratives, the influential autobiographies of black radicals in the 1960s and 1970s, the vital role life writing played in the women's movement: these represent the liberatory politics of autobiography, its "potential to be the text of the oppressed and the culturally displaced" (Swindells 7). In the 1990s that political project expands to consider trauma, human rights violations, and the role testimony and self-narration might play in assuaging them.[19] At the same time, however, the politics of life writing was swinging in the other direction as theoretically motivated literary critics condemned it for its failure to appreciate the incomplete, fragmented, undecidable, contingent, and aleatory subjectivities described by the likes of Lacan, Derrida, Althusser, Foucault, and Butler.[20] Anything less was politically quiescent, retrograde, and naïve.[21]

This homologous thinking that correlates form and politics remains intact through the memoir boom of the late twentieth and early twenty-first centuries. Memoir's most vocal critics, for example, link it to neoliberalism, viewing it as a symptomatic form of the entrepreneurial individualism and millennial narcissism infecting contemporary culture today.[22] On the other hand, Daniel Worden contends that memoir can reveal the "material limits" of contemporary life, functioning as "an aesthetically inflected ideology critique" (174) that "estrange[s] us from ourselves and make[s] visible the structures that produce our subjectivities, the rules that bind us to a way of life that is in constant crisis yet also shows no sign of ebbing" (176). Julie Rak also challenges those who view memoir as inherently narcissistic and thus apolitical, arguing

---

19. A key text for this project is Shoshana Felman and Dori Laub's *Testimony.*

20. See, for example, Paul de Man's "Autobiography as De-facement."

21. The exception here would be postmodern autobiography, which does incorporate the lessons of critical theory into its exposition of the self. *Autobiography & Postmodernism*—a collection edited by Kathleen Ashley, Leigh Gilmore, and Gerald Peters—and Sarah Townsend's *True Relations* describe the many ways in which postmodern experimentalism can be a boon to autobiography.

22. See, for example, Walter Benn Michaels's "Going Boom" and Leigh Gilmore's "American Neoconfessional." To be fair, Gilmore, a long-time advocate of autobiography, only connects the recent "neoconfessional" turn in memoir to neoliberalism.

instead that "memoir is a way of discovering the lives of others, not of redis-covering or obsessing about the self" (8). Borrowing from Lauren Berlant's notion of "affective citizenship," Rak views memoir as a "citizenship technol-ogy" (210), a means of producing an "affective belonging to a community" (139). The politics that follow from this conception of memoir are democratic and communitarian, but as Rak acknowledges, memoir's affective citizenship, grounded in the desire for an intimate belonging that supersedes one's relation to the state, doesn't necessarily entail a clear and obvious politics. Instead, the politics of memoir for Rak are "sometimes radical and sometimes conserva-tive." The memoir form "creates new ways to imagine affective ties, justice, and even new ways of being social," but also "reinforces normative ways of thinking and being" (213).

Here, once again, we find the vacillating value of the form-politics homol-ogy. Although Rak recognizes this vacillation, the homologous relation between form and politics still shapes her thinking. But what if the vacilla-tion of the form-politics homology demands more than an openness to fluc-tuating political valences? What if we started from the idea that there is no meaningful relationship between politics and aesthetic form? What if, rather than embracing the always doubled political valence of form, we tried instead to discover new forms, new ways of thinking and being, that might become available once we abandon that relationship altogether? It's the difference between, on the one hand, concluding that our current inability to determine "whether a given thought system or aesthetic form is progressive or reac-tionary" requires newly compromised, or perhaps dialectically synthesized, forms of both-ness, or, on the other hand, concluding that we must abandon homology altogether and start thinking differently. The second path is scary because it requires us to relinquish what we think we already know about the political relevance of literary form, even about politics itself. The second path might lead to a dangerously depoliticized aestheticism. And yet, if homologi-cal thinking remains vacillatingly indeterminate, it's hard not to see it as little more than a counterproductive liability for any political project, progressive or reactionary. In this book's first chapter, I will suggest that Sheila Heti's and Chris Kraus's life writing braves this second path. In particular, Kraus's work offers the case study as a form of self-narration that can't be homologized to politics even as it refuses to be dismissed as mere aestheticism. The generic mode of selfhood, which emerges in Heti and Kraus as an alternative to both autonomous and heteronomous modes of being in the world, allows them to conceive politics in a whole new way.

By the beginning of the twenty-first century, the obsolescence of the form-politics homology also begins to affect metafiction, understood here as fiction that self-consciously reflects on and interrogates its own aesthetic conditions of possibility. Earlier in the twentieth century, modernism embraced reflexive self-criticism as a generative aesthetic practice. Although it grows increasingly self-conscious as the decades pass, it more or less avoids eating its own tail.[23] Modernism's reflexivity, in other words, remains productive. Even when Beckett fails again, he fails better. For someone like Clement Greenberg, this is a purely aesthetic project. These self-reflexive forms only function subversively within the institution of art itself. Much more bullish on modernism's political potential, however, Jameson views the period's reflexive interrogation of its own aesthetic conditions of possibility as a form of Utopian thought, suggesting that modernism's self-conscious pursuit of new forms "echoes . . . the hopes and optimism of that great period dominated by the Second International" (*Postmodernism* 313). For Jameson, modernism's Utopian politics are of course in direct contradistinction to postmodernism's political impotence, manifest in "metabooks which cannibalize other books, metatexts which collate bits of other texts" (96).[24] In the postmodern era, self-conscious art collapses in on itself, losing any ability to speak productively to the sociopolitical domain.

Linda Hutcheon corroborates Jameson's account, but also narrows it, suggesting that the political impotence Jameson ascribes to postmodern culture in general really only applies to the autotelic forms of American surfiction and the French *Nouveau Roman*. For Hutcheon, in fact, these forms don't even count as postmodern but are instead examples of "late modernist extremism" (*Poetics* 52), or elsewhere, "late modernist radical metafiction" (108). Hutcheon brackets out these depoliticized forms so she can instead champion the political potency of "historiographic metafiction," a blend of historical reference and aesthetic reflexivity that deploys irony as a mode of political critique.[25] Because Jameson grounds his take on these developments in the material and economic conditions of late capitalism, however, he sees Hutch-

---

23. See Greenberg's "Modernist Painting."

24. It's worth remembering that the self-reflexive interrogation of art's conditions of possibility becomes tautologously nonproductive in the postmodern era because of a "heightened . . . reification [that] penetrates the sign itself," effectively making "reference and reality disappear altogether" (*Postmodernism* 96). And that "heightened reification" is, of course, a result of the changing historico-economic conditions of "late capitalism" that preclude aesthetic autonomy and art's political effectivity. The materialist metafiction of the novels I examine in the second chapter actually embrace the fully reified sign shorn of reference but deploy it as the constructive building block of entirely new worlds.

25. Also see Hutcheon's *Narcissistic Narrative*, where she acknowledges but also defends metafiction against the charge of preening, apolitical narcissism. Emphasizing metafiction's political power, Hutcheon writes, "If self-reflecting texts can actually lure the reader into participating in the creation of a novelistic universe, perhaps he can also be seduced into action—even direct political action" (155).

eon's distinction between political historiographic metafiction and apolitical autotelic metafiction as specious. Once "the culture of the simulacrum comes to life in a society where exchange value has been generalized to the point at which the very memory of use value is effaced" (*Postmodernism* 18), there's no point in trying to squeeze a meaningful politics out of art's ironic posture toward the world. Thus, David Foster Wallace suggests by the early 1990s that "irony *tyrannizes* us" (*E Unibus Pluram* 67), while metafiction, that most ironically self-conscious of postmodern forms, is like "lovers not being lovers. Kissing their own spine. Fucking themselves" ("Westward" 332).[26]

As has been well documented,[27] authors and critics have worked hard over the past three decades to avoid such formal masturbation. (Although if memoir really is *the* literary form of the twenty-first century, we may have just replaced one form of autoeroticism with another.)[28] Interestingly, as I discuss in this book's second chapter, one such attempt to love more than just ourselves includes something of a doubling down on metafiction itself, an effort to reconnect metafiction to the world by emphasizing the ontological materiality of the text.[29] Crucial to this project is the complete abandonment of any homologous relationship between metafictional form and politics. As we've seen, the political valence of texts that interrogate their own conditions of aesthetic possibility oscillated throughout the twentieth century, but the homologous logic that insisted on some kind of necessary relationship between form and politics persisted. More recently, however, among those authors innovating metafictional form beyond its death in the Wallace-inspired 1990s, we've seen the complete disarticulation of self-reflexive form from political value. In fact, the rehabilitation of self-reflexive form in these texts—I will focus in particular on Salavador Plascencia's *The People of Paper*, Percival Everett's

---

26. Outside of his fiction, Wallace acknowledges that metafiction has been aesthetically useful, pushing art beyond its limits to previously undiscovered domains. But when one interviewer contends that some metafictional techniques have "very real political and historical applications," Wallace refuses to take the bait and instead chalks up the successes of metafiction to the few artistic geniuses—Borges, Nabokov, Coover—with the vision and talent to innovate aesthetically (McCaffrey 135).

27. See, for example, Robert L. McLaughlin's "Post-Postmodern Discontent" and *Postmodern/Postwar—and After.*

28. The journey from Wallace's self-fucking postmodernists to Walter Benn Michaels's neoliberal subjects who "really want . . . to be fucked" is short and direct ("Fifty Shades" 31).

29. This project is distinct from Wallace's own doubling down on metafiction in "Westward the Course of Empire Takes Its Way" where, as he tells Larry McCaffrey, he wanted to amplify metafiction until it exploded so he could then build a humanist aesthetic from the rubble (McCaffrey 142). The ontologization of the texts discussed in chapter 2 is also distinct from the kind of ontological preoccupations Brian McHale takes to be an index of postmodernism in *Postmodern Fiction.*

Percival Everett by Virgil Russel, Ben Marcus's *Notable American Women,* and Jonathan Foer's *Tree of Codes*—depends on and is only made possible by that productive disarticulation.

Finally, a few words on historical fiction and its concomitant realisms. The homology between form and politics dominates theories of the historical novel beginning with Georg Lukács's influential work on the form. Working within a Marxist framework that views historical consciousness as the sine qua non of meaningful social, economic, and political change, Lukács contends that historical fiction is particularly well-suited for producing that consciousness in its reading subjects. In particular, the historical novel's realism allows it to portray "the broad living basis of historical events in their intricacy and complexity, in their manifold interaction with acting individuals" (*Historical Novel* 43). Lukács's historical novel treats history as more than the interaction of nation-states or a chronology of significant events, and it understands its characters not as transcendental Romantic subjects, but as agents and effects of historical change. Tellingly, however, Lukács locates the historical novel's peak political potency in the nineteenth century. Writing his analysis in 1936 and 1937, in the midst of the rise of European fascism, he has little faith that the early twentieth-century historical novel—which he calls "the historical novel of democratic humanism"—will be as successful as its nineteenth-century predecessors. "Modernization and abstractness in the portrayal of historical characters," he complains, makes the historical novel of his age too preoccupied with a present disconnected from history (339). Such books fail to overcome their "immanent tendency to turn the past into a *parable of the present*," leaving readers with a thin sense of their embeddedness in the larger socioeconomic antagonisms of historical change (338).

Lukács's diagnosis forecasts what Jameson will later describe as the complete erasure of all historical sense under postmodernism's late-capitalist economic regime. E. L. Doctorow's *Ragtime,* for example, which Jameson views as the postmodern historical novel *par excellence,* is a "seemingly realistic novel" that "is in reality a nonrepresentational work that combines fantasy signifiers from a variety of ideologemes in a kind of hologram" (*Postmodernism* 23). Consequently, the novel evinces a "crisis in historicity" (22) that "short-circuit[s] an older type of social and historical interpretation which it perpetually holds out and withdraws" (23). Doctorow's work might address political themes and ideas, but the novel itself cannot be said to be political in any meaningful way. Retaining the homologous logic but reversing the argument, Linda Hutcheon argues that *Ragtime*'s postmodern experiments "alter received historical opinion" but in no way "evade the notions of historicity or historical determination" necessary for politics (*Poetics* 18). Thus, for Hutcheon, *Ragtime* still functions as a trenchant "critique of American democratic ideals" because it replaces the historical centers of US power with marginalized women, immigrants, and African Americans (61).

Clearly, then, one's inclination to view postmodern historical fiction as politically potent depends in large part on how one imagines politics. For Jameson, individuals require a historically grounded sense of the larger material conditions of which they are a part. For Hutcheon, politics involves including the excluded and ironically undermining the institutions that rely on and reproduce overly stable notions of historical truth. As we've already seen with Wallace's critique of postmodern metafiction, however, by the early 1990s, after the end of history, many fiction writers concluded that Hutcheon's project of self-consciously ironic critique had run its course.[30] The historical novel doesn't disappear, and it remains residually postmodern for quite some time, but any homologous connection it might have to politics dissipates.[31] The form grows increasingly disarticulated from politics, leaving Jameson to argue, somewhat perversely, that today only the speculative futures of science fiction have the capacity to provide a historical sense of the present.[32] I see his point: there's no history left that hasn't been swallowed up by the consumerist culture of spectacle, image, and profit, but the future, precisely because it doesn't exist yet, isn't quite as susceptible to those corrupting forces. But I'm going to let Jameson keep his sci-fi futurity, and in this book's third chapter I'll instead examine a set of recent historical novels—Jonathan Lethem's *Dissident Gardens*, Dana Spiotta's *Eat the Document*, and Rachel Kushner's *Telex from Cuba* and *The Flamethrowers*—all of which, in their treatment of revolutionary activities large and small, attempt to hash out a new path for contemporary historical fiction. In particular, I'll show how these books wrestle with the historical novel's disarticulated relationship to politics, with Kushner's *Flamethrowers* ultimately engineering a new mode of realism, which I'll call *gestural realism*, that not only repurposes historical fiction, but also supersedes a core

---

30. The young men in Jeffrey Eugenides's *The Virgin Suicides*, for example, who attempt to think historically about a set of suicides that defined their childhood in the early 1970s, capture the struggle to produce significant historical understanding at the end of the twentieth century. Although their lives are surrounded by History (the Greco-Turkish war, World War II, the racial revolts in Detroit), their authorship of the past never escapes the lobotomized confines of a suburban consumerist culture oblivious to the world economic forces shaping reality at home and abroad.

31. See Huehls, "Historical Fiction after the End of History," for a more detailed account of the fate of the historical novel at the end of the twentieth century and the beginning of the twenty-first.

32. See Jameson's "Historical Novel Today." He also makes this argument throughout *Archaeologies of the Future*.

impasse in contemporary revolutionary thought between immanent and transcendent forms of protest.

Not coincidentally, these three literary forms—life writing, metafiction, and the historical novel—were victims of the same "inverted millenarianism" that proclaimed the ends of art, theory, and revolution. Linda Anderson's introduction to autobiography speculates, for example, that theory's intervention in the form over the course of the 1980s could amount to "the death of autobiography," although she also emphasizes, as will I, its many "ghostly returns" (14). Suggesting that literature's propensity for self-reflection can only be "terminal," David Foster Wallace predicts that metafiction will end in literary "Armageddon" (McCaffrey 134). And Jameson sees fit to ask if it's even possible to write a historical novel under the conditions of contemporary capitalism. In each case, these literary forms are abandoned, they've come to an end, because they no longer provide the potent politics they once promised. Autobiography ends up reinforcing the very reified subjectivities feminists oppose. And later, memoir confirms the entrepreneurial individual constitutive of neoliberal hegemony. Metafiction fiddles while Rome burns, lacking the referential capacity to show us even what it means "to be a fucking human being" (McCaffrey 131). And the historical novel, working only with "a host of names and an endless warehouse of images," has little chance of making history appear to its contemporary readers (Jameson, "Historical Novel Today" 263). And yet, as the twenty-first century progresses, these literary forms don't actually die. Some instantiations of these forms accept their political impotence. Others double down on the form-politics homology and insist on their continued purchase on the political. *Art, Theory, Revolution,* however, is interested in a third set of twenty-first-century texts that take these various ends as a reason to abandon the form-politics homology altogether. These texts ask: What can life writing, metafiction, and the historical novel be and do when they reject homologous thinking? What new modes of value production become available when the disarticulation of form from politics functions not as literature's limit but as its grounding condition of possibility—that is, when the collapse of the form-politics homology doesn't simply designate a text's failure to be properly political but instead opens up a new domain within which literature can operate?

Generality

There is no simple or single answer to these questions. However, in my exploration of a wide swath of twenty-first-century literature, I have found one idea appearing over and over again in various forms: generality. Many contemporary authors, perhaps exasperated by the vacillations of the form-politics homology and working from the assumption that there is no necessary relationship between form and politics, are exploring generality as a nonhomological mode of value production. But what exactly is generality? Why is its mode of value production nonhomological? And what forms of value does it produce instead?

To start answering those questions, I want to begin with a footnote from Laurent Berlant's *The Female Complaint.* In a discussion about Sara Ahmed's take on the dangers that generality poses to feminism, specifically its tendency to erase particularity and difference, Berlant observes: "Ahmed's work tends to equate universalist arguments with generalist ones, as has mine and much else: but in this book I argue that the logic of the general is quite different from that of the universal, in that the general is an experience of social belonging that is embodied and has qualities, as opposed to the universal, which has always been defined" (284). Although my thinking about generality differs somewhat from Berlant's, I want to emphasize the distinction she makes here between generality and universality. They are, as she says, categorically different logics that produce value in entirely different ways. When she states that universality "has always been defined," she means that its parameters are predetermined and fixed, and it's that definitional fixity that makes universality and its partner, particularity, mutually exclusive concepts. Universals are, by definition, not particular, and vice versa, which is why, for example, Ahmed worries that an overly generalized feminist politics will blot out female particularity. They can't coexist. By distinguishing between universality and generality, however, Berlant suggests that Ahmed would be correct to worry about universality erasing particularity, because those concepts adhere to a mutually exclusive logic, but she need not be similarly concerned about generality, which does not. Instead, generality for Berlant (and here she's discussing the genre of female sentimentality as an example of generality) is "an aesthetic structure of affective expectation, an institution or formation that absorbs all kinds of small variations or modifications while promising that the persons transacting with it will experience the pleasure of encountering what they expected, with details varying the theme. It mediates what is singular, in the details, and general about the subject" (4). Again, the female-sentiment component of Berlant's take on generality is not immediately germane to my project, although it not only resonates with the version of generic female subjectivity that we will see in Heti and Kraus, but it also demonstrates that these abstract philosophical concerns remain pertinent to a diversity of political spheres, including those oriented around questions of subjectivity and identity. More immediately relevant to my theorization of generality is Berlant's account of an ongoing process of negotiation or mediation between singularity and generality that never requires the kind of definitional fixity that would make the singular-general relationship mutually exclusive. That's why Berlant contends that the singular-general relationship subscribes to an entirely different logic than the particular-universal relationship: the former escapes the logic of mutual exclusivity that defines the latter. Consequently, it would be incorrect to conceive generality as merely a compromised position between particularity and universality, or as a particularity that has come close to universality but can't quite close the deal. Instead, generality adheres to its own unique set of requirements and produces value in its own distinct way.

In "On Interpretation," the second book of his *Organon*, Aristotle writes, "Some things are universal, others individual. By the term 'universal,' I mean that which is of such a nature as to be predicated of many subjects, by 'individual' that which is not thus predicated" (Aristotle, np). This foundational idea of Aristotelian logic—correlating particulars with subjects and universals with predicates—remains a crucial touchstone for Western philosophy. In his 1903 Harvard lectures on pragmatism, however, Charles Peirce tellingly misquotes Aristotle and claims that "that which is of such a nature as to be predicated of many subjects" (*quod aptum natum est prædicari de pluribus*) is actually the way Aristotle defines "the general." Here, Peirce transforms Aristotelian universality into generality in an effort to find philosophical precedence for his own argument that "perceptual judgments involve generality," not universality (94). The act of making a claim about something that we perceive, Peirce maintains, involves developing a generality out of singularities, not applying a preexisting universal concept to a particular. Clearly distinguishing between universality and generality, Peirce adds, "Had I . . . asserted that a perceptual judgment could be a universal proposition, I should have fallen into rank absurdity." Why, exactly, would such a claim be absurd? Because "perceptual judgment is the cognitive product of a reaction," and "reaction is existence" (96). Universals precede perceptual judgment; generalities are born from it. Peirce does allow that, within the parameters defined by general propositions, "a universal proposition can be necessarily deduced" (97), but he insists that the predicative claims we make about the world, derived as they are from phenomenological experience and "reaction with the environment," can only be understood as generals, not universals (352).[33]

---

33. Peirce discusses the phenomenological basis of his philosophical pragmatism in his opening two lectures, "Pragmatism: The Normative Sciences" and "The Universal Categories."

Peirce's distinction between universality and generality, along with his understanding of generalities as the predicates of perceptual judgments of experience, are expanded further in John Dewey's *Logic: The Theory of Inquiry*. Like Peirce, Dewey thinks that logical discourse tends to mistakenly essentialize predicative qualities into universals because it incorrectly thinks of predicative qualities as inhering immutably in a given object of inquiry. In Aristotle, for example, the sentence "Callias is a man" indicates that Callias, an individual, exemplifies the universal quality of manhood. The predefined universal is imported and applied to Callias. Or as Dewey explains, this approach produces knowledge according to "*a priori* principles fixed antecedently to inquiry and conditioning it *ab extra*" (12). Instead (and this is why he, like Peirce, describes logical predicates as generals rather than universals), Dewey understands predicates as the "conditions which have been ascertained during the conduct of continued inquiry to be involved in its [inquiry's] own successful pursuit" (11). Thus, logical forms "are a generalization of the nature of the means that must be employed if assertibility is to be attained as an end" (16).[34] Unlike the a priori and self-evident logic of universality, then, Dewey offers a logic of generality that is conditions-based, processual, and ongoing.

In addition to establishing the "radical difference" between universality and generality, Dewey further elaborates his own approach by distinguishing between two different kinds of generality: a generality of kinds and a generality of means/operations (254).[35] The former, which he also describes as "generic" generality, gives us our taxonomic sense of types, classes, and species. The latter form of generality, which captures the conditions-based ongoingness of Dewey's distinct take on generality, concerns "possible ways

---

34. This idea echoes the definition of form that Kramnick and Nersessian's "Form as Explanation" offers. For them, form is disciplinary-specific and inquiry-relative, which is why it's a mistake to view it as anything more than "the explanation through which it comes into view and whose ends it serves" (651). Dewey admits that his understanding of predicative generality might sound circularly paradoxical to some, but he says it's only paradoxical if we assume that all propositions "are purely declaratory and are final and complete in this declaratory capacity" (178). But "the problem takes on a very different aspect," he suggests, "if it be admitted, even as a hypothesis, that what [propositions] declare is the need and advisability of performing certain operations as means of attaining a final subject-matter which may be groundedly asserted. For upon this basis, the idea that propositions are factors in determining the very subject-matter they are about is exactly what is to be expected instead of being paradoxical" (179).

35. I am using Dewey's language here, but he also, confusingly, names the generality of kinds "generic" and the generality of means/operations "universal," even though the first half of the *Logic* is devoted to differentiating between generality and universality. His use of "universal" in this context is of course very different from the *a priori* universality of rationalist philosophy that he attacks earlier in the project, but to avoid any confusion, I will be sticking with "kinds" and "means/operations."

or modes of acting or operating" (264) or "being" (260). By way of example, he explains the difference like this: "When it is said, for example . . . , that 'this object falls within the category of machines,' something more is meant than that it is included within the kind *machines*. What is meant is that it exemplifies the principle or order of principles by which *being* machinery is defined" (273). The generality of "the category of machines" is generic generality and the generality of the "order of principles by which *being* machinery is defined" is means/operational generality. According to Dewey, philosophy has ignored the generality of means/operations involved in being machinery in favor of the generic understanding of the kind of thing a machine is. "Classic theory transformed ends attained into ends-in-themselves. It did so by ignoring the concrete conditions and operations by means of which the fulfilments in question are brought about" (177). But "classic theory" gets things perfectly backwards since, at least by Dewey's account, we only gain our understanding of kinds through a continuum of inquiry governed by a generality of means/operations. Our generic knowledge of kinds is not an "ultra-mechanical" process of "placing, mentally, a number of singulars in a row and then throwing out unlike qualities until a number of 'common' qualities remains" (269).

Instead, given the "contingent nature of existential material" (264), Dewey describes a reciprocal relationship between means and ends, operations and kinds, grounded in the ongoing process of inquiry, which requires "treating the general propositions that are formulations of ways of action as *hypotheses*—a mode of treatment that is equivalent to treating the formulated modes of action as *possible,* instead of as required or necessary. This way of treating conceptions has its direct impact also upon formation of kinds. For it demands that grounds for them be searched for, and the grounds must be such as to satisfy (inclusively and exclusively) the requirements of the hypothesis that has been adopted and employed" (266). If, however, one discovers a singularity that challenges these general modes of action, that singularity simply becomes "the antecedently conditioning means to further inquiries" (196). This process of ongoing modification and recalibration explains why, if one accepts Dewey's thinking about the *two* forms of generality, the singular-general relationship is never mutually exclusive. Instead, singular and general are always reciprocally informing and shaping each other.

None of the texts I discuss in the following chapters conceives generality in precisely this way. None of my authors is a closeted Deweyan; none explicitly engages the philosophical distinction between universality and generality; none even uses this specifically philosophical language. After all, my archive of contemporary fiction is concerned with the messier worlds of art, literature, subjectivity, and politics while Dewey's work, intervening in the history of

Western philosophy, attempts to model logic on scientific inquiry. Nevertheless, I find Dewey's thinking about the singular-general relationship quite useful because it provides a philosophical basis for some of the core features that
emerge from my archive of contemporary fiction that engages the conceptual
antinomies of art, theory, and revolution. More specifically, Dewey helps us
understand how the singular-general relationship:

- refuses the logic of mutual exclusivity
- assumes the historical contingency of its materials
- derives more than just immanent value from ongoing modes of being
- categorizes and flattens out knowledge (into kinds and means), but not to
  the point that it's entirely homogenized (universalized) away

Most crucially for my archive of authors, these features of the singular-general relationship resist reduction to the form-politics homology. The forms of
value emanating from singular-general relationships are modal, ongoing, and
conditions-based, which makes them not particularly conducive to homological thought, which, as Dewey says of Western philosophy more broadly,
hypostatizes certain concepts as "external ideals and standards" when those
concepts should be more properly understood as the "generalized results" of
"the very operations of inquiry" (178).

We find such hypostatization, for example, in Caroline Levine's search for
"more just forms." Already knowing what justice looks like, it's easy to go
out and locate it in a specific form. And according to Dewey, such concepts
aren't entirely unhelpful. Rather than predetermining their value, however, he
suggests that we should instead appreciate that "their meaning is exemplified
in their further use, and is also clarified and modified in this use" (178).[36] In
her own work on generality, Levine clearly recognizes this facet of generality.
"Unlike universalizing statements," she observes, "generalizations can be provisional and deliberately limited to certain classes or contexts," they "work as
'open rules' that may be checked or altered by new instances" ("Model Think-

---

36. This passage from Dewey reminds me of the pragmatism running through Ludwig
Wittgenstein's *Philosophical Investigations*: "For a *large* class of cases—though not for all—in
which we employ the word 'meaning' it can be defined thus: the meaning of a word is its use
in the language" (§ 43). Wittgenstein develops this definition of meaning as use, along with his
ideas about language games and family resemblances, to counter what he describes in *The Blue
and Brown Books* as philosophy's "craving for generality" (17). When Wittgenstein talks about
generality, however, he is thinking about a hypostatized approach to value much more akin to
what I've been describing as universality, while his redescription of meaning as use aligns nicely
with Dewey's description of means/operations generality.

ing" 636).[37] This ongoing provisionality slips away, however, when Levine makes her "deliberately transhistorical and transcultural argument about politics and form," an argument that relies, curiously, on a notion of form's immutable value: "If forms have general properties that they carry with them wherever they go, then it follows that *we can make predictions about how political forms will work wherever they take shape*" (640). Here Levine hypostatizes form and its "affordances," making it easy for her to argue, for example, that the form of Christina Rosetti's "Goblin Market"—which "model[s] rhythms of difference and rest, routines of orderliness and sensuous satisfaction, and varying degrees of likeness and difference" (648)—exemplifies the "ideal rhythm" of labor time (649).

By my reading, however, the singular-general relationship precludes such "transhistorical and transcultural" claims, even as it avoids the radical relativisms of mere particularity. It foils homological thinking's attempt to confidently link form and politics and insists instead on a much more provisional and qualified approach. This is what we will see in the contemporary US fiction about art, theory, and revolution that I engage over the next three chapters. Although no single author presents a unified theory of the singular-general relationship, we will, in general, find a variety of ongoing, reciprocal relationships between singularity and generality that sidestep the mutual exclusivity of particularity and universality. Forms of generality in these texts are generalized out of singularities, and singularities are, in turn, derived from generalities.[38] Singularities, in other words, are always constituting, reshaping, and even expanding the field of generality. (Dewey calls this the *generality of means/operations*.) At the same time, in a reciprocal fashion, the field of generality provides a discrete set of terms, concepts, or other variables that we draw on, assembling and reassembling those variables in different ways, to produce singularities. (Dewey calls this *generic generality*.) Crucially, the value of that singularity has nothing to do with its potential universalizability. Instead, the singularity's value is a function of its relative relationship to other

---

37. Anna Kornbluh offers a Marxist-materialist take on the same idea: "Human beings make—emergently, unwittingly, spontaneously—the forms on which their lives depend" (5).

38. Singularity has its own idiosyncratic conceptual history, so it's important to distinguish my use of the term here from other forms the concept has taken in the past. When I talk about singularities, I am not thinking of them in the Deleuzian sense, which leaves them in the realm of the virtual, a site of labile potentiality; nor as Michael Hardt and Antonio Negri borrow the concept from Deleuze to indicate the irreducible difference of individual subjects, their core, irreplaceable this-ness or haecceity; nor am I imagining singularity in the way that systems theorists use it to describe a minor variance that produces a massive effect. Instead, I use singularity to name the specificity of a given assemblage born from configuring various components and variables of a general field.

singularities born of the same generality, as well as its relative relationship to the broader field of generality from which it has been composed. In other words, the value of a singularity derives from its specific configuration of the general's available components while the value of the general derives from its absorption and accommodation of singularities, in an ongoingly provisional way. This is what Berlant means when she says that generality "mediates" what is singular and general about the subject.

In the first chapter on art's dominant conceptual forms, for example, Sheila Heti and Chris Kraus replace a mode of aesthetic value production centered on questions of formal autonomy and heteronomy with one based on the generic forms of genre. A genre's generality comprises the discretely bound, preexisting set of tropes, rules, formats, character types, plot devices, and so forth. And any given genre work stands as a singularity, its value stemming from the unique way an author culls, configures, and deploys the genre's general set of variables. In this way, the value of a generic singularity is not representational; it's not based on its ability to point to, index, or connect directly to the world. Rather, its value is a function of the singularity's distinct configuration of the generality's various components—the relative relationship between the singular and the general as well as between one generic singularity and any others born from the same generality. For Heti and Kraus, this generic mode of value production works better in an age marked by form's disarticulation from politics. Realizing that very little distinguishes her from anyone else in the world, for example, Heti's art abandons the logic of autonomy and heteronomy in favor of a fully generic model of female subjectivity. Kraus embraces a similar aesthetic, but, worried about the potential overdetermination of genre, she also introduces the generalizations of case study as a way to ensure that genre's generality remains flexible and ever-expanding. Her work generates singularities that expand the domain of generic generality, thereby ensuring that its ends never end up hypostatized as ends-in-themselves.

In the second chapter on theory's self-reflexive forms, we'll see an array of authors embracing a constructive form of generality to escape the recursivity that attends theory's demand that thought must think its own conditions of possibility. Rather than subjecting their own texts to that reflexive mandate and the ensuing recursions of value that follow from it, Plascencia, Marcus, Everett, and Foer treat the main tropes and concepts from theory's heyday— the death of the author, the chain of signifiers, present absence, *différance,* the writerly text—as the constructive building blocks of their literary works. In so doing, they effectively strip theory of its insistent reflexivity and make it a generality, just another thing in the world with some but not universal value. This in turn allows them to use those general building blocks to construct distinctly singular novels that appear, on their face, similar to the experimental postmodern metafiction of the late twentieth century, but which I will argue function in precisely the opposite way. Rather than making the deconstructive move of transforming world into text, these novels from Plascencia, Marcus, Everett, and Foer make the constructivist move of transforming text into world. They are able to do so, I argue, by reimaging theory's "truths"—particularly its commitment to reflexivity—as historically contingent, general phenomena rather than as universal features of thought and language. The result is a version of truth that can be generally but never universally true.

In the third chapter on revolution, Rachel Kushner's *The Flamethrowers* will, in both its representational content and narrative form, recommend replacing immanent and transcendent forms of revolutionary practice with gestural forms. Gestures, conceived in Kushner's text as a preexisting set of generic movements and actions, exist as a kind of human stock footage, one of many *langues* we'll see throughout *Art, Theory, Revolution*. As with the generic and the general, the value of gesture results from the way a given movement or configuration of the body draws on our shared, common knowledge of that human stock footage. While immanent and transcendent forms of revolutionary practice establish their significance by claiming a universal purchase on the world (e.g., if revolution were more immanent it would be more successful, or vice versa), the value of a gesture stems from its similarity to and difference from the general storehouse of potential human gestures, as well as its relative relation to other gestures taken from the same storehouse. For Kushner, this gestural mode establishes a more revolutionary relationship among people than either immanent or transcendent forms can.

Thus, the generic, the constructive, and the gestural emerge from my readings of contemporary US fiction about art, theory, and revolution as three forms of generality that produce value out of the singular-general relationship rather than through any formally homologous relation they might bear to politics. My authors develop these general forms as they engage a set of conceptual antinomies—between aesthetic autonomy and heteronomy, first- and second-order thought, and immanence and transcendence—that have caused the form-politics homology in the fields of art, theory, and revolution to grow vacillatingly undecidable. They then offer these forms of generality as interventions in and corrections to the conceptual limitations of the form-politics homology as it has functioned in those fields. Moreover, because the novelists discussed here develop these forms of generality through their own innovations in literary form, they also intervene in the form-politics homology as it has operated in literary studies, replacing the older literary forms of life writing, metafiction, and historical fiction with the more general literary forms of case study, theoretical literalism, and gestural realism. Finally, alongside these literary forms of generality, the primary texts discussed throughout *Art, Theory, Revolution* offer a notably limited and qualified account of politics as a thoroughly ad hoc practice grounded in the reciprocal ongoingness of the singular-general relationship. Although generality is not in itself political, my archive of texts also suggests that it might be shortsighted to think of its many forms—the generic, the constructive, and the gestural—as entirely apolitical. They're not not political, although thinking of them as such also requires new understandings of the political itself, understandings which might not even register as political to many on both the left and the right. Each chapter offers examples of what this changed notion of the political might look like, and a coda on Mark Bradford's visual artworks, particularly his 2017 installation "Pickett's Charge" at the Hirshhorn Museum in Washington DC, thinks even more concretely about how this generalized politics which is not one might be materialized and mobilized in the world today.

CHAPTER 1

Art, Life Writing, and the Generic

The end of art has obviously not brought art to an end. For years after its 2015 opening, visitors still had to make reservations at the Broad contemporary art museum in downtown Los Angeles months in advance. Nearly three million people visit the Museum of Modern Art (MOMA) in New York City every year. Tourists loiter outside Frank Gehry's Santa Monica home, snapping souvenir photos. Alexander Rodchenko has his own hashtag on Twitter. My sons learned about Pollock, Matisse, Warhol, and Picasso in preschool. Art is everywhere, and people really seem to love it.

Of course, that's one of the primary reasons that so many scholars and critics have declared Western art's demise. Where's the potency in a Kandinsky brushstroke when it's been integrated into the preschool curriculum? Whither the aesthetic when a visit to the Met is just another stop on a New York City tourist itinerary, sandwiched somewhere between Times Square and paddle-boating in Central Park? Or when some of the world's most elite artists exhibit their work in the lobbies of high-rise office buildings?

When Arthur Danto declared in 1984 that art had ended twenty years earlier, with the 1964 exhibition of Andy Warhol's Brillo Boxes at Stable Gallery in New York City, he offered a slightly different take on the popularization and commodification of the art object.[1] For Danto, the Brillo Boxes marked art's

---

1. Other declarations of art's demise include Donald Kuspit's *The End of Art*, Cuauhtémoc Medina's "Contemp(t)orary: Eleven Theses," and Chris Campanioni's *Death of Art*. Noël Carroll's *Theories of Art Today* offers a collection of essays responding to the end of art at the turn

end because they represented the moment that art and commodities could no longer be meaningfully distinguished from each other. Rather than viewing that indistinguishability as evidence of art's capitulation to the market, however, Danto presented it as a Hegelian triumph, as "the sacramental return of the thing to itself through art" (*Beyond* 136). Privileging being over representation, or in Danto's language, manifestation over expression, art frees itself from meaning and interpretation to become simply the thing that it is. No longer bound by representational imperatives, art after Warhol is free to be anything at all—pop culture, video, performance, social interaction, whatever. "The age of pluralism is upon us," Danto writes. "It does not matter any longer what you do, which is what pluralism means" ("End of Art" 57).

As this invocation of pluralism suggests, Danto's thinking about art's end has a definite political valence. Artists are "liberated" (*Beyond* 9) from the overdetermined strictures of art history and tradition while art's radical pluralism suggests its "egalitarian," democratizing commitments (137). Art's formal heteronomy—that is, its openness to the world, its becoming life—erases hierarchies and allows it to engage politics and society more directly. Or as Danto puts it, after Warhol, "art can be externally dictated to, in terms either of fashion or of politics, but internal dictation by the pulse of its own history is now a thing of the past" (9). Of course, as Ben Davis observed while eulogizing Danto in 2013, art's primary external dictator for at least the past several decades has been capital. Warhol might have opened art's doors to the world, but the world has bum-rushed art ever since, reducing the political potential of its egalitarian pluralism to the cold neutrality of market forces. This idea, that art has been permanently tainted by capital, is a much more common explanation for art's demise. Sianne Ngai asserts, for instance, that "the slackening of tension between autonomous art and the commodity form is the one development that has arguably had the greatest impact on the development of twentieth-century art overall" (58). Roger White, a contemporary artist and critic, even felt capital's encroachment in art school at Columbia: "It was unclear," he writes, "where academia left off and the art market began. The minute we'd set foot in our first seminar room, we were all already inside the industry" (3).[2] Or, the egalitarian pluralism of art's heteronomy also proved to be the ideal condition for the triumph of the marketplace.

Flipping the political valences and reclaiming the art object from capital's heteronomy, Nicholas Brown champions an aesthetic that asserts its autonomy from the external dictation of a market quick to commodify art. "The isola-

---

of the millennium. Berel Lang's *The Death of Art*, which includes Danto's famous essay "The End of Art," provides one from fifteen years earlier.

2. White depressingly reports that art "was discussed openly and seriously as an asset class and a portfolio diversifier, young artists as investment opportunities" (4).

tion of an autonomous field," Brown asserts, is "the necessary condition of possibility (within market society) for the production of any artwork" (19). Such autonomy derives from a work's "immanent purposiveness" (13), the set of "internal norms" and "ambitions" that the "self-legislating" art object gives itself (31). Here we find a return to that "internal dictation" that Danto's pluralistic vision once saw as "a thing of the past." An art object's intentional form, its internally defined rasion d'etre, rescues it from external dictation by the market, fashion, politics, and even the audience. Formal autonomy replaces heteronomy. Art becomes art, not life, and its politics are saved from capital's corrupting influence. Thus, in much the same way that Danto lends a democratizing, egalitarian political valence to the heteronomous end of art under Warhol, Brown correlates formally autonomous art with its own specific political forms. Acknowledging that autonomous "works of art have no political efficacy of their own" and are not "emancipatory," Brown nevertheless suggests that "under current conditions, [they have] a politics" (37). Since the "current conditions" Brown has in mind are those of contemporary capitalism, autonomous art's "politics" are necessarily anticapitalist. The autonomous art object's resistance to commodification manifests a formal intentionality that makes disagreement and difference possible, which is important for Brown and many others in his *nonsite* orbit who view antagonistic difference—particularly class inequality—as the indispensable foundation for any meaningful political debate and practice.[3]

For my purposes here, the specifics of Danto's and Brown's arguments are less important than their broader homologous structure. Danto aligns art's formal heteronomy with a certain political impulse, and Brown does the same with art's formal autonomy. Both see a homologous relation between art's formal disposition toward the world and a particular set of abstract political formations. To be sure, the conceptual and abstract nature of their art-politics homologies keeps their political claims relatively modest. No one is arguing that collage's forms are more politically progressive than portraiture's, that sculpture manifests utopian impulses that performance never could, or that a video installation will move an audience to revolutionary action. Rather, for both Danto and Brown there's a shared sense that art's formal relation to the world—either its full-blown intercourse with the world (heteronomy) or its studied, intentional separation from it (autonomy)—looks similar, on an abstract, conceptual level, to various forms that structure and motivate politi-

---

3. See, for example, Walter Benn Michaels's *The Beauty of a Social Problem*.

cal thought (e.g., equality, hierarchy, interconnection, democracy, community, disagreement, opposition, or antagonism).[4]

Danto and Brown are of course not the first to homologize art's formal autonomy and/or heteronomy to political forms and concepts. Ever since Kant's influential theory of aesthetic autonomy severed beauty from all motivated interest and aligned art's formal autonomy with an absence of political concern, art's relative autonomy and heteronomy have been the primary formal categories through which scholars, theorists, and artists have articulated Western art's politics, or lack thereof. Coleridge, for example, reversed Kant's thinking about aesthetic autonomy, viewing it as a radically transformative power that synthesizes opposites and projects utopian possibility. Many avant gardists of the early twentieth century, on the other hand, grounded their work in direct opposition to aesthetic autonomy, which they viewed as a bourgeois construct apolitically separated from life and the world.[5] Theodor Adorno's *Aesthetic Theory* proposes a dialectical relationship between autonomy and heteronomy, suggesting that art heteronomously touches society politically only by first autonomously removing itself from society (252–53). But the socially heteronomous, along with its attendant politics, are purged altogether from art by mid-century critics like Clement Greenberg and Michael Fried, both of whom require art's formally autonomous severing from the world. Then, as we've already seen, Danto contends that such severing is impossible after Warhol makes art coextensive with the world, while contemporary thinkers like Brown and Michaels argue for its return.

The point of this admittedly loose genealogy is not to trace the orderly development of the art-politics homology over time, but instead to highlight the complete *lack* of development when it comes to determining the political valences of autonomous and heteronomous art in the Western aesthetic tradition. History helps us see that the art-politics homology is highly contingent, always vacillating, and never stable. Sometimes formal heteronomy aligns with

---

4. To be sure, this homologizing move isn't always so tempered. Take, for example, Walter Benjamin, who claims in "The Work of Art in the Age of Mechanical Reproduction," found in *Illuminations,* that his favored heteronomous aesthetics are "completely useless for the purposes of Fascism" but are very "useful for the formulation of revolutionary demands in the politics of art" (218). Or conversely, think of Walter Benn Michaels arguing, via Brecht, that the aesthetic beauty of autonomous art can help us "feel" the economic inequalities of contemporary capitalism (*Beauty* 39).

5. However, even as early twentieth-century avant-gardists asserted art's necessarily heteronomous connection to the world, they also resisted the world's instrumentalization of art by developing a more politically charged, and ultimately anticapitalist, version of aesthetic autonomy. See the third chapter of Peter Bürger's *Theory of the Avant Garde* for a thorough explanation of the avant-garde's complicated relationship to aesthetic autonomy.

a leftist, egalitarian politics and autonomy doesn't; at other times the reverse is true. Sometimes the vacillation even occurs within the same work of art. This was the case with Brecht's experimental theater, for example, which Adorno condemned for being too heteronomous and didactic, Lukács chastised for being too autonomous and not didactic enough, and Benjamin championed for being the perfect balance of autonomous experiment and heteronomous engagement with the world.[6] Or sometimes there's universal agreement on an art object's relative autonomy or heteronomy but disagreement about its corresponding politics. For example, Nicholas Bourriaud views the heteronomous commitments of relational aesthetics as an "angelic programme" that creates community and "re-stich[es] the social fabric" (36), while Claire Bishop reads those same heteronomies as evidence of relational aesthetics' neoliberal complicity (14). Given the contingent fluctuations of the art-politics homology, however, it's perfectly plausible to imagine Bishop making the opposite argument in a different sociohistorical conjuncture. As she readily acknowledges, "The meaning of artistic forms shifts in relation to the uses . . . made of these forms by society at large, and as such they have no intrinsic or fixed political affiliation" (30). Thus, the art-politics homology that correlates formal autonomy and/or heteronomy with specific political formations is itself heteronomous to the extent that its ongoing vacillations indicate that its alignments of art and politics are always historically contingent.

Jacques Rancière has a name for this situation in which art's "autonomy and heteronomy are linked as two sides of the same coin" (Tanke 78).[7] He calls it art's "aesthetic regime," and he views it as a very distinct way of thinking about art and its relation to the world that should be distinguished from what he terms art's "ethical" and "representative" regimes. Each of art's three "regimes," according to Rancière, conceives the relationship between art and the world differently. Under an ethical regime like Plato's, art's "ontological veracity, or lack thereof," and the im/morality that follows from it, govern all thinking about that relationship (Deranty 120). Because a painting of a bed will never *be* an actual bed, much less the Form of a bed, Plato views it as ontologically fallen, untrue, and potentially corrupting. Under a representative regime like Aristotle's, the ethical regime's demand that art be ontologically equivalent to the world is replaced with an investment in art's capacity to

---

6. A thorough account of the debates over Brecht can be found in Shannon Jackson's "What Is the 'Social' in Social Practice."

7. See Johanna Drucker's *Sweet Dreams* for an analysis of contemporary art that views this duplicity as leading to inevitably complicit art. For Drucker, however, complicity isn't necessarily a bad word. Also see Rachel Greenwald Smith's *On Compromise* for a smart critique of Drucker's position on complicity.

represent the world. Aristotle demands that representations plausibly mirror the world, but he does not need them to be the world.

Under the aesthetic regime, however, investments in art's ontological and representational relations to the world are replaced with a concern for art's autonomous separation from or heteronomous engagement with the world. "The life of art in the aesthetic regime," Rancière writes, "consists precisely of a shuttling between these scenarios, playing an autonomy against a heteronomy and a heteronomy against an autonomy" (*Dissensus* 132). This shuttling, in turn, produces a corresponding vacillation in art's political significance. After listing a number of political claims grounded in aesthetic autonomy and/or heteronomy, for example, Rancière observes, "Each of these positions may be held and has been held. This means that there is a certain undecidability in the 'politics of aesthetics'" (133). Or, echoing Jameson's claim that "we are no longer in the position of evaluating whether a given thought system or aesthetic form is progressive or reactionary," Rancière elsewhere asserts that the aesthetic regime "suspen[ds] . . . every determinate relation correlating the production of art forms and a specific social function" (138). Crucially, he doesn't say that the aesthetic regime's blurring of autonomy and heteronomy, art and life, makes art apolitical. Rather, he merely observes that the "undecidability" of the art-politics relationship guarantees that "art promises a political accomplishment that it cannot satisfy," while "those who want it to fulfil its political promise are condemned to a certain melancholy" (133). For Rancière, then, the vacillation of the form-politics homology doesn't signal the end of art. Such ends only arrive, he says, when autonomy or heteronomy is "pushed to the extreme" and placed in a mutually exclusive relationship with the other (132). Instead, according to Rancière, the vacillation between aesthetic autonomy and heteronomy, and the attendant vacillation of the form-politics homology, simply define the baseline condition of art today.

Two contemporary female authors, Sheila Heti and Chris Kraus, explore these art-life dynamics of the aesthetic regime, refusing, like Rancière, to overdetermine the relation into a rigid art-politics homology. At the same time, however, their work doesn't content itself with the aesthetic regime's indeterminate vacillation between autonomy and heteronomy. Instead, their texts—Sheila Heti's *How Should a Person Be* (2010) and Chris Kraus's *I Love Dick* (1997), *Aliens & Anorexia* (2000), *Torpor* (2006), and *Summer of Hate* (2012)—approach the question of art in terms of its singularity and generality rather than its relative autonomy and heteronomy. In this way, their work resists the homologous thinking that would locate a corresponding politics in art's autonomous and/or heteronomous form and instead develops an alternative framework for thinking about art in terms of its singularity and generality.

Doing so also yields an approach to politics that is reluctant to find specific political value in any particular aesthetic form. Consequently, politics in these works is nonideological, contingent, and fleeting.

Both Heti and Kraus develop their thinking through forms of life writing that innovate the relationship between literary textuality and performance while at the same time reconceiving the nature of female selfhood. They explore the problem of being a person in the world, in other words, through the language of aesthetic autonomy and heteronomy. Their deeply personal inquiries into female being are reinforced by extended meditations on art and the role art might play in mediating selfhood. In fact, for both Heti and Kraus, art is one of the things they might be. And as inhabitants of the aesthetic regime, they approach the possibility of being art, of making their lives art, through the autonomy/heteronomy debate. Thus, instead of asking whether or not and how art captures life representationally, they ask: can life become art; should art become life; could art and life ever intersect with each other in a meaningful way?

As I will demonstrate, however, neither Heti nor Kraus is particularly satisfied with the answers that this autonomy/heteronomy framework makes available to them. Consequently, I will also detail their common effort to reimagine art, female life writing, and the self it describes, outside the conceptual contours of autonomy and heteronomy.[8] Finding little value in an ever-vacillating art-politics homology and recognizing that "every determinate relation correlating the production of art forms and a specific social function" has been suspended, both, albeit it in very different ways, embrace a singular-general model of value production for both art and the self. Here's the argument in a nutshell: Heti's work replaces autonomous/heteronomous models of selfhood with a generic female subjectivity out of which singularities emerge. This model runs into trouble when the available forms of generic female subjectivity are limited, overdetermined, or just outright sexist. Working to expand the available forms of generic female subjectivity, Chris Kraus treats female life writing as case study, a form that insists on the generalizable (but not universalizable) truth value of singular female experience. Added together, Heti moves from general to singular, drawing on a generic notion of humanity to produce her singular self, and Kraus moves from singular to general, using the singular content of her individual life to produce case studies that expand the overall category of general female experience. In this way, Heti and Kraus replace the autonomy/heteronomy framework that grounds the

---

8. Kingston-Reese's *Contemporary Novelists* also stages a conversation between Heti's and Kraus's work, suggesting that their texts "designate new aesthetic categories for the struggles of living aesthetically today" (133).

aesthetic regime's vacillating art-politics homology with the singular-general relationship, which they employ as a new way to think about the value of art, female selfhood, *and* women's life writing. In turn, because this singular-general model of value production resists being homologized to politics conventionally conceived, the generalized forms of self and art that we find in Heti and Kraus become the basis for new ways to inhabit the world that also demand new ways to think about the nature of politics today.

Autobiography and Life Writing

Heti's and Kraus's respective engagements with the art-life relationship depart significantly from a long literary tradition that has historically conceived that relationship as a representational problem.[9] In what follows, I will use the term "autobiography" to refer to works that think about this relationship representationally, as a matter of accurately representing life in art, and I will use the term "life writing" to refer to works that think about this relationship aesthetically, in Rancière's sense of the term, as a question of whether and how art and life can and should intersect, overlap, or become each other.[10] The Heti and Kraus texts that I will be discussing here are perhaps most precisely described as "autofiction," a particular subgenre of life writing in which authors appear as characters in their texts, a text's settings and events are taken from the author's life, and texts frequently include an account of their own production.[11] "Autotheory" would be an equally apt designation, especially if we follow Lauren Fournier's recent account of the genre as a distinctly feminist project of "performative life-thinking" (14). Regardless of the moniker we choose to refer to Heti's and Kraus's work, their common violation of what Philippe Lejeune calls the "autobiographical pact"—that is, the guarantee that a text's author, narrator, and protagonist are identical—is foundational to their life writing projects. Their texts also violate what Lejeune describes as autobiography's "referential pact"—an agreement, "coextensive with the autobiographical pact"—which guarantees that autobiography "provide[s] infor-

9. They are, of course, not alone in this departure. Rather, they are part of a larger trend at the end of the twentieth century and the beginning of the twenty-first that challenges autobiography's conventions and assumptions.

10. In making this distinction, I am following the lead of Laura Marcus, who notes in *Autobiography* that the term "life writing" has replaced "autobiography" in the past decades to accommodate a proliferation of generic forms, including fiction, experimenting with self-textualization (110). Those literary experiments have moved contemporary life writing beyond the representational concerns of autobiography.

11. See Hywel Dix's *Autofiction in English* for a wide-ranging treatment of the genre.

mation about a 'reality' exterior to the text" (22). Once these two pacts are broken, life writing becomes a primarily aesthetic project interrogating the boundaries between art and life, not a representational one.

Even before autobiography's representational concerns gave way to life writing's aesthetic ones, however, autonomy and heteronomy were already crucial concepts for the genre. As many critical accounts of the history of autobiography in Western culture detail,[12] autobiography was initially perceived as an autonomous representation of a universally exemplary autonomous life. As Laura Marcus explains in *Auto/biographical*, "The autonomous status of autobiography is based on its separation from forms of history-writing" (5), a separation intended to reinforce "the oppositions between self and world, private and public, subjectivity and objectivity, the interior spaces of mind and personal being and the public world, including that of the literary market-place" (4). The case for this autonomous conception of autobiography, which correlates "the psychological unity of the human mind and the aesthetic unity of the written text" (181), was made most influentially by Georges Gusdorf, a French scholar whose 1956 essay "Conditions and Limits of Autobiography" didn't appear in English until James Olney included it in his foundational collection of essays, *Autobiography*, published in 1980. According to Gusdorf, "Autobiography properly speaking assumes the task of reconstructing the unity of life across time. This lived unity of attitude is not received from the outside," Gusdorf insists, but rather, it is "man" whose "intervention . . . structures the terrain where his life is lived and gives it its ultimate shape" (24). Such an internally dictated project is justified by a belief in the universal exemplarity of the individual's sovereign, autonomous life. As Linda Anderson explains, "According to this view, generated at the end of the eighteenth century but still powerfully present in the middle of the twentieth, each individual possesses a unified, unique selfhood which is also the expression of a universal human nature" (5).

Although this autonomous/universalist model of autobiography does not overtly homologize itself to a specific political orientation, the critiques of that model—leveled throughout the twentieth century's concluding decades by feminists, racial minorities, and other marginalized populations—most certainly read it as an ideologically conservative maintenance of the white,

---

12. See, for example, Laura Marcus's *Autobiography* and *Auto/biographical Discourses*, Linda Anderson's *Autobiography*, and the introduction to Sidonie Smith and Julia Watson's *Women, Autobiography, Theory*.

patriarchal status quo.[13] And with that critique, heteronomous particularity and its attendant politics of difference overhaul autobiography. For the heteronomous model of autobiography, selves are created through discourse, not just represented by it; individuals are shaped by the world and the interconnected relations they have with each other; and identity is always fractured and incomplete, never unified, whole, or total.[14] Or as Anderson characterizes this decades-long shift from an autonomous to a heteronomous model of autobiography: "In this view the subject is constituted by gender but also by other divisions and representations which belong to specific histories and locations" (103). Given this proliferation of particularized subject positions, it's not surprising that scholars and critics correlate the heteronomous model of autobiography to a politics of difference. Julia Swindells exemplifies this move when she writes in 1995 that "autobiography now has the potential to be the text of the oppressed and the culturally displaced, forging a right to speak both for and beyond the individual. People in a position of powerlessness—women, black people, working-class people—have more than begun to insert themselves into the culture via autobiography, via the assertion of a 'personal' voice, which speaks beyond itself" (7).[15] The particularity of voice that heteronomous autobiography makes possible, in other words, mirrors the drive for democratic inclusion and equal rights motivating feminist, racial, and other minoritarian political projects of the time.

Heteronomy's critique of autonomous autobiography's claims on universality completely reoriented the genre around a social justice politics motivated by equality, inclusion, and liberation. However, the problem of representativity—the question of whether, how, and for whom a given individual life might be exemplary—remained. The heteronomous model successfully challenged the white, male claim of universal representativity, but it could not "avoid equally contentious claims to representativity, the problem of speaking *as* or speaking *for* that continually returns and which seems impossible to resolve in any

---

13. Foundational texts making this critique include Sidonie Smith and Julia Watson's *De/ Colonizing the Subject,* Hertha Wong's *Sending My Heart Back across the Years,* Sidonie Smith's *Subjectivity, Identity, and the Body,* Leigh Gilmore's *Autobiographics,* Kenneth Mostern's *Autobiography and Black Identity Politics,* and Barbara Rodriguez's *Autobiographical Inscriptions.*

14. It's worth noting that this heteronomous model draws not only from the critique leveled by those previously excluded from autobiography's tendentious universality but also from the poststructural critique of autobiography made most famously in Paul de Man's "Autobiography as De-facement."

15. Related work on testimony makes similar claims for the political potency of highly particularized self-narratives. See, most influentially, Shoshana Felman and Dori Laub's *Testimony: Crises of Witnessing in Literature, Psychoanalysis and History.*

final way" (125).[16] In other words, the terms of representativity shifted: whereas the autonomous form of autobiography claimed that a particular life exemplified universal life, heteronomous forms claimed that an individual life could be representative of a larger collective. But the struggle to justify the move from an individual life to a broader set of lives, even when individual life was conceived intersubjectively and relationally, didn't disappear with heteronomous autobiography's critique of universality. Authors of such texts were still seen to be speaking as a representative member of a collectivity. They weren't claiming *universal* representativity, but they were making a structurally similar move that simply reiterated the same logic on a narrower scale. Thus, debates about intersectionality, inclusion and exclusion, and who can speak for whom remained as pressing as ever, even after autobiography had embraced the proliferation of heteronomous subject positions.[17]

This is the way autobiography thinks about the politics of autonomy and heteronomy under a representational regime. Underpinned by the autobiographical and referential pacts, it trusts that lives are being truthfully represented, and on the basis of that representational veracity, it treats those lives as representative. If the represented life is viewed as autonomous, a problematically universalizing politics accrues to it; if the represented life is viewed as heteronomous, a more progressive politics of difference accrues to it, although that politics also struggles with the same problem of representativity that compromises the autonomous/universal model.

Unable to resolve the problem of representativity—that is, the relationship between particular and universal, particular and collective—authors begin producing works that challenge the autobiographical and referential pacts and the representativity they imply. As Linda Anderson puts it, the key question facing would-be authors of autobiography at the end of the twentieth century was whether "the self [could] eschew its representativeness, its role of 'speaking for others,' and still have something of political significance to say" (111). In an attempt to answer that question, authors begin exploring other functions that the genre might serve. Autobiography expands into life writing; the aesthetic regime supplants a representational one; and authors begin exploring alternative conceptions of selfhood and the political implications that follow from them.[18]

---

16. This passage in Anderson summarizes an argument found in the first chapter of Nancy Miller's *Getting Personal*.

17. "Other Subjects," the third chapter of Anderson's *Autobiography*, offers a good overview of the problem of representativity in heteronomous life writing.

18. I am telling an admittedly simplified, linear story about the development of autobiography over the course of the past few decades. I do not mean to suggest that all authors abandon the project of representation in favor of a more aesthetic project. Rather, I am only trying to capture a shift in focus, emphasis, and possibility over time. Raymond Williams's thinking in

This is where Heti and Kraus come in, writing in the thick of this turn-of-the-century literary landscape that is pivoting from representational to aesthetic concerns. To be sure, both writers frequently speak the residual language of representativity and speculate about the exemplarity of female life: "One good thing about being a woman is we haven't too many examples yet of what a genius looks like," Sheila wryly muses (4). But both are also committed to forms of life writing that escape representativity, its motivating belief that lives have representational meaning and value, and the notion that good life writing represents that meaning and value to readers. The "I" in Kraus's *Aliens & Anorexia,* for example, is particularly taken with the Squat Theater, a Hungarian experimental theater group that relocated to New York City in the 1970s, because, as two of its members explain, "in our performances we manifested an existence that overrode its representation" (79).

This kind of language signals the emergence of an aesthetic regime of life writing that replaces the representational regime of autobiography. Under the aesthetic regime, autonomy and heteronomy remain important concepts, but they now refer to the aesthetic form of the text itself, not just to the lives the text describes. This is how Danto and Brown imagine aesthetic autonomy and heteronomy in the debate I staged at the beginning of the chapter, only now the art object in question is the life-writing text. In turn, the politics homologized to autonomy and heteronomy also change. In place of a politics of representational difference, we now have an aesthetic politics grounded in the relative autonomy and heteronomy the text bears to the world.

Unsurprisingly, though, we find the same vacillating arguments about that aesthetic politics as we saw earlier in the various and variable political arguments made about autonomy and heteronomy more broadly. Walter Benn Michaels, for example, views most life writing, including Heti's *How Should a Person Be?,* as irredeemably heteronomous and overly attached to personal voice, individual experience, and the naïve belief that those things matter. Describing memoir as the neoliberal genre *par excellence,* he argues that memoir's formal heteronomy—its shameless incorporation of the world—only reinforces the instrumentalized entrepreneurialism of neoliberalism's *homo œconomicus* ("Going Boom"). On the other hand, Michaels champions Maggie Nelson's *Jane: A Murder,* suggesting that "its ambition to be 'perfect' in a way no person ever can be" evinces a formal autonomy entirely severed from the world about which the text ostensibly speaks (*Beauty* 3). For Michaels, this kind of work, which "refuses the politics of personal involvement," manifests an anticapitalist politics that makes "today's objective social conditions" visible

---

Marxism and Literature about emergent, dominant, and residual cultural forms is closer to the way I intend my loose history of the genre.

(172). And yet, under the aesthetic regime, the opposite arguments are equally plausible: autonomous life writing that is all art and no world is too apolitical, but heteronomous life writing's compelling attachments to the world make its art politically significant. Daniel Worden makes this argument, for example, when he observes that "the first-person voice in literature," "striv[ing] to articulate alternative models of subjectivity," might effectively counter neoliberalism's "idealization and isolation of the entrepreneurial individual as the benchmark of success" (164). Thus, Worden is bullish on heteronomous life writing's capacity to articulate "a more material orientation toward reality that emphasize[s] economic and political limits" (163). As we saw earlier, the point here is not to suggest that one argument is more correct than another, but to observe the vacillation in any form-politics homology that takes art's formal autonomy and heteronomy as the primary source of its politics.

Just as Heti and Kraus speak the language of representation and representativity while also thinking beyond it, they are also thoroughly enmeshed in this aesthetic discourse of autonomy and heteronomy: "I want my life to be a work of art," Sheila claims (73). And in *I Love Dick*, Hannah Wilke, who "is a model for everything [Chris] hope[s] to do" (172), "willingly became a self-created work of art" (213). Ultimately, however, as I will now begin to demonstrate by turning first to Heti's *How Should a Person Be?*, Heti and Kraus engage these representational and aesthetic discourses in an effort to reimagine art, female selfhood, and its writing not as particulars valued for their broader representational value, nor as autonomous and/or heteronomous beings valued for their separation from or connection to the world, but instead as singularities that contribute value to and derive value from a broader generality. This approach foils the politically homologous thinking that marks the representational and aesthetic approaches, and makes available an alternative and highly contingent take on the relation between art and politics.

Heti's Arts of the Self

It's significant that Heti's "novel from life" asks *how* a person should *be*, not what a person should do, how a person should treat others, or even how to be a person. Hers is an aesthetic question, not a political, ethical, or practical one, and it requires an aesthetic answer. As Sheila discovers over the course of the novel, however, the language of aesthetic autonomy and heteronomy provides inadequate answers. Gradually recognizing that inadequacy, Sheila reimagines the how-ness of being as generic, a generalized mode of being distinct from the aesthetic discourse of autonomy and heteronomy, which proves salutary to both Sheila and her art. The generic serves as a form of generality that replaces aesthetic autonomy, heteronomy, and the vacillating politics that attach to those concepts.

For the bulk of the novel, however, Sheila's attempt to determine how a person should be remains stuck in the autonomy-heteronomy duality. At first, Sheila is all heteronomy. She would watch others "to see what they were going to do in any situation, so [she] could do it too." "I was always listening to their answers," she explains, "so if I liked them, I could make them my answers too" (1). And when others watch her, she hopes that they like her only for whom she appears to be, not for whom she is. "No one has to know what I think," she says, "for I don't really think anything at all, and no one has to know the details of my life, for there are no good details to know" (3). As Sheila moves into adulthood, however, this openness to and for others becomes dangerous, permitting one jealous ex-boyfriend to script a disturbing play about her life: "In the final scene I kneeled in a dumpster—a used-up whore, toothless, with a pussy as sour as sour milk—weakly giving a Nazi a blow job, the final bit of love I could squeeze from the world." Lacking autonomy, the script "lodge[s] inside [her] like a seed that [she] was already watching take root" (25).

To countervail the shame and embarrassment that follows from these heteronomous attempts to "patch [her]self together with [her] admiration for the traits [she] saw so clearly in everyone else," Sheila tells herself instead, "*It's time to stop asking questions of other people. It is time to just go into a cocoon and spin your soul*" (5). Even though she knows "that personality is just an invention of the news media . . . that character exists from the outside alone . . . [and] that inside the body there's just temperature" (2), Sheila nevertheless desires some form of internally dictated autonomous being that is first and foremost identical with itself rather than with the world. She doesn't want to be a composite representation of the world; and she doesn't want to be defined by her relationality to it. She wants autonomy, not heteronomy. But she also doesn't want an autonomy that is naïve, narcissistic, or self-reflexive, and she doesn't want it to come at the expense of meaningful externalities: friends, love, politics, work, and so on. To help Sheila walk this tightrope, Heti turns to art, writing Sheila's attempt to determine how a person should be as an allegorical journey through late twentieth- and early twenty-first-century Western art.

First, Sheila tries on the heteronomy of relational aesthetics, a subset of participatory art that undoes conceptualism's dematerialization of the art object only to reimagine it as an interactive experience that necessarily includes an audience.[19] Or as Nicolas Bourriaud explains of relational aesthetics, "The role of artworks is no longer to form imaginary and utopian realities, but to actually be ways of living and models of action within the existing real" (13). Viewing "the spread of the supplier/client relations to every level of human life" as art's "enemy," relational aesthetics suggest that people should be interactive, connected, and social, without any profit motive (83). Sheila agrees, renouncing a play she's been writing "because it's not in the service of [her] life" (71), which she instead conceives as deeply relational: "Life feels like it's with Margaux—*talking*—which is an equally sincere attempt to get somewhere, just as sincere as writing a play" (82). Realizing that Sheila plans to use their conversations as material for her play, however, Margaux, feels exploited and instrumentalized by the relationship, a problem that echoes the primary critique of relational art: namely, that it's dangerously complicit with the entrepreneurial economic status quo it supposedly contests.[20] After all, corporations and governments want to increase participation, be more inclusive, and forge affective relations too. Or as Claire Bishop argues, relational art's impetus to "social inclusion" is "less about repairing the social bond than a mission to enable all members of society to be self-administering, fully functioning consumers who do not rely on the welfare state and who can cope with a deregulated, privatized world" (14). To be sure, most participatory artists intend the opposite, but given its formal ephemerality and commitment to heteronomous determination, such work remains susceptible to co-optation. So if the signifiers of social participation flirt with the instrumental as much as the utopian, the for-profit as much as the communitarian, then perhaps a more directly political version of heteronomous art is in order.

In the text, this position is occupied by two of Sheila's friends in the theater world, Ben and Andrew. Dissatisfied with the absence of meaningful work the theatrical arts afford, they conclude that "talk is cheap" and set off for Africa where they realize that there are millions of people living in shacks who "are smart and, you know, are people" (162). While traveling, they hatch a plan to

---

19. Participation is different from performance in that witnessing and experiencing a performance is not the same as participating in it. In a June 2012 interview with Adam Robinson, Heti explains that she "was thinking a lot about relational aesthetics and artists like Rirkrit Tiravanija when [she] was writing the book." She wanted "to write a book that could be undergone the way life is undergone; not a book understood by the author and given to you, but undergone by the author and undergone by the reader." As will become clear, Heti's investment in relational aesthetics is not necessarily at odds with my generic reading of the novel.

20. See Liam Gillick and Maria Lind's "Participation" for a take on participatory art that pegs its emergence directly to "the effects of the service economy and its post-Fordist methods of work organization" (207). Claire Bishop's *Artificial Hells* tells a similar story.

write a play that gives voice to many of the women they meet abroad, thereby using art to confront and address "the injustice of the circumstances some people are born into versus others" (165). Whereas participatory art counters social violence and injustice by staging ethical and affective interactions, this type of activist art wades into the violence, forcing its audience to bear witness in the hopes of effecting meaningful change. And yet, as Maggie Nelson astutely observes in *The Art of Cruelty*, because activist art "predetermine[s] what . . . we should have been looking at . . . and, by extension, what is frivolous or wrong to look at in its place," such art substitutes an artist's outrage at injustice for the injustice itself (26). Little surprise, then, that Andrew and Ben's play ends up being about themselves discovering injustice, not the injustice African women suffer. As they explain to Sheila and Margaux over dinner, they can't figure out how to "build a bridge from [their] story to another story that [they] think is important to tell, then tell that story somehow" (167). They can't write themselves off the stage.

These are the novel's two heteronomous aesthetic modes: participatory, relational art and activist art. Together, they give us a chiasmic conflation of art and life. Participatory art turns life (i.e., talking, interacting, socializing) into art. Activist art turns art into life (i.e., politics, violence, injustice). Both transformations rely on a formal homology between art and politics that neither can determine or maintain. Participatory art intends its relational forms to mirror nonhierarchical community, but their ephemerality also leaves participatory art vulnerable to instrumentalization and complicity. Activist art deploys the immediacy of exposure to incite political outrage in its audience, but its righteous hubris runs the risk of reinscribing rather than redressing political injustice. Recognizing that these heteronomous modes of art and being fail to deliver stable and secure value, Sheila investigates more autonomous forms.

First, she tries on medium specificity, a concept Clement Greenberg used back in the 1960s to defend modern art from the heteronomous threat of kitsch and commercialization. As Greenberg writes, if each art could "determine, through its own operations and works, the effects exclusive to itself," then "each art [would] be rendered 'pure,' and in its 'purity' find the guarantee of its standards of quality as well as of its independence" (755). Once painting understands exactly what makes painting painting, in other words, the value and significance of a given painting can be measured accordingly, and painting's value becomes autonomous, internal to itself. Although, as we've seen Danto argue, Warhol's pop art shattered the autonomy of medium specificity by ignoring the history of art's "internal dictation" and erasing the boundaries between art and non-art, the idea returns at the end of the twentieth century as new media—digital and otherwise—expand the artist's palette.[21] Sheila expands it even further when, in pursuit of a pure, medium-specific aesthetic autonomy, she decides to become a blow-job artist. Looking around at her "contemporaries," Sheila can't help but observe that "we live in an age of some really great blow-job artists. Every era has its art form. The nineteenth century, I know, was tops for the novel" (3). The deadpan irony here about the historical decline of artistic media is tongue-in-cheek, but only partially, as later in the novel readers find Sheila holed up in her boyfriend's house, "working on [her] blow jobs, really trying to make them something perfect." "I started feeling proud, like I was doing something useful in the world," she reports, "and not for one moment did I think to myself that I should be doing something more old-fashionedly important, like finishing a play" (155). This pastiche of the "perfect" blow job is what the autonomy of medium specificity looks like after Warhol, after the end of art.

In one last attempt to find a more autonomous mode of being, Sheila works diligently to turn herself into an art object. To that end, her friendship with Margaux fulfills her long held desire to be "friends with a painter who would make [her] into an icon that people would admire" (93). But when Margaux paints her, Sheila is disappointed to learn that Margaux has replaced the painting's original title, *Genius,* with the notably less iconic *House for a Head.*[22] And Sheila eventually realizes that "it is cheating to treat oneself as an object, or as an image to tend to, or as an icon. It was true four thousand years ago when our [Jewish] ancestors wandered the desert, and it's as true today when the icon is ourselves" (183). As with the perfecting of the blow job, the heteronomous intrudes once again, and the aesthetic icon, far from being autonomously self-sustaining, becomes for the other: "We have found that, in our freedom, we have wanted to be like coke to the coke addict, food to the starving person, and the middle of the night to thieves" (184). In other words, Sheila's iconic autonomy is passive and consumerist. She's an object inserted into the world, and her value is a function of the world's affection, desire, and maybe even jealousy for her. This is not an aesthetic autonomy by which the art object constantly, and intentionally, asserts its difference and independence from the world. Rather, as icon, Heti's autonomous soul is easily "sould."[23]

---

21. For an expansive reconsideration of medium specificity in the digital age, see Sabeth Buchmann, "The (Re)Animation of Medium Specificity in Contemporary Art." Also see work from Rosalind Krauss, who made a career defending medium specificity in more Greenbergian terms. "The abandonment of the specific medium spells the death of serious art," she warns in *Perpetual Inventory* (xiii).

22. You can see the painting here: https://thenewinquiry.com/reality-fiction/.

23. Sheila reports, with some concern, that she frequently mistypes "soul" as "sould" (5).

These two attempts to determine how a person should be via autonomous aesthetic modes—medium specificity and an embrace of the art object's inherent iconicity—don't fare much better than the heteronomous aesthetic modes discussed above. Here, art strives to avoid being conflated with life, but the heteronomous world always intrudes. In the case of medium specificity, the whole world intrudes to assert the banal homogeneity of all media forms. In the case of the icon, commodity fetishism intrudes to assert the impossibility of aesthetic isolation. Add to those the ephemerality of relational art (talking with Margaux) and the narcissistic complicity of activist art (white men in Africa), and we have a quadruple threat—irrelevance, commodification, ephemerality, and complicity—not just against contemporary art but also against the formal project of being a person in the twenty-first century.

Generic and Singular Selves

This tendency for autonomous and heteronomous forms to turn into each other might justify a more dialectical approach to things. After all, even Adorno, one of the twentieth century's most ardent champions of autonomous art, offers a thoroughly dialectical account of the art object's relative autonomy and heteronomy: "The double character of art—something that severs itself from empirical reality and thereby from society's functional context and yet is at the same time part of empirical reality and society's functional context—is directly apparent in the aesthetic phenomena, which are both aesthetic and *faits sociaux* [social facts]" (252). Adorno offers a dialectical version of the autonomy-heteronomy relation because of what he sees as the ineluctable fact of material production—that's a heteronomy that just won't ever go away: "Scarcely anything is done or produced in artworks that does not have its model, however latently, in social production. The binding force of artworks, beyond the jurisdiction of their immanence, originates in this affinity" (236). By this account, art doesn't achieve autonomy by severing itself from the world, as Michaels suggests. ("The production of art's difference from the world . . . counts as the work it does in the world," he writes [*Beauty* 172].) Rather, the artwork becomes autonomous by letting the heteronomous world into it. Thus, in a perfect reversal of Michaels's formulation, for Adorno, "The work is social and historical through and through: only thus can it become autonomous" (Jameson, *Late Marxism* 185).

Sheila, however, is not a dialectical thinker. Her life is a muddled mess of autonomy and heteronomy, and she's not going to theorize a determinate relation between the two. Instead, her approach to autonomy, heteronomy, and the specific art-life relationship each entails looks a lot more like Rancière's nondialectical approach to those concepts. For Rancière, heteronomy, or "art becoming mere life," and autonomy, or "art becoming mere art," are just two extreme scenarios between which the life of art constantly shuttles (*Dissensus* 132). Thus, rather than putting "each back in its own place" (183), Rancière blurs them into a unified field undergoing constant reconfiguration, effectively replacing art's discourse of autonomy and heteronomy with what he elsewhere calls "the distribution of the sensible."[24] This concept refuses to think about art as separate from, or as standing in some other complicated relationship to, the world: "There is no 'real world' that functions as the outside of art," Rancière insists. "Instead, there is a multiplicity of folds in the sensory fabric of the common, folds in which outside and inside take on a multiplicity of shifting forms, in which the topography of what is 'in' and 'out' are continually criss-crossed and displaced by the aesthetics of politics and the politics of aesthetics. There is no 'real world.' Instead, there are definite configurations of what is given as our real, as the object of our perceptions and the field of our interventions" (148). In lieu of the firm conceptual distinctions between autonomous and heteronomous modes of being, here we only find a "shared surface," common to both, where "functions slide into one another," yielding art-life configurations that remain irreducible to the mutually exclusive logic that drives so much work on the relationship between art and politics (*Future of the Image* 106–7).

Sheila embraces a similar outlook when she declines the autonomy-heteronomy framework that shapes the bulk of her investigation into how a person should be and instead adopts a practice borrowed from Margaux's mother. As Sheila explains, it's a "technique in which, whatever problem you came across in your life, you were just supposed to throw up your hands and say, *Who cares?*" (6). Sheila practices this technique a lot, most productively when meditating on her first boyfriend's malicious prediction that she would spend the last moments of her life "kneel[ing] in a dumpster . . . weakly giving a Nazi a blow job." As I've already noted, this prophecy initially devastates Sheila, and it also sets her up to think about the problem of being as a battle between autonomy and heteronomy: will she allow herself to be defined heteronomously by the outside world, or will she discover an autonomous self

24. See Rancière's *The Politics of Aesthetics*, particularly pages 12–19. There, Rancière explains that "the distribution of the sensible" names "the system of self-evident facts of sense perception that simultaneously discloses the existence of something in common and the delimitations that define the respective parts and positions within it. . . . This apportionment of parts and positions is based on a distribution of spaces, times, and forms of activity that determines the very manner in which something in common lends itself to participation and in what way various individuals have a part in this distribution" (12).

that resists the boyfriend's heteronomous prediction? However, reconsidering the prediction later in life, in a chapter titled "What is Freedom?," she breaks from that logic and instead, imagining life as "a multiplicity of folds in the sensory fabric of the common," asks, "*Who cares?* If someone has to wind up, at the end of their long life, kneeling in a dumpster before a Nazi, it might as well be me. Why not? Aren't I human? Who am I to hold myself aloof from the terrible fates of the world? My life need be no less ugly than the rest" (274).

And with that simple "Who cares?" Sheila connects herself to "the rest" and embraces her generic humanity. Crucially, this is not capitulation to heteronomy. She isn't becoming as others view her but is instead recognizing that there are any number of ways she might be, any number of ways she might configure and distribute her sensible. The value of her self doesn't derive from who she is (autonomy) or what society has made her (heteronomy) but from the way she does or does not embody any of the various types of generic being available to her as a common person in the world. Or as Sheila observes, "We are gestures, but we less resemble an original painting than one unit of a hundred thousand copies of a book being sold" (185). Thus, when Sheila takes a good close look at herself, she concludes that "[she's] done as little as anyone else in this world to deserve the grand moniker *I*. In fact," she says, "apart from being the only person living in this apartment, I'm not sure what distinguishes me" (187). The point, of course, is that nothing distinguishes her. At least, nothing that matters. But it's precisely because the distinctions of the individual self don't matter that she turns to the general, to the other 99,999 copies of the human book being "sould." Not because they're selves like us; but precisely because they're not-selves like us too. The connection is not to another self, but to the general forms of selfhood that emerge when we say *Who cares?* It's a connection that is not an identification. It's a generic or species mattering, a form of mattering that comes from not mattering at all. You get to be a one, but not the one. A singularity, but not an individual.[25]

Throughout *How Should a Person Be?*, Heti explores singularity through the character of Margaux. But while Sheila develops an understanding of her own genericness only after pursuing and then dismissing autonomous and heteronomous modes of being, she develops an understanding of Margaux's singularity only after first considering but then dismissing her representative exemplarity. That's because, when Sheila and Margaux first meet, Sheila is struggling to complete a play commissioned by a feminist theater company— struggling because she doesn't actually know anything about women: "What

---

25. Judith Butler articulates a similar notion of subjectivity in *Frames of War*. Although for her, the subject's "radical substitutability and anonymity" stems from a shared, generalizable precariousness predicated on our apprehension of life's grievability (14).

women had to say to one another, or how a woman might affect another, I did not know" (41). Viewing her relationship with Margaux as a possible solution to this representational impasse, Sheila records their conversations, hoping they will provide representative examples of the kinds of things that women say. Despite Margaux's misgivings, Sheila justifies her recording project with a convenient theory: "Most people live their entire lives with their clothes on, and even if they wanted to, couldn't take them off. Then there are those who cannot put them on. They are the ones who live their lives not just as people but as examples of people. They are destined to expose every part of themselves, so the rest of us can know what it means to be a human" (60). In short, Sheila denudes Margaux so that Sheila doesn't have to be representatively naked herself. After a massive falling out with Margaux, however, Sheila eventually realizes that people aren't representative examples of people. They're just people. "Margaux was not like the stars in the sky," Sheila observes. "There was only one Margaux—not Margauxs scattered everywhere, all through the darkness. If there was only one of her, there was not going to be a second one." She isn't an example of anything other than herself. She's singular. But because Sheila "had never wanted to be one person, or even believed that [she] was one, [she] had never considered the true singularity of anyone else" (300).[26]

This conception of singular being complements Sheila's theory of generic being—that is, her idea that humans "less resemble an original painting than one unit of a hundred thousand copies of a book being sold" (185). Singularities like Margaux emerge from the generic generality when they draw on the set of specific gestures that are available to "the human type" (184). Thus, Sheila says that humans aren't unique, like "an original painting," but are rather singular configurations, which, in many ways, aren't all that different from the other 99,999 copies of the human type. In other words, as a singularity, Margaux's most distinguishing feature is neither her representativeness (singularities aren't representative examples of a larger collective or universal) nor her originality (singularities can't be original because they are derived from the general). Instead, it's her one-ness, the simple fact that she is a singular iteration of generic humanity. "*You are only given one,*" Sheila realizes, and "the one you are given is the one to put a fence around" (300).

---

26. "When I was younger," Heti explains in an interview with Madeleine Schwartz, "I always really wanted to abstract life. More and more as I get older I realize that this abstraction is totally devoid of life. It's missing something true about life. Every situation is different from every other situation. There is always the temptation to have some big abstract answer, but life is not abstract. That is inaccurate" (6).

Heti's Novel Play

It matters, then, that Margaux's actual words—her singular words—make their way, not into Sheila's play, but into Heti's "novel from life," which is itself structured like a five-act play, with a substantial chunk of the text written as a play that includes dialogue and stage directions:

> *Margaux eats the toast with jam.*
>   MARGAUX
> It still seems like you might do something in the next day that's remarkable.
> Maybe that's what the play could be about.
>   SHEILA
> (*anxiously*) What? Saving the day?
>   MARGAUX
> Something remarkable.
>   SHEILA
> (*uncertain*) Yeah.
>   *Long pause. Margaux is staring out the window.*
> What? What are you thinking? (69)

In addition to these transcribed conversations presented as theatrical text, Heti includes apparently verbatim emails from Margaux, which, rather than functioning as representative examples of the kinds of things women say to each other, are instead intended to register as the actual words that one woman did say to another woman.[27]

These formal innovations should be read in the context of twentieth-century theater's complicated relationship to textuality, a relationship that bears directly on questions about theater's relative autonomy and heteronomy.[28] His-

---

27. Reading Heti's novel as a paradigmatic example of what he calls "affective neorealism" (as opposed to "storytelling neorealism"), Lee Konstantinou argues that the text's inclusion of "unvarnished audio recordings, emails, and other affective records of body-to-body contact" allow it to "construct a fantasy that the novel might become a self-justifying or self-vouchsafing *document,* a document that gives us not the reality effect but reality" (119). Kingston-Reese makes a different argument, viewing Heti's use of transcription as "a strategy for playing out the failure of things to become real" (113).

28. It might seem surprising to imagine that Heti is engaged in these conversations, but she's a novelist-critic who comes out of the theater world and has even explained that she actively conceptualizes writing as "a form of acting" (quoted in Marcus, *Autobiography,* 120). Further suggesting the contemporary relevance of these debates, Margaux wryly observes, after suggesting to Sheila that she might feel blocked because she's been commissioned to write a play, that "theater hasn't caught up from a 1930s awareness" (68).

torically, textuality has been seen as a way for playwrights to achieve aesthetic autonomy by curtailing the various heteronomies of theatrical performance: the presence of an audience, the need for live actors, the collaborative process of theatrical production, the range of inflections and interpretations actors bring to their lines, and so forth. As Sarah Townsend explains, these many theatrical heteronomies have made the idea of "theatrical 'autonomy' . . . especially precarious and fraught," although that doesn't mean that plenty of playwrights haven't pursued it, frequently by insisting on the primacy of the text (3). Most famously, of course, Michael Fried uses the idea of theatricality as a way to explain why certain artworks fail to achieve aesthetic autonomy. Because "art degenerates as it approaches the condition of theatre" (830), Fried writes, "the success, even the survival, of the arts has come increasingly to depend on their ability to defeat theatre" (831).

Although they were not necessarily aiming "to defeat theater" in quite the way Fried has in mind, Martin Puchner describes an array of modernist playwrights (Mallarmé, Joyce, Stein, Yeats, Brecht, and Beckett) who deployed antitheatrical "modes of textual representation that explicitly foreclose[d] any act of impersonation" (16). These authors viewed impersonation as problematically heteronomous since live acting makes it impossible to know for sure "which gestures and movements are part of the artwork and which ones are the result of accidents on the stage" (6). In pursuit of greater aesthetic autonomy, these playwrights compose antitheatrical closet dramas—plays that forego an audience and aren't written for the stage, but which also aren't poetry or prose. Such highly textualized work should be juxtaposed, Puchner argues, to the avant-garde theater, which embraced heteronomous theatricality, "as well as everything associated with it, such as collaborative production, collective reception, distraction, and riotous audiences" (11). As Erika Fischer-Lichte explains, a defining feature of avant-garde theatricality was a move away from textuality, away from the notion that "the artistic character of performance was primarily affirmed through the performance of literature, through the dramatic literary text that was supposed to steer and control performance." Instead, the avant-garde "fundamentally redefines the dynamic between the literary dramatic text and performance. No longer does the text steer, control, and legitimize performance. Rather, the text becomes one material among other materials—like the body of the actor, sounds, objects, et cetera—each of which the performance manipulates or adapts, thereby constituting itself as art" (80–81).

Given this conceptual history, then, it's significant that Sheila (and Heti[29]) takes a play commissioned for the stage and turns it into a novel written to be

---

29. In her interview with Adam Robinson, Heti confirms that she, like Sheila, once struggled to finish a play that a feminist theater commissioned her to write about women.

read, but also that the novel written to be read looks like a play, but not a play intended for the stage. Instead of producing "a true work of art, a real play," as the feminist theater company has requested, Sheila writes a book about her decision not to, which nevertheless includes, in part, the play that it's not (40). ("I want you to finish your play," an exasperated Margaux tells Sheila. "Does it have to be a play?" Sheila asks. "No," Margaux confirms [262].) As an example of the antitheatrical textualization of theater, we could read *How Should a Person Be?* as a play for aesthetic autonomy. Conversely, as an example of the theatricalization of the novel, we could read it as a move toward aesthetic heteronomy.[30] Or, given that neither of those descriptions is quite accurate, we could throw up our hands and say, Who cares? As with Sheila's quest to determine how a person should be, maybe aesthetic autonomy and heteronomy are the wrong concepts for thinking about the formal aesthetics of Heti's antitheatrical textuality/antitextual theatricality. Perhaps there's a way in which Heti's life writing engages the same singular-general model of value production that she proposes for female selfhood. After all, her "novel from life" doesn't stand as an exemplary representation of a life; it doesn't performatively embody a life; and it doesn't present itself as an autonomous work of art severed from the world. Instead, it's a play wrapped inside a novel—a singularity that's also, quite literally, "one unit of a hundred thousand copies of a book being sold" (185). The play-novel question, then, is just as off-point as the autonomy-heteronomy question. The book is a muddled mess of both, play and novel, in a way that redistributes readerly sensibility, making it possible to see life as neither representation nor performance but instead as both singular and general simultaneously.[31]

This approach also allows Heti to sidestep the politics that might otherwise be homologously ascribed to a work aiming to achieve either aesthetic autonomy or heteronomy through the manipulation of the relationship between text and performance.[32] The antitheatrical modernists, for example, favoring aesthetic autonomy out of a fear that "the theater would actually provide a forum in which the constitution of [normative] public opinion

---

30. In "Notation after 'The Reality Effect,'" Rachel Buurma and Laura Heffernan contend that Heti's work offers "relatedness [as] the antidote to representativeness" (89). To be sure, Sheila values her relationship with Margaux and even understands selfhood as relationally constituted. But that doesn't mean that Heti is countering Sheila's "reified idea" (91) of autonomous art with her heteronomous relations with Margaux, thereby "dissolv[ing] the hard division between life and literature" (90). After all, as we've already seen, Heti's novel is deeply skeptical of both autonomous and heteronomous modes of value production.

31. Kingston-Reese describes this simultaneity as a "vacillation" between real and ideal (132); I'm suggesting that the vacillation is superseded by the singular-general relationship.

32. Although it obviously doesn't prevent her from being (mis)read in this political way, as Michaels does when he locates a neoliberal logic at the heart of *How Should a Person Be?*

might take place," believed that their separation from the social sphere would facilitate a more forceful indictment of it (Puchner 11). More comfortable with the heteronomous contingencies of performance, however, the theatrical avant-gardists sought to provoke audiences out of their normative, bourgeois sensibilities by incorporating the audience into theatrical productions (Fischer-Lichte 81). In other words, both sought to challenge conservative mindsets, thwart social mores, and undermine normative political assumptions, but each also thought that only *their* formal aesthetic could achieve those goals and that the opposing formal aesthetic was directly at odds with their achievement because of its complicity with the reactionary status quo. Working hard to avoid the mutually exclusive thinking at the heart of these form-politics homologies, *How Should a Person Be?* resists being homologized to a clear and obvious politics in the way that theatrical, heteronomous performances and antitheatrical, autonomous representations have tended to be. Instead, by replacing the debate between text and performance with a singular-general approach to value production, Heti offers what Margaux describes as a form of "complete meaning in art that is even better than political meaning" (172).

A Kind-of Politics

What exactly does this mean? What does "complete meaning in art" look like, and how would that be "even better than political meaning"? Instead of maintaining the distinction between formal autonomy and heteronomy and dwelling on the specific politics that emerge from each, Margaux's "complete meaning" indicates a desire to meld them together into a unified field that would render the distinction between them obsolete, just like Heti does with theater and the novel. Art becomes a unified field that produces even more than political meaning when art is understood as continuous with rather than distinct from the world, when, as Rancière puts it, autonomy and heteronomy are not two different and mutually exclusive relationships that art has with the world but are instead just two particularly extreme ways to distribute and redistribute the sensible.

If that unified field is a precondition to "create complete meaning in art," then how exactly does that mode of value production result in a form of value that is "even better than political meaning"? Rancière once again provides an initial model as he suggests that the shared "surface of equivalence" that constitutes the distribution of the sensible might also provide "the formative principles of a new communal life" (*Future* 95).[33] In Rancière's work this reads as both less and more political than politics conventionally conceived as policy disagreement, ideological debate, or structural antagonism. It's less because it demurs from making the kinds of political claims that are legible in contemporary political discourse—claims about identity and difference, race and class, conservative and progressive ideology. And it's more because it manifests a level of radical equality that conventional politics practiced on a left-right spectrum can't attain.[34] Suhail Malik and Andrea Phillips describe this as a generalized politics: "This is not any politics in particular but a phrasing of an indeterminate politics of community as a repartition of the sensible" (124). This in turn makes politics "occasional; nothing is inherently political. More emphatically, that the principle of equality has no content of its own and cannot be assumed in advance of its implementation means that it is an 'empty' notion" (126).[35] In other words, whatever politics emerges out of the distribution of the sensible isn't based on formal homology; the form of the "surface of equivalence" doesn't translate into any specific political form or ideology. Instead, the distribution of the sensible is political whenever it's configured in a way that we understand to be political. That's why Malik and Phillips say it's "occasional."

---

33. The political modesty of this position stems from Rancière's broader approach to philosophy, which consistently avoids the epistemological problems of identity and difference, self and other, subject and object, by focusing instead on distributive logics of inclusion and exclusion. While the former approach pursues a politics of critique oriented toward a horizon of truth, undoing identity with difference or challenging the universality of the object with the representational vicissitudes of the subject, the latter approach aims to describe, and then reconfigure, what we are able to see, say, think, and do without necessarily ascribing any ideological or predetermined political value to that reconfiguration.

34. For a critique of the politics that follow from Rancière's work, see pages 54–67 in Michaels's *The Beauty of a Social Problem*, as well as the long footnote on page 193.

35. The idea of equality as an "empty notion" echoes poststructuralism's reconsideration of universality at the turn of the millennium, articulated most clearly in Ernesto Laclau's *Emancipations* and Judith Butler, Ernesto Laclau, and Slavoj Žižek's *Contingency, Hegemony, Universality*. In those works, Laclau, Butler, and Žižek speak of universality as "spectral," "impossible and necessary," an "empty signifier," a "void," and a "non-place." There is, however, a key difference between Rancière and Laclau, Butler, and Žižek. Emptiness for them is just another instance of poststructural constitutive absence (or, for Žižek, the Lacanian Real), an unbridgeable gap that fuels the irresolvable dialectic between particular and universal, present and future. Rancière's emptiness, however, is the emptiness of a homogenized field of generality. There is no constitutive absence at the heart of Rancière's distribution of the sensible; there is only the openness of potentially new configurations of the sensible. In this way, Rancière's work sidesteps universals and particulars, identity and difference, and the dialectics that so frequently follow from their antinomous relations.

Paolo Virno's work, which shares Rancière's generalized conception of the order of things, makes this politics a bit more concrete. In place of the distribution of the sensible that Rancière imagines as a set of "common denominators" (*Future* 93), an "alphabet of types" (97), and a "surface of equivalence" (99), Virno, borrowing from Marx's *Grundrisse*, offers the "general intellect," which Virno variously describes as a "base which authorizes differentiation" (25); a set of "generic logical-linguistic forms which establish the pattern for all forms of discourse" (35); an array of "common places," which, like a "skeletal structure," "are the woof of the 'life of the mind'" (36); "the cognitive-linguistic habits of the species"; "the generic faculty of language" (56); and a "pre-individual reality" comprising "the biological basis of the species," "language," and "the prevailing relation of production" (76–77). Virno is particularly concerned about the ease with which post-Fordist modes of production harness and exploit these generalized forms of thought, language, and feeling that the general intellect comprises. However, precisely because these generic communicative faculties *precede* and constitute the conditions of possibility for all differential productions of value—post-Fordist or otherwise—Virno sees no reason to abandon them just because contemporary capitalism has appropriated them, making "the life of the mind" the primary source and fuel of affective, immaterial labor under post-Fordist capital. Instead, for Virno, the generic, species-based, linguistic and cognitive faculties that constitute the "general intellect" also provide the set of generic components through which post-Fordist capital might be reconfigured. Because the generic-ness of the general intellect precedes post-Fordist capital's appropriation of it, it offers a space for conceptual retreat. Thus, Virno advocates a politics that exits from post-Fordism's particular configuration of the general intellect, returns to the generic, and then develops new configurations out of that preexisting generality. This isn't an anticapitalist politics that resists or opposes post-Fordism with a different set of beliefs or ideologies about the way the world should be; it's an anticapitalist politics that uses the same constitutive components of the general intellect that post-Fordism exploits, but does so in newly reconfigured ways. This, it seems to me, is one way to understand what Margaux might mean when she talks about a form of meaning that is "even better than political meaning." Instead of art that homologously indexes political meanings and values that we already know and understand, Margaux pursues an aesthetic that draws on a generic generality to produce new meanings that don't necessarily fit into established political frameworks. These meanings don't seem political on their face, but they could prove politically significant precisely to the extent that they exceed what we currently understand as political. This is the way in which they might be "even better than political meaning."

Virno admits that these new reconfigurations of the general intellect, these new distributions of the sensible, will most likely be highly individualized, or to use my language, singular. But again, freed from homologous logic, there's no basis for ascribing a specific politics to that individualism. It's not necessarily bourgeois, neoliberally entrepreneurial, or disturbingly Ayn-Rand-ian just by virtue of being individual. Instead, "the crucial point," Virno insists, "is to consider these singularities as a point of arrival, not as a starting point; as the ultimate result of a *process of individuation,* not as solipsistic atoms" (76). Language, the foundational generality of the general intellect, is key to this process of individuation out of the generic: "The passage from the pure and simple ability to say something to a particular and contingent utterance" is, for Virno, the process of moving from *langue* to *parole,* from general to singular.[36] Because of the generic foundation of this "process of individuation," the singularity who emerges out of the generality of the general intellect speaks not as an "I" but as "a one" (77). Like Sheila, this singularity is no less ugly than, and is only made possible by, "the rest." Most importantly, this mode of generic value production renders nonsensical the homologous thinking that correlates specifically autonomous and/or heteronomous forms with a specific politics. The formal relation a given configuration or singularity bears to the world can't entail a specific politics once the value of that given configuration or singularity stops being a function of its formal autonomy and heteronomy and starts being a function of its distinct reconfiguration of a set of generic variables. It can be political, but much as Malik and Phillips describe Rancière's politics as "empty," it's not *necessarily* political or homologously political. It won't necessarily index a liberal or conservative, anticapitalist or capitalist, progressive or reactionary, politics.

In theory, the form of politics that emerges from Virno's thinking about the general intellect seems promising. His capacity to imagine a politics beyond politics, to conceive a form of value production that is "even better than political meaning," helps us think about what politics might look like in an age defined by the disarticulation of form from politics. And yet, to return momentarily to Heti's "novel from life," we would be justified in wondering, first, how exactly do we access the distribution of the sensible, the general intellect, the *langue* of life? And second, as seems to be the case with Heti, what if the generic forms one has access to are all "shit" (277)? Heti answers the first question—how to access the generic—with her *Who cares?* epiphany.

---

36. Virno borrows the concepts of *langue* and *parole* from Ferdinand de Saussure's "Course on General Linguistics." "Langue" for Saussure names the general field of language—all the letters, sounds, rules, words, etc.—that we draw on whenever we speak or write. "Parole" names any singular instance of language use.

The ability to reimagine the self as a singular collection of general variables effectively undoes the particularized self-importance of the unique individual and her relationship to the collective. But what about the fact that Heti's *Who cares?*, far from opening up new realms of possibility and modes of being, simply allows her to feel comfortable with the idea of blowing a Nazi in a dumpster? If your *langue* is filled with such horrible forms, what's the use of rendering oneself generic?

To be fair, Virno actually suggests that when we speak as "a one" rather than an "I," we have recourse to a general field of language far greater than a given *langue*: "the act of *parole* does not exclusively depend on the determined *langue* . . . ; rather, it stands in relation to a generic *faculty* for speaking" (77). And elsewhere he describes the generic domain as an "exuberance of possibilities," a "virtual abundance," and a "surplus" (70–71).[37] Practically speaking, however, as Heti's work clearly indicates, that virtual abundance might not always be available, especially if you're a young woman trying to make it as an artist or writer in the big city. It might be hard to feel all that exuberant about one's generic possibilities. Put differently, Heti helps us see that, in practice, the generic remains susceptible to the overdetermined circumscriptions of genre, which means that it might not be enough to retreat into and then reconfigure the constitutive components of a generic humanity. In addition, the generic might require constant and active expansion. For its possibilities to be truly exuberant, for its virtuality to be truly abundant, we need to move not just from the general to the singular but also in the other direction, from the singular to the general, so that the myriad ways of being that exist in the world are constantly adding to the general *langue* from which singular lives are composed. For this part of the project, we have to leave Heti behind and turn to the life writing of Chris Kraus, an author who, much like Heti, thinks about forms of life via forms of art, and vice versa. Kraus's contribution to this chapter's larger attempt to conceive politics beyond the homologous thinking that links autonomy and heteronomy with distinct political value involves her embrace of the case study as a potent form of life writing. For Kraus, treating singular female lives as case studies prevents the generic from becoming an overdetermined genre.[38] Kraus's case studies share Heti's singular-general take on female life, but they are at pains to expand the boundaries of generic

---

37. This move of Virno's, his attempt to out-*langue* langue, strikes me as excessively exuberant and unnecessarily virtual.

38. This take on genre as dangerously overdetermined does not necessarily comport with contemporary theories of genre that emphasize and champion its flexibility. See, for example, Theodore Martin's *Contemporary Drift* and Jeremy Rosen's *Minor Characters Have Their Day*. I do not intend to indict genre in the same way Kraus does, or offer a theory of genre that emphasizes its strictures. Thus, even though "generic" is frequently used as the adjectival form of "genre," I'll be distinguishing between the two terms because Kraus does the same in her work.

female life to include absolutely everything. Or as Eileen Myles has written in praise of Kraus's first novel, "When *I Love Dick* came into existence, a new kind of female life did, too" (15).[39]

Case Study against Genre

This new kind of female life, the life Kraus presents across four novels-from-life stretching from *I Love Dick* in 1997 to *Summer of Hate* in 2007, only emerges after a concerted battle against the overdeterminations of genre. In *Torpor,* for example, we find Sylvie Green living in Thurman, New York, with her husband Jerome in the late 1980s.[40] Feeling herself succumb to the "New Traditionalism"—the process by which previously unruly twenty-somethings abandon the project of changing the world and instead begin to create families—Sylvie realizes that she's fulfilling the genre expectations embodied in the contemporaneously hit television show *thirtysomething* (24–25). Further seduced by the rustic tropes of upstate New York—the "dark green shutters with their crescent moons . . . the wide-plank maple floorboards" (206)—her life bears an unsettling resemblance to the autumnal scene of smiling dogs, soaring pheasants, and vibrant foliage depicted on the Rheingold beer sign she used to stare at while drinking at the Ear Inn in New York City (30–31). Hiking with Jerome at Brant Lake, she realizes that "the promise of the sign had been fulfilled" (31). But that fulfilled promise of the "Perfect Life" never gives her life substance, and she begins to notice other people her age "building actual lives they seemed to take quite seriously" (206).

We find the same genre overdetermination in the dynamic between Chris and Sylvère in *I Love Dick,* a text that begins with a sushi dinner they share with Dick, "an English cultural critic who's recently relocated from Melbourne

---

That doesn't mean, however, that genre can't also be understood as a compelling and productive form of generality. It's just that in Kraus genre is conceived as overly pre- and proscriptive.

39. Heti has also praised *I Love Dick,* commenting in an interview with Kraus in *The Believer,* "I know there was a time before I read Chris Kraus's *I Love Dick* (in fact, that time was only five years ago), but it's hard to imagine; some works of art do this to you."

40. The Chris-Kraus character in each book changes names. In *I Love Dick* and *Aliens & Anorexia* she is Chris Kraus; in *Torpor* she is Sylvie (Kraus's real-life husband's name is Sylvère Lotringer, so in this case, Kraus has given the Chris-Kraus character the feminine version of her husband's name); and in *Summer of Hate* she is Catt. This obviously thwarts any attempt to read the texts autobiographically, although significant parallels between Kraus and her characters exist. Consequently, I will treat the four different female protagonists in the four different books as loosely the same person. Character details and plot events are repeated and overlap across all four texts in a way that encourages such a reading.

to Los Angeles," in Pasadena, California, on December 3, 1994.[41] After dinner, Chris and Sylvère are nervous about driving to their house in the mountains because of impending snow,[42] so Dick invites them to spend the night at his place. Chris feels like Dick has been making eyes at her over dinner, and back at his house, after more drinks, he seems to be flirting. Nothing happens, but that night she dreams about Dick, and when she and Sylvère wake up in the morning, he's mysteriously gone. For Chris, Dick's absence evokes the lover who slips out unannounced after a one-night stand. Convinced that she and Dick have just shared a "Conceptual Fuck," Chris becomes obsessed with Dick and all that has (or has not) passed between them (21).

Back home, Chris's obsession draws in Sylvère as well, if only because their marriage has suddenly become more alive, more sexual, than it has been in years. They begin writing "Dear Dick" letters (none of which is ever sent) charting the growth of this idée fixe that something deep, complex, and intense occurred that night at Dick's house. Although Chris sees her writing as an opportunity to begin taking her life "quite seriously," she initially only feels qualified to tell "The Dumb Cunt's Tale," the generic story of a woman orbiting around men, their ideas, and their passions (27). Sylvère reinforces this feeling, reimagining himself and Chris as Charles and Emma Bovary while searching for the best genre category to describe Chris's writing: "Adultery in Academe, John Updike meets Marivaux . . . Faculty Wife Throws Herself at Husband's Colleague." As far as Chris is concerned, however, Sylvère's prescriptive attempt to fit their situation and her writing into a predetermined category "presumes that there's something inherently grotesque, unspeakable, about femaleness, desire" (138). This persistent attempt to render her experience and feelings as genre reduces Chris's life to a prewritten, already legible form. But Chris is not performing genre fiction. She isn't writing "Lonely Girl Phenomenology" (137). Instead, as she insists to Dick, "What I'm going through with you is real and happening for the first time" (138). In other words, it's a singularity that can't be understood according to genre convention or character type.

Having escaped the overdeterminations of genre, however, the absolute singularity of Chris's experience also runs up against the tendency to view male artists as "presenters of ideas" and female artists merely as "presenters of themselves" (178). In other words, deeply personal life writing like Chris's is easily dismissed as overly particularized, quirky, or idiosyncratic. It's only

---

41. The real-life Dick is Dick Hebdige, author of, most famously, *Subculture: The Meaning of Style* (1979).

42. They are living in southern California during Sylvère's sabbatical from Columbia, but they shortly return to their home in Thurman, New York, which is where *Torpor*'s Sylvie and Jerome live.

read for its "confessional-therapeutic connotations," and its representational relevance is presumed to extend only to those with a similar set of experiences (Kraus, *Where Art Belongs* 82–83). "To be female still means being trapped within the purely psychological," Chris writes to Dick. "No matter how dispassionate or large a vision of the world a woman formulates, whenever it includes her own experience and emotion, the telescope's turned back on her. Because emotion's just so terrifying the world refuses to believe that it can be pursued as discipline, as form. Dear Dick, I want to make the world more interesting than my problems. Therefore, I have to make my problems social" (196). Chris's challenge, then, which is also Kraus's task in all four of her novels-from-life, involves making the singular larger than itself. Or, as Chris understands Hannah Wilke's work to be asking: "If women have failed to make 'universal' art because we're trapped within the 'personal,' why not universalize the 'personal' and make it the subject of our art?" (211). Far from purging self from text, then, Kraus descends into the self, but only to produce a text, a work of art, that is substantially more than that self. Kraus's relentless chronicling of personal feeling escapes the individualized specificity of the Rousseauian confessional subject, instead yielding a text with a strong claim on the literary, philosophical, and artistic.

Crucially, Kraus doesn't universalize the personal by simply assuming, as centuries of male artists have, that their personal experiences exemplify universal truths.[43] Instead, the extensive and intimate personal disclosure we find in her texts functions "not as personal narcissism but as a means of escaping the limits of 'self,'" as a decreation of the self that arises when the whole self, in all its chaotic glory, is exposed in art (*Where Art Belongs* 83). This is why it would be incorrect to understand this as a representational project committed to the exemplarity of the self. There is no "self" in Kraus's work. Or, as she explains to Dick in an attempt to account for the intense content of her letters, the notion that "art supercedes what's personal" is "a philosophy that serves patriarchy well and [she] followed it more or less for 20 years." After meeting him, however, she's charting an entirely different course (230).

One of the guiding lights of her new pursuit is the early twentieth-century French philosopher Simone Weil, who observes, "The chief element of value in the soul is its *impersonality*" (*Aliens* 70). For Kraus, critics' and scholars' failure to understand the committedly impersonal nature of Weil's writing explains why they consistently misread her anorexia as a symptom of a mas-

---

43. Elsewhere in *I Love Dick*, Chris suggests that many male authors use the third person to suggest the universality of the experiences their texts represent, but she views "the 'serious' contemporary hetero-male novel [as] a thinly veiled Story of Me, as voraciously consumptive as all of patriarchy" (72). Chris's use of the first person rends that veil, admitting the personal even as it doesn't content itself with the *merely* personal.

ochistic narcissism they see fueling her work, as a particularizing specificity mitigating the significance of her philosophical thought. For Kraus, however, there's no reason not to treat her anorexia as a philosophical concept in its own right. "So long as anorexia is read exclusively in relation to the subject's feelings towards her own body," Kraus writes, "it can never be conceived of as an active, ontological state" (162). But if Weil's philosophical goal involves destroying the "I" to understand the *impersonal* truth of the human, or what in Heti I described as generic humanity, then we have to read her anorexic "self-destruction . . . as strategic" (50). In Kraus's work, the same is true of her protagonists' intense emotions, chaotic feelings, and erotic desires, which, like Weil's anorexia, one might be tempted to read as symptoms of a masochistic narcissism fueling Kraus's work, but which actually ground her attempt to think feeling as a philosophical project, as a path to a more generalized conception of the human. Kraus identifies a similarly impersonal sensibility in Paul Thek's installation art, which "argu[es] for a state of decreation, a plateau at which a person might, with all their will and consciousness, become a thing," and also in sadomasochism, which she describes as "the only yardstick left for measuring the will-to-decrease" (70).

Initially, when Chris and Sylvère are both writing letters to Dick in an effort to engage him in a loosely conceived performance art project about their growing obsession, the writing doesn't decrease the self. These are the letters—catalogued in "Scenes from a Marriage," *I Love Dick*'s first of two sections—that Sylvère understands via his preconceived genre categories, but against which Chris eventually rebels when, unbeknownst to Sylvère, she sends Dick a fax asking if they can meet privately. Up until this point, Sylvère understood himself to be coauthoring a performance art project with Chris, but after Chris sends the secret fax, "Sylvère couldn't help thinking Chris had betrayed the form they'd both invented" (67). But sensing that "writing is the only possible escape to freedom" (78), Chris has already begun thinking quite differently about the project, and in the text's second section, "Every Letter is a Love Letter," her letters to Dick become a platform for self-decreation through radical self-exposure. Chris explains the idea in a letter to Dick responding to his writing about art: "I disagree with you, obviously about the frame. You argue[44] that the frame provides coherence only through repression and exclusion. But the trick is to discover *Everything* within the frame" (133).[45]

---

44. I suspect that Chris has in mind here the fifth chapter of Hebdige's *Subculture*.

45. *I Love Dick* includes a brilliant discussion of an R. J. Kitaj painting, *John Ford on His Deathbed*, that aptly exemplifies a frame that includes everything. "The painting," Chris explains, "is a chronicle of a life's events . . . but these events are splayed like life, chaotic and abstracted. All the dissonance is drawn together in a frame that can contain them not through

The frame is one clear way that works of art assert their aesthetic autonomy.[46] By excluding everything outside the frame, the artwork separates and distinguishes itself, establishing its formal aesthetic autonomy from the heteronomies of life and world. Sylvère speaks this language when he complains that Chris has "betrayed the form" of their project, and Chris even speaks this language when she tells Dick that she wants to pursue emotion "as discipline, as form." But Chris's desire to include everything inside the frame also indicates that she has a slightly different understanding of aesthetic form and the disciplinary frames that delineate it. Including everything inside the frame undoes the mutually exclusive relationship between aesthetic autonomy and heteronomy. If you take the totality of a singular life and put it inside the frame, then you're not just refusing to distinguish between autonomy and heteronomy, you're also claiming a broader significance for the idiosyncratic particularity of your life, the kind of broadly meaningful significance usually reserved for the aesthetically autonomous artwork. This approach blows past any dialectical balancing or synthesizing of aesthetic autonomy and heteronomy, and instead imagines a "surface of equivalence" where each has collapsed into the other, thereby rendering the distinction moot. Including all of Chris's singularities—her obsessions, idiosyncrasies, desires, and emotions—inside the frame allows them to signify more broadly, as form, or as contributing to a more general understanding of the human type. In this way, Chris's writing adds to the *langue* of life, contributing new content to an already capacious distribution of the sensible and thereby expanding possible ways of being.

For Kraus, the form that's best able to include "*everything* in the frame," the form that can expand the *langue* of life in a way that might give Heti more life options than fellating Nazis, is the case study.[47] In fact, while Sylvère and Dick can only read Chris's life as a set of genre conventions, Chris wants to name her collection of letters *I Love Dick: A Case Study* (153). The case study is the opposite of genre. If genre provides a set of predetermined forms through which individual experience becomes codified, then the case study offers the totality of a specific case as an opportunity to discern the generic generalities it embodies. Those larger generalities are then added to the already existing set of knowledge we have about ways of being in the world, and life changes accordingly. Or as one social science handbook on case study observes, "People can learn much that is general from single cases. They do that partly because they are familiar with other cases and they add this one in

---

magic but through Ford's formidable self-invented will" (202–3). Kraus could very easily be writing about her own work here.

46. See Walter Benn Michaels's "The Force of a Frame."

47. Lauren Berlant's "On the Case" explicitly links case study methodology to a general/singular mode of value production.

thus making a slightly new group from which to generalize, a new opportunity to modify old generalizations" (Stake 85).[48] This isn't a particular functioning as an exemplary representation of the universal; it's a singularity expanding a general field of knowledge.[49] Crucially for Kraus's project, because the case study can only expand the general when it has all the facts, once it captures the totality of an experience, it welcomes the chaotic messiness of the personal. Everything counts. As Chris explains to Dick over an awkward dinner, "The more particular the information, the more likely it will be a paradigm." If "the only way to understand the large is through the small," then it becomes crucial that the small not only include everything but also that it achieves complete honesty (154). Despite including everything, then, the case study achieves a formal coherence that points us toward a broader generality. It's a formal mode by which the individual understands herself as part of "the rest" and asserts the broader, philosophical significance of her life by adding it to the general field. By "universaliz[ing] the 'personal' and mak[ing] it the subject of . . . art" (*I Love Dick* 211), by "examin[ing] things coolly, [by] thrust[ing] experience out of one's own brain and put[ting] it on the table," by "refusing the realm of abject memoir/confession . . . [and] treat[ing] female experience universally" (*Video Green* 63), by "handl[ing] vulnerability like philosophy, at some remove" (*I Love Dick* 208), Kraus's work expands the possible ways that people, and art, might be in the twenty-first century.[50]

One of the primary techniques Kraus deploys to understand the large through the small involves the deft manipulation of temporality in her work. Although each novel ostensibly treats a discrete timeframe from Kraus's life, within each frame, she unmoors time and history from the lived chronology of her life and manages to "discover *Everything* within the frame." Because she doesn't really adopt this approach until halfway through *I Love Dick,* the first half of the novel proceeds chronologically, according to the dated letters she and Sylvère write to Dick. The dates continue in the second half of the novel, but the content each date frames includes entire decades of time and history,

---

48. See the double issue of *Critical Inquiry,* vol. 33 (Summer and Fall 2007), edited by Lauren Berlant, that investigates the form and function of case study across many disciplines. As Berlant writes in her introduction to the first issue, "The case is always normative but also always a perturbation in the normative" ("On the Case" 670). That doubleness is what I hope to capture by conjoining Heti and Kraus in this chapter. Heti struggles with normativity while Kraus perturbs it.

49. In this spirit, Kraus explains in an interview with Anna Poletti that her writing could be read as anthropology (133–34).

50. As Kraus's language in these passages suggests, she obviously doesn't adhere to the distinction between universal and general that I'm trying to maintain throughout this book. I'd suggest, though, that when she talks about "treating female experience universally," she means something akin to what I'm describing as an expansion of a generalized notion of humanity that abjures the logic of particular and universal.

or what Rancière might describe as "a multiplicity of folds in the sensory fabric of the common." In these later letters, the emotional intensity she feels for Dick becomes a jumping off point for amalgamating a diverse array of meditations on art, culture, history, and geography—that is, everything.

To take just one example, a chapter in *I Love Dick* titled "Route 126" begins outside the letter form, with conventional narration, but the text is still directed at Dick: "It's taken me eleven months to write this letter since our visit. Here's how it began" (140). We then read the beginning of a letter dated February 24, 1995, followed by a brief justification of the letter's temporal and physical expansiveness: "Ann Rower says 'When you're writing in real time you have to revise a lot.' By this I think she means that every time you try and write the truth it changes. More happens. Information constantly expands" (140). After this explanation, we find the actual letter, properly dated January 17, 1996, eleven months after the initial letter. The content of that letter begins three months prior to her ever encountering Dick (September 1994), on a plane to Guatemala where Chris will meet and interview a hunger striker, Jennifer Harbury. Chris narrates some of the Guatemala trip, digressing frequently into the history of the Guatemalan civil war, and then in the next section, the letter returns to the present ("This letter's taken almost a year to write . . .) but then immediately slips into an indeterminate moment in the past that begins the narration of the one time she went to Dick's house and they had sex ("On Thursday night I got off a plane from JFK to LAX. I was going to your house" [144]), although that story also quickly digresses: "Eleven weeks ago I'd tailed your gorgeous car along 5 North . . ." (145). Consequently, when, on the next page, she writes, "And now I'm heading out to visit you again alone," the specific temporal moment that "now" references has grown difficult to pin down. No mind, however, since we are promptly transported back to Guatemala, with more digressions into Harbury's past, and then further back to 1940s California, and then 1980s suburban California, discussing the dumping of corpses that inspired *Poltergeist,* which reminds her of Chicano farm workers, which leads her to Rigoberta Menchu's childhood, the national Condor Preserve, and something Nancy Barton recalls about a project that Nan Border made in 1982 about the unsolved murders of eight female hitchhikers. Then, onward to a discussion of the Feminist Art Program at CalArts that Miriam Shapiro founded in 1972, and then back to driving to see Dick, but then back to Guatemala. It really goes on and on like this, and we find the same temporal parataxis in *Aliens & Anorexia* and *Torpor* as well.

While it would be easy to dismiss this as schizophrenic idiosyncrasy (in much the same way that Simone Weil's work is dismissed for its female maladies), this is precisely what Kraus means by case study. The digressions and dislocations, the snippets and snatches, are all part of the *everything* that Kraus packs into the frame, as evidenced when she writes of an overlooked rural New York artist named William Bronk: "While the works in Bronk's collection might seem disparate, they are actually parts of one large body created by a clusterfuck of influence" (*Video Green* 47). And taken together, Bronk's collection "proved that a life full of meaning can happen anywhere, even in this isolate town." This, she says, is "what poetry offers us: a world defiant of bureacro-porn, where people exist and everything counts" (49). And it's precisely by bringing together this *everything* in one amalgamated clusterfuck of a structure that the work decreates the boundaries of the individual—abstracting the specificities of her time and place—and opens up onto more general truths.

Maggie Nelson finds important precedent for such work among the New York School poets, particularly its female members such as Barbara Guest, Bernadette Mayer, Alice Notley, and Eileen Myles. For Nelson, these poets, along with the painter Joan Mitchell, practice a distinctly female form of abstraction generally associated with the New York School—Nelson calls it "the feminine abstract" (*Women* xix)—that transmutes "a flood of personal details" (xviii) into "primary, originary forms" (xxii). Much as we saw in Heti, such abstraction only becomes possible once you accept that your individuality makes you generic, not unique. Eileen Myles captures this in her claim to be "writing out of female anonymity" (xxvi), and Chris echoes the sentiment in a letter to Dick: "For years I tried to write but the compromises of my life made it impossible to inhabit a position. . . . Embracing you & failure's changed all that [']cause now I know I'm no one. And there's a lot to say" (221). This is Chris's "Who cares?" moment. "Is there any greater freedom," she wonders, "than not caring anymore what certain people in NY think of me?" (81).[51] Or as Nelson puts it, disavowing the notion that everyone is special and important allows authors of female abstraction to capture "the fact of feeling" rather than the specificity of individual emotion (104). In effect, being nobody serves as the foundation for accessing and expanding the broader, more general truths of humanity that provide life meaning beyond its singularity. The decreated individual isn't exemplary or representative but is instead a wellspring for expanding who we are and what we can be.

Politics after Formal Homology

But do any of these generalized abstractions resonate politically? After all, Nelson indicates that the path to a generalized truth of humanity runs directly

---

51. Remember that Heti's "Who cares?" moment comes in a chapter titled "What Is Freedom?"

through "not caring," a major theme that she identifies at the heart of the New York School aesthetic. From Frank O'Hara's "lack of interest in affecting, much less revolutionizing, the culture at large" (69) to Myles's self-negation and debasement, which we've of course also seen in Kraus, who explicitly describes her feelings for Dick as a case of "not giving a fuck" (28), the absolute refusal to take the self seriously (even as the self is immersed in serious stuff) makes possible this deft move from the personal to the general. But does it also permit a similar move from the personal to the political?

Not exactly—at least, not in any way that might homologously link the case-studied self to an easily recognizable political position or set of commitments. After all, at one point Chris actually justifies her embrace of case study with an icky echo of neoliberal selfhood, telling Dick, "I want to own everything that happens to me now. . . . Because if the only material we have to work with in America is our own lives, shouldn't we be making case studies?" (155). Here Chris seems to accept the *homo œconomicus* model of neoliberal subjectivity, equating case study with an entrepreneurial self-fashioning responsible for, among other things, the contemporary gig economy. But owning everything that happens to her and treating her own life as building material doesn't necessarily mean that she's adopting a neoliberal sense of self. After all, *homo œconomicus* believes in the absolute and inherent value of the self, while Kraus makes the opposite claim, insisting on the completely empty value of her own life. Like Sheila, she knows she's no one. Moreover, the meaning and value of the "everything" included in the case study stems from the act and fact of its inclusion, not from homologously correlating it with something that it's not, like politics.

In other words, case study isn't going to tell us what something means, how it should be valued, whether it's right or wrong, or even how we should feel or think about it. It will, however, show us how and why things happen, how and why things have the values they have. When it comes to a more political concern like the subjugation of women, for example, Chris suggests that the case study offers a way to "expose the conditions of our own debasement" (*I Love Dick* 211), "to reveal the circumstances of one's own objectification" (215). But exposing conditions and revealing circumstances is a primarily descriptive, neutral project. It's not so much an indictment or a critique, much less a utopian vision, as much as it's a way of understanding how we arrived where we are. But for Chris, that counts as politics: "Politics means accepting that things happen for a reason," she writes. "There's a causality behind the flow and if we study hard enough it's possible to understand it. Can politics be articulated in a way that's structural, electric, instead of being dug up again, the boring bit at the bottom of the barrel? I think the clue to this is simultaneity, a sense of wonder at it: that the political can be a PARALLEL SOURCE

OF INFORMATION, & more is more: adding an awareness of politics, how things happen, to the mix can just enhance our sense of how the present is exploding into Now Time" (133). Like the empty, occasional politics of Rancière's distribution of the sensible and Margaux's "even better than political meaning," here politics has no particular ideological value because it's just more of the everything. It's an understanding of "how things happen," not the value things have. If you can really get at the all of something—the framed *everything* of the case study—then you actually have a shot at understanding why things happen as they do. In an example provided in *I Love Dick,* for instance, Chris claims that Henry Frundt's *Refreshing Pauses,* a case study of the Guatemalan Coca-Cola strike in the 1980s, offers "a total reconstruction of events through documents and transcripts" that allows readers "to understand everything about corporate capitalism in third world countries" (53). Again, the case study isn't offering particulars that are representative or exemplary of a universal but is instead providing singularities that help us understand the how and why of broader, more general conditions.

But what might it mean for politics to have similar concerns—for political discourse to replace its interest in whether or not current conditions are right or wrong, just or unjust, progressive or reactionary, with an attempt to understand how and why the current conditions have the values they have? Instead of correlating our world with specific ideological valences, politics would involve generalized understanding derived from the careful study of the world. Homologous thinking grants political significance to a given aesthetic form. (Autonomous art, by severing itself from the world, is anticapitalist; or, participatory art, precisely because it requires audience participation, is radically democratic.) But a politics derived from forms of generality, a politics grounded in the how and why of the world, doesn't stake out a position on capitalism, radical democracy, or any other political/ideological form. As a form without any corresponding politics, case study makes this kind of non-homologizing politics of generality possible. Form thus becomes irrelevant as an index of political value, but it remains a potent way to produce an understanding of conditions and circumstances while revealing new truths about the world.

CHAPTER 2

Theory, Metafiction, and Constructivism

Over the past several decades, declarations announcing the end of theory have proliferated as widely as those declaring the end of art. Terry Eagleton's *After Theory* (2003) is perhaps the most famous example, but really, since at least December 1987, when a *New York Times* headline about Paul de Man announced, "Yale Scholar Wrote for Pro-Nazi Newspaper," we have been inhabiting theory's long, hand-wringing twilight.[1] Before I go any further, I should be clear that I'm using "theory" here to name the particular version of deconstructive poststructuralism popularized and institutionalized in US English departments after 1970—a distinct vein of theory responsible for what we now refer to more generally as the linguistic turn in literary and cultural studies.[2] So even though theory and poststructuralism aren't synonymous, and

---

1. Even before the Paul de Man scandal, scholars were anticipating, or perhaps wishing for, theory's demise. See, for example, Walter Benn Michaels and Stephen Knapp's "Against Theory," from 1982, and Howard Felperin's polemical *Beyond Deconstruction: The Uses and Abuses of Literary Theory*, published in 1985.

2. Those announcing theory's demise share this understanding, as we find just as many authors proclaiming the end of poststructuralism and/or deconstruction as we do the end of theory. Thus, in addition to Terry Eagleton's *After Theory*, Thomas Docherty's *After Theory*, Paul Bové's *In the Wake of Theory*, Martin McQuillan's *Post-Theory*, Michael Cook's "The Death of Theory," Jennifer Howard's "The Fragmentation of Literary Theory," and Stephen Metcalf's "The Death of Literary Theory," we find Jeffrey Williams's "The Death of Deconstruction, the End of Theory, and Other Ominous Rumors," Wendell Harris's *Beyond Poststructuralism*, Tilottama Rajan and Michael O'Driscoll's *After Poststructuralism*, and Colin Davis's *After Poststructuralism*.

even though the critical deployment of poststructuralism was often reductive, more caricature than commitment, I'll be using "theory" as shorthand for a cluster of poststructural concepts—the death of the author, the chain of signifiers, *il n'ya pas de hors texte* [there is nothing outside the text], present absence, *différance*, the writerly text—that circulated widely over the course of the twentieth century's concluding decades. The death of theory, then, names the waning influence that these poststructural concepts had for anyone working—as theorist, critic, or author—in language and literature at century's end.

These various theoretical concepts follow from poststructuralism's mandated reflexivity. The insistence that thought think itself—that meaning, knowledge, and understanding constantly interrogate their own conditions of possibility—leads to a set of conceptual forms marked by indeterminacy, deferral, and a blurry relationship between world and word, reality and representation. This reflexive mandate lies at the heart of poststructural theory. (As I'll explain later, it also lies at the heart of postmodern metafiction.) In the essay that effectively births poststructuralism out of structuralism, for example, Derrida deconstructs and moves beyond structuralism by folding structuralism back on itself, demanding that it think its own conditions of possibility, or what Derrida describes as "the structurality of structure" ("Structure" 279).[3] If structuralism is a theory that describes the production of value within closed structures, then Derrida demands that structuralism consider the structures that produce *its* value. What structures the structures? According to Derrida, once structuralism asks this question and reflexively applies its own insights to itself, structuralism will realize that its supposedly closed structures have no logically justifiable foundation and are actually predicated on an evasive absence, an unaccounted-for blind spot at their center. The structure that acknowledges this ineradicable absence, that admits its ungrounded grounding, becomes poststructural: or, a structure that, having reflected on its own structurality, incorporates its recognition of the constitutive absence at its center into its own self-understanding. That's what I mean by mandated reflexivity.

For Roland Barthes, such reflexive thinking is not just required by poststructuralism; it's the defining aspect of theory itself. As he explains in a 1971 interview with Stephen Heath:

> Julia Kristeva's work is considered theoretical; it *is* theoretical. However, it is
> considered theoretical in the sense of *abstract, difficult*, because it is believed

---

3. Explicitly engaging Ferdinand de Saussure's *Course in General Linguistics*, Derrida also delivers a foundational deconstruction of structuralism in *Of Grammatology's* second and third chapters.

that theory is abstraction and difficulty. . . . But of course 'theoretical' doesn't mean 'abstract'; from my point of view, it means *reflexive,* i.e., turning back on itself: a discourse that looks back on itself is thereby a theoretical discourse. After all, the eponymous hero, the mythical hero of theory could be Orpheus, precisely because he is the one who looks back on what he loves, even at the risk of destroying it; in looking back at Eurydice, he makes her vanish, he kills her a second time. This retrospection *must be done,* even at the cost of destruction. ("Interview" 144)

Here Barthes not only correlates theory with reflexivity, but he also mandates reflexivity *at any cost.* The destruction of love, of knowledge, of philosophy: small prices to pay for the larger truths (about the absence of foundational truth) such reflexive interrogation makes possible. Working from Barthes's understanding of theory, then, we can say that the end of theory describes the end of a very specific kind of intellectual reflexivity. Not just self-consciousness or self-awareness, but an act of self-reflection that undoes the intelligible coherence of the object being reflected *and* the act of reflection itself—like an uroboros, which, upon swallowing its own tail, finds itself punctured and spiraling, a symbol not of unified wholeness but of the impossibility of wholeness. The end of theory is the end of that hall-of-mirrors spiraling, the end of a folding back that unmoors, or even destroys.

This chapter will be particularly interested in the way theory's end, the decline of mandated reflexivity, plays out in contemporary fiction. If much postmodern fiction from theory's heyday embraced this mandated reflexivity, how does fiction respond after the end of theory, when reflexive thought is no longer the sine qua non of intellectual rigor? As I'll describe at length in what follows, I focus on contemporary fiction written after the end of theory that nevertheless integrates an array of theoretical forms and concepts into itself. Why, if theory is supposedly dead, do we still find its concepts alive and well in so much contemporary fiction? Are authors today, writing after the end of theory, using theory in a different way than it was used by authors writing in an earlier age of peak theory? The short answer: yes. The long answer: just as we saw the conceptual impasse between aesthetic autonomy and heteronomy induce a vacillation in the relation between aesthetic form and politics that prompted many to herald the end of art, thereby setting the stage for authors like Sheila Heti and Chris Kraus to rethink the politics of aesthetic form in terms of singularity and generality, theory's insistently reflexive forms, once homologously linked to an illusion-busting, emancipatory politics, also suffer a vacillation in the form-politics relationship, prompting many to declare the end of theory and setting the stage for contemporary authors to rethink the potential politics of theory's forms in constructive rather than deconstructive terms.[4]

In the period of theory's dominance stretching from the 1970s to the beginning of the 1990s, literary fiction pursued its own reflexive mandate, manifest most notably in the proliferation of experimental metafiction: John Barth's *Lost in the Funhouse* (1968), John Fowles's *The French Lieutenant's Woman* (1969), Raymond Federman's *Double or Nothing* (1971), Angela Carter's *The Infernal Desire Machines of Dr. Hoffman* (1972), Ishmael Reed's *Mumbo Jumbo* (1972), Robert Coover's *The Public Burning* (1977), Italo Calvino's *If on a Winter's Night* (1979), Umberto Eco's *The Name of the Rose* (1980), Salman Rushdie's *Midnight's Children* (1981), Kathy Acker's *Great Expectations* (1982), J. M. Coetzee's *Foe* (1986), Paul Auster's *New York Trilogy* (1987), Trey Ellis's *Platitudes* (1988), A. S. Byatt's *Possession* (1990), Tim O'Brien's *The Things They Carried* (1990), and Jeanette Winterson's *Written on the Body* (1992), to name a few. These texts are actively reflexive. They heed theory's demand that language interrogate its own conditions of possibility, and their metafictional forms follow directly from that interrogation. "At this point the story grows obscure," we read in the final pages of Auster's *City of Glass,* a sentence that collapses word and world by simultaneously referring to the story the narrator traces inside the text and to the fiction we hold in our hands (200).

Now, I'm not suggesting that Paul Auster was so inspired by *Of Grammatology* that he sat down and wrote *City of Glass.* In fact, in a 1993 interview with Chris Pace, Auster claims to have never even read Derrida. Thus, although some scholars view "postmodernist metafiction as a programmatic thematization . . . of post-structural theory" (Quendler 121), it is perhaps more accurate to view "poststructuralism and metafiction" as "reciprocal[ly] relevant" (Currie 3, 8).[5] Best to say that theory influences metafiction in different ways and in varying degrees depending on the author. As far as novelist and critic David Lodge is concerned, for example, poststructural work from the likes of Derrida and Lacan is "so opaque and technical in its language that the first glance—baffled, angry, or derisive—is likely to be the last one" (148). On

---

4. In its broadest terms, then, these authors' constructive deployment of otherwise deconstructive theoretical concepts aligns with those "projects of building" (as opposed to the "ubiquity of unsettling and unmaking" that defines contemporary theory and criticism) that Anna Kornbluh champions in *The Order of Forms* (4).

5. Also see Katie Muth's "Postmodern Fiction as Poststructuralist Theory." Muth doesn't focus on metafiction per se, but she makes a compelling case for the profound influence of poststructuralism on "anti-realist" literary experimentation like Acker's. Also see Josh Toth's *The Passing of Postmodernism,* which notes the "hardly . . . coincidental co-development of anti-foundationalist and language-focused sentiments" in both poststructural theory and postmodern metafiction (42).

the other hand, the self-reflexive narrator in John Fowles's *French Lieutenant's Woman* observes nearly two decades earlier that the novel he's writing "cannot be a novel in the modern sense of the word" because he "lives in the age of Alain Robbe-Grillet and Roland Barthes" (80). Regardless of the level of direct influence, however, we can safely say that theory and metafiction in the final decades of the twentieth century were both committedly theoretical to the extent that both were, to use Barthes's language, discourses that looked back on themselves reflexively, even at the risk of deformation and destruction. Metafictional authors weren't necessarily *applying* poststructuralism to fiction, but they were awash in the same pool of intellectual history that viewed reflexivity as compulsory intellectual practice.

Over the course of the 1990s and well into the twenty-first century, however, both theory and fiction grew less theoretical, in the reflexive sense of that term. As theory waned, so too did postmodern metafiction. In the literary field, one important trigger for that decline is surely David Foster Wallace's 1993 "E Unibus Pluram," which famously registers Wallace's exhaustion with metafiction, indicting its reflexivity as little more than a wry, hip pose complicit with televisual consumer culture. As many before me have discussed, Wallace's call for a literature that "treat[s] of plain old untrendy human troubles and emotions in U.S. life with reverence and conviction" (81), prompts a turn in contemporary fiction toward realism, memoir, genre fiction, and historical fiction.[6] But I'm less interested in the various realisms that develop in theory's wake than I am in a collection of texts that, even after the end of theory, continue to look a lot like postmodern metafiction without actually being postmodern metafiction. These texts bear all the markings of theoretical (i.e., reflexive) metafiction—opaque signifiers, dead authors, worlds reduced to text, deferred or indeterminate meanings, and empowered readers—without any of the loopy reflexivity that we find in the likes of Auster, Barth, Calvino, Ellis, Federman, Rushdie, and so on. Turning against the linguistic turn, this new generation of authors deploys these now-dead theoretical conceits to achieve literary ends that are entirely antithetical to those pursued by an earlier generation of postmodern metafiction writers. Instead of collapsed foundations and endless play in a world of pure, textual artifice, these texts use the well-known tropes of poststructural theory as the tools and building blocks for various forms of unreal realism, for speculative fictions that contribute to the composition rather than the deconstruction of the world. I'll be describ-

---

6. For good descriptions of these various turns, see Alison Shonkwiler and Leigh Claire La Berge's *Reading Capitalist Realism*, Madhu Dubey's "Post-Postmodern Realism?," Robert McLaughlin's "Post-Postmodern Discontent," Andrew Hoberek's "Literary Genre Fiction," Lee Konstantinou's "Neorealist Fiction," and Günter Leypoldt's "Recent Realist Fiction."

ing this distinct deployment of theoretical conceits as "theoretical literalism." We can find this literal approach to theory's undead forms in texts such as Laird Hunt's *The Impossibly* (2001); Percival Everett's *Erasure* (2001), *I am Not Sydney Poitier* (2009), and *Virgil Russell by Percival Everett* (2013); Ben Marcus's *Notable American Women* (2002) and *The Flame Alphabet* (2012); Nicole Krauss's *The History of Love* (2005); Salvador Plascencia's *The People of Paper* (2005); Jonathan Safran Foer's *Everything is Illuminated* (2002), *Extremely Loud & Incredibly Close* (2005), and *Tree of Codes* (2010); Junot Diaz's *The Brief and Wondrous Life of Oscar Wao* (2007); David Foster Wallace's *The Pale King* (2011); Mat Johnson's *Pym* (2011); Ben Lerner's *Leaving Atocha Station* (2011), *10:04* (2014), and *The Topeka School* (2019); Ruth Ozeki's *A Tale for the Time Being* (2013); Rachel Cusk's *Outline* (2014); and George Saunders's *Lincoln in the Bardo* (2017). At first glance, many of these books about books look quite similar to the postmodern metafiction of the 1960s, '70s, and '80s. And yet, we would be incorrect to think that these contemporary authors bear the same relation to theory as their postmodern forebears. Writing after the end of theory, in the wake of mandated reflexivity, these authors decline to turn theory's conceptual forms against fiction itself. They refuse to collapse world into word and instead use theory's increasingly defunct concepts to innovate forms of contemporary fiction that highlight the material presence and positive effects of language.

The End of Theory

So why exactly does theory, at least in its poststructural, necessarily reflexive form, wane in the 1990s?[7] Scholars have proffered many explanations. In 1998 Marjorie Levinson argued that, in the final accounting, "the pursuit of reflexive knowledge"—which, at the time, she viewed as "axiomatic for scholarship in the humanities"—had not produced significant tangible outcomes ("Posthumous" 266). In a similar vein, Rey Chow observes that the differences marking lived experience (i.e., hierarchical and oppressive differences that designate the inequalities of class, race, geography, sexuality, etc.) could

---

7. In *Theory after "Theory,"* Derek Attridge and Jane Elliott describe theory's "afterlife," a ghostly, poststructural residue that continues to haunt critical thought, but they also note the new commitments—affect, things, ecology, spirituality—that theory has adopted since its poststructuralist heyday (1). Also see Jason Potts and Daniel Stout's *Theory Aside,* a collection that explores the paths that theory could have taken but didn't. It's also worth noting here that some scholars continue to engage and deploy poststructural methodologies well after theory's end. See, for example, Julian Wolfreys's *Literature, In Theory.*

not be incorporated and resolved into the signifying chain of differences that defined theoretical thought (184). Theory, like politics, might be preoccupied with difference, but the thinking just never translated successfully to more material concerns. Add to these critiques a gradual shift in the humanities' preferred objects of study—from texts, signifiers, ideology, and meaning, to biology, technology, science, and bodies—along with the increasing irrelevance of theory in an age of big data (why speculate theoretically when algorithms and data structures can deliver quantifiable truths?), and theory's decline feels almost inevitable and unsurprising.

Without mitigating the significance of these various explanations for the end of theory, I want to focus in particular on how the truth of truth's inaccessibility—the message of radical openness and indeterminacy distilled from poststructuralism's constitutive absences and deconstructed centers—gradually stopped registering as emancipatory and radical, and began instead to appear complicit and conservative. Even as influential scholars such as Henry Louis Gates Jr., Judith Butler, Edward Said, Gayatri Spivak, and Homi Bhabha successfully enlisted poststructural theory to political ends (at least conceptually), others were observing that theory's fluid chains of signifiers and other antifoundational forms looked disturbingly similar to the unbridled flow of global capital in a neoliberal age.[8] Those same poststructural forms of thought homologously linked to liberatory politics were just as easily linked by formal homology to the logic of late capitalism. In this way, theory experienced a vacillation in its form-politics relationship similar to the one the previous chapter described in the field of art: for some, the antifoundationalism resulting from theoretical self-reflexivity looked like a progressive strike against the ossified hierarchies of thought that perpetuate injustice and inequality, but for others that same antifoundationalism created a world of indeterminate value ripe for exploitation by increasingly financialized forms of capital. Consequently, once the "theoretical landscape [was] no longer united by the perception of a definitive link between epistemological indeterminacy and political freedom," Elliott and Attridge explain, a commitment to theory began to seem potentially at odds with a commitment to social justice, liberty, and equality (4).[9] According to Jeffrey Nealon, this potential correlation between

---

8. Fredric Jameson makes an early version of this point throughout *Postmodernism*, and it's a major focus of Jeffrey Nealon's *Post-Postmodernism*. Also see Brian Massumi's "Perception Attack" and Elizabeth Povinelli's "The Persistence of Hope."

9. Of course, theory had to fight hard to establish its politically leftist *bona fides*, as its dense abstractions, at first glance, appeared entirely apolitical. See Barbara Christian's "The Race for Theory" for a paradigmatic indictment of theory's inherently apolitical, and perhaps even racist, logic.

theory and capital has only intensified in the ensuing decades. Observing that "the glory years for humanities theory in North America coincided with economic neoliberalism's rise" (171) and that "the dominant logic of economics in the neoliberal revolution years has in many ways been isomorphic . . . with the cultural logic of the humanities and the rise of theory" (173), Nealon ultimately concludes that "theory is neoliberal" (174).

If, as Nealon suggests, theory has, over the course of a couple of decades, entirely reversed itself, ricocheting from one formal homology (between poststructural forms and liberatory politics) to another (between poststructural forms and neoliberal politics), then how should we conceive the political value of theory? For Nealon, the replacement of one homologous relationship with another requires us to operate within the reality of the new homology between theory and neoliberal capital. It's so totalizing and inescapable that there's no point trying to think outside it. Revealing and critiquing the homology no longer has any political effect, and so rather than worrying or expressing moral outrage about it, Nealon follows Jameson's lead and treats it as "axiomatic," as the necessary "starting point," "not the conclusion of," our contemporary cultural analyses (176). That all seems basically correct to me, but instead of accepting this new homology ("theory is neoliberal") as our current, axiomatic condition of possibility, I want to view the ease with which the homology between theory and liberatory politics turned into a homology between theory and neoliberalism as evidence of the problems with homologous thinking in general. If the homology between theory and liberatory politics that supercharged humanities scholarship in the 1980s and early 1990s can so easily register as a homology between theory and neoliberalism in the 2000s and 2010s, then perhaps the original homology was never as viable as we thought. Theory's vacillating form-politics homology might even lead us to conclude, not that we should accept as axiomatic today's apparent homology between theory and neoliberalism, but that we should work to conceive theory's value in new, nonpolitically homologous ways. The many authors and theorists discussed in this chapter do just that, primarily by developing more general forms of thought—which I will describe as being constructivist in nature[10]—that sidestep the politically homologous thinking that defined theory's rise and eventual fall.

Or, we should take such vacillation in the political valence of theoretical forms of thought as evidence that the implications—political and otherwise—of theory's mandated reflexivity are (and always were) contextually and

---

10. I use "constructive" here in the most common sense of the word, to indicate a building up or adding to. I don't intend any connection to constructivist art and/or architecture. I might also have used the word "positivist," except for all the baggage that word carries with it.

historically contingent. In the 1970s and '80s, when essentialist thinking still permeated left-wing political projects, theory's antifoundationalism seemed to push that work in more radical directions. Today, however, when indeterminacy and slippery signifiers reign, when technology and capital unmoor referential stability and undermine all systems of coherent value production from the moment a child caresses her first screen, it's not surprising that theory's reflexive forms appear perfectly complicit with the neoliberal economic dominant.

This idea, that theory might be historicized and its shifting political valences explained accordingly, seems obvious, but it's actually quite at odds with the overarching, universalizing project of theory and its deployment in the decades of its late twentieth-century ascendance. Of course, in its proper form, poststructural theory deconstructed universals and annihilated metaphysics. In its practical deployment, however, there was always this inclination for scholars to treat poststructural insights as metaphysical, universal truths. "*That's* not how meaning works," they'd tell us, "*This* is how meaning works." This habit of turning the indeterminacy of metaphysics into a metaphysics of indeterminacy is what Stanley Fish refers to as the "anti-foundationalist paradox"—the temptation to treat the absence of foundations as a new foundation, or, our desire to tell our students, "Ye shall know that truth is not what it seems and *that* truth shall set you free" (Quoted in Hutcheon, *Poetics* 13). As Fish's ironic quip suggests, this tendency to make a metaphysics of the antimetaphysical, a foundation of the antifoundational, also emerged as a desire to ascribe a necessary and inevitable political outcome to theory's mandated reflexivity: freedom. But of course, we should no more make a metaphysics of theory's form-politics homology than we should of its antimetaphysical claims. Over the course of the 1980s and early '90s, it was perhaps just too tempting not to, particularly since theory at the time was consistently assailed for its apparently apolitical abstractions. But now that the politics of theory's forms have reversed themselves, flipping from freedom to neoliberal complicity, we can see just how nonsensical it is to ascribe anything more than a *historically contingent* politics to any given form of theoretical thought. There is no necessary or inevitable relation between form and politics. There is nothing inherently political about any given conceptual form. Rather, the relationship between form and politics can be configured and reconfigured in different ways at different times, but nothing political follows necessarily from theory's specific forms.

The passage from Barthes with which this chapter began, where he insists that theory's reflexive turning back on itself "*must be done,* even at the cost of destruction," actually displays an awareness of theory's historical contingency even as it implies that theory's reflexive truths are more true than previous forms of truth. If we keep reading, Barthes admits that he views theory's mandated reflexivity "as corresponding to a very definite historical phase in Western societies." (That's the historical contingency bit.) But then, a Hegelian metaphysics intrudes when he describes that phase as "a scientific phase, a phase in the wisdom of our society (a phase eminently superior, of course, to the infantile phase that coexists with it and consists in not reflecting on language, in speaking without turning language back upon itself, in manipulating a kind of simpleton's language: obviously, this refusal to turn language back upon itself is an open invitation of major ideological impostures)" ("Interview" 144). To the extent that Barthes recognizes the formal demands of theoretical thought as a historical phase, he acknowledges its nonuniversalizable contingency. But to the extent that he views this phase as "eminently superior" to all earlier phases, even granting it the political power to avoid and reveal the "ideological imposture" of "simpletons," he's clearly tempted to make a metaphysics, and a critical politics, of theory's reflexive mandate.

If you view theory's self-reflexive conceptual forms as "eminently superior" to a more "infantile phase" of thought, however, then when they gradually become the preferred forms of neoliberal capital, you're going to have quite a mess on your hands. But if you understand theory's reflexive mandate as a contingent conceptual formation, as generally but not universally true, then you also realize that any homology between politics and theory's forms is similarly contingent and certainly not the result of some necessarily political feature of theoretical reflexivity. In turn, when those forms begin to align more with neoliberal capital than with radical forms of leftist freedom, the end of theory isn't so much a crisis as it is just another historically contingent phenomenon, another thing happening in the world. It might even be an opportunity to reimagine theory's value beyond the homologous relations its conceptual forms may or may not have with political thought.

The End of Metafiction

The theoretically inclined literature of the period hews to a similar course. Instead of the metafiction of the 1970s and '80s that heeded theory's reflexive mandate and rigorously interrogated its own conditions of possibility, fiction at the turn of the twenty-first century began to treat metafiction's reflexive imperative as a historically contingent phenomenon. As we've already seen in the above discussion of theory's decline, authors of metafiction writing at the end of the twentieth century also confront a vacillation in the form-politics homology that an older generation of authors sought to establish between metafiction's formal challenge to "the fundamental structures of narrative fiction" and its attendant revelation of the "fictionality of the world outside the literary fictional text" (Waugh 2). Converting its critique of "outworn literary conventions into the basis of a potentially constructive social criticism" (11), earlier champions of metafiction didn't just attack literary realism, they challenged status quo reality itself. (William Gass, credited with first using the term *metafiction,* defines it as "fiction which draws attention to itself as artefact to pose questions about the relationship between fiction and reality" [25].) Highlighting the political potential of reflexive thought, for example, Robert Siegle offers a full-blown endorsement of metafiction's liberatory political potential: "The oppressed at the moment they achieve a reflexive or revolutionary sense of themselves—the two often amount to the same thing—begin to see the class in power as comic in its pretentiousness, ensconced in power only by the vagaries of chance, and naively unaware how fragile, arbitrary, and temporary is its place in the ultimate scheme of things" (244).

Needless to say, this reflexive/revolutionary consciousness never quite materialized, which is why a contemporary author like Percival Everett looks back at this project not just as a contingent historical phenomenon, but also as a little ridiculous. In *Erasure,* for example, Everett stages a conversation between a self-proclaimed champion of "postmodern fiction," Davis Gimbel, and a very skeptical interlocutor. Reluctant to abandon the political promise of metafictional form, the experimental postmodernist insists, "I have unsettled readers. I have made them uncomfortable. I have unsettled their historical, cultural and psychological assumptions by disrupting their comfortable relationship between words and things. I have brought to a head the battle between language and reality. But even as my art dies, I create it without trying" (37). In part, Gimbel's metafictional art is dying at the end of the twentieth century because it never "unsettled" readers in the ways he asserts. Naïve, ideologically mystified readers weren't picking up experimental postmodern fiction in the first place. But also, as Josh Toth explains, the antifoundational politics associated with metafiction's reflexive forms were never reliably leftist and always had a tendency to turn into their opposite. Arguing that "postmodernism's very strategies have become . . . aligned with the very thing they sought to undermine: fundamentalism (in all its forms)" (113), Toth suggests that the "failure of postmodern metafiction" is "a failure to avoid becoming or, at the very least, *seeming* entangled in the totalizing impulse . . . it claimed to repudiate" (116). "The corrosively self-reflexive works of postmodernism,"

Toth concludes, are "necessarily haunted by the very specter they attempted to exorcise: the specter of a telos, the specter of positivism, the specter of humanism" (136).[11]

Consequently, in much the same way that theory's mandated reflexivity comes to be seen as a contingent historical phenomenon rather than a universal truth, contemporary fiction writers also gradually turn away from metafictional reflexivity and find new ways to approach both theoretical and literary reflexivity. This turn is just another way to talk about the difference between the set of books, discussed by Judith Ryan in *The Novel after Theory*, which "incorporate theory," "reflect on it, complicate it, and sometimes go beyond it" (7),[12] and the set of books, discussed by Nicholas Dames in "Theory and the Novel," which describe but do not reproduce "the slippery nature of signs" (165). It's also the difference between what I've elsewhere described as "the theory novel" (those texts from the late 1960s, '70s, '80s, and early '90s that practice theory's mandated reflexivity) and the "post-theory theory novel" (those theoretically literal texts written since the late 1990s that deploy poststructural concepts without buying into their antifoundational, aporetic implications).[13]

As Dames explains in his review of an array of such novels—Teju Cole's *Open City* (2011), Jennifer Egan's *A Visit from the Goon Squad* (2011), Ben Lerner's *Leaving the Atocha Station* (2011), Sam Lipsyte's *The Ask* (2010), Lorrie Moore's *A Gate at the Stairs* (2009), and Jeffrey Eugenides's *The Marriage Plot* (2011)—this second set of texts often quite easily absorbs theoretical concepts into a typically realist literary mode. In these novels, Dames suggests, we see realism fighting back against theoretically informed, experimental metafiction, capturing and describing theory's slippery signifiers in the fixed and forthright prose of conventional realism. Dames thus sees the incorporation of poststructural themes and concepts into these novels' content as realism's ultimate defanging of theory. The result—a "strangely conservative and undialectical postmodern utopia" (159)—renders theory "just another thing-in-the-world," "no longer the key to all the world's things" (163–64).

Jeffrey Eugenides's *The Marriage Plot*, a novel with the kind of self-reflexive title that might lead readers to expect a narrative preoccupied with the arti-

---

11. Also see Jeffrey Williams's *Theory and the Novel*, which offers an interestingly conservative take on literary reflexivity, viewing it as a way "to disseminate and propagate an *ethos* of literature, of 'the literary life,' a drive and desire for literature, and finally to reproduce the system of relations of the institution of literature" (22).

12. Ryan's title is a bit confusing. To clarify, she examines the effect theory has on novels (the novel once theory appears on the scene), not the novel after the end of theory, which is where my interest lies.

13. See Huehls, "The Post-Theory Theory Novel."

fice of its own conditions of possibility but which actually turns out to be a perfectly conventional and straightforward piece of realist fiction, exemplifies Dames's point. Opening in the apartment of the allusively named Madeleine Hannah, an undergraduate English major at Brown University in 1982, the novel's opening sentence invites us to "look at all the books" (3). Primarily an exercise in metonymic character development, we are meant to understand that the nineteenth-century novels artfully adorning Madeleine's bedroom—Austen, Dickens, Eliot, and the Brontës—effectively bespeak her true nature. Counterposed to these novels heavy on plot and character, we find the canon of high theory—Derrida, Barthes, Baudrillard, Lyotard, and Foucault—linked to Leonard Bankhead and the semiotics class where he and Madeleine meet and fall in love. (Barthes's *A Lover's Discourse* plays matchmaker.) Mitchell Grammaticus, the religious studies major who stands as the third vertex in *The Marriage Plot*'s rather scalene love triangle (he never stands a chance against the darkly brooding Leonard), carries an entirely different canon in his backpack: William James, Thomas Merton, Saint Teresa, and Paul Tillich. Having pegged each character to a distinct reading list, Eugenides follows the generic conventions of the nineteenth-century marriage plot to stage a three-way conversation among Enlightenment humanism (Madeleine), post-structural epistemology (Leonard), and religious belief (Mitchell). While Derrida, Barthes, and Baudrillard unmoor Madeleine's literary assumptions in the classroom, Leonard's eccentricity and passion challenge her normative thinking in the bedroom. Or, Leonard's seduction of Madeleine allegorizes theory's late twentieth-century seduction of conventional humanistic inquiry, and Mitchell isn't even enrolled in the class.

Before *The Marriage Plot* ends, however, Leonard's corrosive depression unravels his marriage to Madeleine and he disappears into the Oregon outback. Madeleine and Mitchell do get together, but their single sexual encounter signals Madeleine's decision to let Leonard go more than it does any feelings she has for Mitchell. Perhaps most revelatory of all, we learn that Leonard once took a religious studies course with Mitchell and actually takes Mitchell's faith quite seriously. Or, to crudely allegorize once more: Theory and Religion acknowledge that they have more in common than they initially imagined, but the Novel realizes that it doesn't need either of them to thrive. The life-changing truths about the indeterminacy of meaning, desire's constitutive lack, and the impermanence of authorship that fuel Madeleine and Leonard's love prove to be little more than historically contingent phenomena—just some things in the world rather than the truth of all the world's things.

Consequently, despite being a book filled with books, *The Marriage Plot* never becomes a book about books. The fiction refuses to become metafiction;

it never succumbs to theory's reflexive blandishments. Eugenides steeps his novel in the foundational theoretical texts of poststructural theory, but *The Marriage Plot* refuses to consider the ramifications those works have for its own production of value. The novel's many books thicken our understanding of character and setting, metonymically indexing particular types of students at a specific moment in US intellectual history, but they never implicate the novel itself. Eugenides investigates textuality symptomatically, not reflexively.

On the rare occasion that textual reflexivity does threaten to implicate *The Marriage Plot,* the effects remain internal to the text. All potential recursivity is suppressed. Struggling to live with Leonard's depression, for example, Madeleine observes: "The experience of watching Leonard get better was like reading certain difficult books. It was like plowing through late James, or the pages about agrarian reform in *Anna Karenina,* until you suddenly got to a good part again, which kept on getting better and better until you were so enthralled that you were almost *grateful* for the previous dull stretch because it increased your eventual pleasure" (345–46). Because *The Marriage Plot* lacks any such arduous passages of its own, however, it's difficult to parse the relationship between this reflection on novels and the novel we're reading. *The Marriage Plot* never achieves the self-consciousness required for its fictions to become metafictions. It's as if *The Marriage Plot*'s realism leaves it utterly un-self-aware of the fact that it, too, is a novel. Eugenides simply declines to go there.

Similarly, at the conclusion of *The Marriage Plot,* which is also the conclusion of the novel's marriage plot, Mitchell asks Madeleine if her undergraduate research on the marriage plot turned up "any novel where the heroine gets married to the wrong guy and then realizes it, and then the other suitor shows up, some guy who's always been in love with her, and then *they* get together, but finally the second suitor realizes that the last thing the woman needs is to get married again, that she's got more important things to do with her life? And so finally the guy doesn't propose at all, even though he still loves her? Is there any book that ends like that?" (406). Mitchell here perfectly describes *The Marriage Plot*'s marriage plot up to this diegetic moment: Madeleine and Leonard married; Mitchell traveled abroad; Leonard committed suicide; and now, Mitchell has returned. Having followed "the other suitor" script to the letter, Mitchell wonders, effectively professing his love for Madeleine by not professing his love for Madeleine, if this would make a good ending to a novel. Entirely ignoring the metafictional implications of the fact that Mitchell's hypothetical marriage plot perfectly describes the plot of her own life, Madeleine answers, "No, I don't think there's one like that," although of course there is, because we've just read it. Mitchell practically begs Madeleine to realize that she's in a novel, but Madeleine demurs. Refusing to give up, Mitchell then asks her if she at least thinks this hypothetical scenario might make a good ending to a marriage plot. Delivering the novel's final word, in a truncated echo of Molly Bloom, Madeleine affirms, "Yes," what Mitchell describes might make a compelling ending to a marriage plot. And so ends the marriage plot of *The Marriage Plot*. But here again, even as Mitchell's hypothetical conclusion to a speculative marriage plot coincides with the actual conclusion of *The Marriage Plot*'s marriage plot, the text never turns back against itself. Madeleine refuses the seductions of Mitchell's mirrors and the iterative convolutions that such reflections might entail never materialize. Instead, such reflexivity collapses into Madeleine's "yes" and simply stands as a conveniently clever way for Eugenides to end his novel. Just as Leonard, institutionalized for depression, realizes that "the smarter you were, the *worse* it was," *The Marriage Plot* indicates that the contemporary novel might be better off not spending too much time reflecting on itself as such (254).

In addition to realist novels like *The Marriage Plot*, however, the contemporary literary landscape includes another set of novels, which also refuse theory's reflexive mandate but do so in more formally experimental ways. The rest of this chapter will focus on some of these experimental works (Salvador Plascencia's *The People of Paper*, Percival Everett's *Virgil Russell by Percival Everett*, Ben Marcus's *Notable American Women*, and Jonathan Foer's *Tree of Codes*), which, at first glance, might be mistaken for good, old-fashioned, postmodern metafiction. I highlight these texts from Plascencia, Everett, Marcus, and Foer, then, because they aren't just absorbing theory into realism as Eugenides, Cole, Lipsyte, and Egan all do. Instead, these authors recognize the obsolescence of the homology between reflexivity and freedom, but they don't turn to realism and abandon theory altogether. Rather, they actively engage theoretical concepts in new ways that allow their novels to think beyond that homology and the political principles and formations on which it depends. To be sure, it would be easy to read these novels through a poststructural lens, revealing the opacity of their signifiers, the elusive ephemerality of their authors, the deferral of their meanings, and their collapse of the boundary between word and world. But this would be a misreading, a failure to appreciate that these fictions continue to engage theoretical concepts, but they do so literally, not reflexively. They resist applying the conclusions and implications of those concepts to themselves and instead innovate new, experimental literary forms out of those concepts. These texts construct instead of deconstruct, signify without *différance*, transmit value instead of undermining its possibility, and embrace the possibility of unreal realisms instead of dismissing realism altogether. Theory, in other words, provides these authors a toolbox of concepts that they draw on to configure the new shape of contemporary experimental fiction. Thus, their distinct, literalized deployment of theory produces *general* but not universal truths—that is, truths that are true in a given place and time because of the distinct way they've been composed and configured. Theory's value in these texts does not derive from its ability to liberate readers from the tyranny of authorship, the fetishization of the signified, or the conservative status quo of realist representation. Instead, it derives from its ability to function as a world-building presence, not a world-destroying absence.

Theoretical Violence

While Barthes insists, in the midst of theory's ascendance, that theoretical reflexivity must be pursued "even at the cost of destruction," Salvador Plascencia's *The People of Paper*, written in the wake of theory's decline, asks whether destruction is perhaps too high a cost. In particular, Plascencia's novel suggests that Derrida's famous line, "Il n'y a pas de hors-texte" [There is nothing outside the text], which collapses world into word, people into paper, might require a level of violence that we'd be better off without.[14] Thus, while some of theory's most popular notions clearly ground the novel's premise and predicate its action, by the conclusion of Plascencia's novel, such broad poststructural concepts will appear obsolete, no longer germane—and even violently counterproductive—to the living of a life. The novel might stage its conflicts in poststructural terms, and deploy formal techniques that embody key poststructural concepts, but it ultimately concludes that little is gained from doing so. The homology between theoretical forms and political liberation doesn't obtain for Plascencia's poststructuralized characters. Despite having learned the reflexive lessons of theory, Plascencia's characters (and the character named Salvador Plascencia who appears in the novel as the author

---

14. As the editors' introduction to the Derrida selection in *The Norton Anthology of Theory and Criticism* points out, this translation is imprecise since it "maintains the inside/outside opposition that the statement in fact aims to overturn" (1682). But as the earlier discussion about the institutional popularization of theory hopefully makes clear, I'm not suggesting that Plascencia read *Of Grammatology* with an eye for such subtle distinctions, or that he even read *Of Grammatology* at all. Rather, as with other concepts like the death of the author and the materiality of the signifier, this idea that nothing exists outside the text—a core conceit of the linguistic turn—has so suffused the institutional culture of the humanities that it's not hard to imagine contemporary authors, particularly those like Plascencia who are the product of esteemed Master of Fine Arts programs, being generally acquainted with the concept in a way that would allow them to deploy it in their writing, which is exactly what I think Plascencia does in The *People of Paper*.

of *The People of Paper*) ultimately resist applying those lessons to their own lives. In effect, Plascencia writes an allegory of thought thinking itself only to conclude that thought doesn't need to. (It's like *The Marriage Plot*, but without the realism.) Far from there being no outside-the-text, Plascencia's characters (and his readers) discover that there is in fact *always* something external to, bigger than, and more real than the text.

In *The People of Paper*, a gang of flower pickers from El Monte, California, goes to war. Led into battle by Federico de la Fe, a chronic bed wetter who arrives in El Monte's carnation fields after traveling from rural Mexico with his daughter, Little Merced, they are not fighting over disputed turf or exploitative labor conditions. They are fighting a "war on omniscient narration," otherwise known as "the war against the commodification of sadness," or a war against the reduction of their lives to text (218). They battle a figure named Saturn, a presence de la Fe first encounters as "a distant force looking down on him" (18) but which gradually grows Napoleonic in its desire to "wipe out whole cultures, whole towns of imaginary flower people" (238). De la Fe sends one of his troops, Smiley, to kill Saturn and liberate the flower pickers from Saturn's omniscience, but when Smiley cuts a hole in California's papier-mâché sky and lifts himself into Saturn's house, he doesn't find the evil tyrant de la Fe had described. Instead, he finds a mopey, lovelorn Salvador Plascencia, author of *The People of Paper*, mourning the loss of his girlfriend, Liz, who has left him for a white man. This introduces a second plot to the novel as Saturn/ Plascencia ramps up his omniscient manipulation of *The People of Paper*'s characters in an effort to prove his potency to Liz and win her back. When she responds negatively to such efforts, Saturn/Plascencia turns his authorial powers against her, reducing her to text before killing her off in the pages of *The People of Paper*.

Collapsing the author and his romantic relations into the novel's fictional world, *The People of Paper* presents itself as paradigmatic metafiction, a dizzying conflation of form and content, reality and fiction, world and word. In this way, everyone inside and outside *The People of Paper* are people of paper. No character embodies this more than Merced de Papel (not to be confused with Merced, de la Fe's wife, or Little Merced, his daughter). The most literal example of a person of paper, she is constructed entirely of paper scraps, and because water makes her soggy and pulpy, she constantly replaces herself with new text. As *différance* personified, she "chronicle[s] everything" (162) but "never allow[s] history to accumulate, her skin changing with the news of the world" (164). In all of these ways and more, *The People of Paper* demonstrates a keen awareness of its conditions of possibility, the pure textuality from which it is built.

And yet, indicating just how easily theory's insights can be used for both liberation and oppression, the novel remains unconvinced by the form-politics homology and explicitly questions the political value of its own reflexive textuality. On the one hand, de la Fe, bent on reclaiming his own conditions of possibility from Saturn/Plascencia's authorship, strives to make his circumstances *more* textual, but on his own terms. He wants the author dead, and if Smiley fails to kill him, Smiley should "steal the plot lines and the hundred and five pages that have been written," "leav[ing] nothing behind but the title page and table of contents" on which he's instructed to write to Saturn/Plascencia, "You are not so powerful" (105). But even as de la Fe fights for a textual world closed off from Saturn/Plascencia's outside authorship and omniscient narration, the closed textual world of the Saturn/Plascencia plot reveals the equally oppressive nature of textual reflexivity. In retribution for Liz's perfidy, for example, Saturn/Plascencia writes her into *The People of Paper* as a treacherous Malinche figure complicit with white settler colonialism. And when his next girlfriend, Cami, also runs off with a white man, Saturn/Plascencia abruptly changes her story inside the text, killing her with bee stings and throwing her off a cliff into the sea where sharks devour her. Texts with no outsides populated entirely with paper people can be dangerous places.

So what does it mean that the closed space of textuality is as violent as it is liberating? Plascencia suggests that what theory so frequently peddles as a playful, freeing indeterminacy is, at the same time, violently oppressive and manipulative. This is the result, as we saw earlier, of a vacillating relationship between theoretical reflexivity and political freedom. The indeterminacy that results from thought thinking its own conditions of possibility can be just as malevolent as it can be empowering. This idea arises most conspicuously when Smiley, always de la Fe's most reluctant soldier, points out to de la Fe that his "war for volition" against Saturn/Plascencia, his pursuit of the freedom he imagines arriving after the author's execution, requires the battalion of carnation pickers to relinquish their own volition to de la Fe.[15] Recognizing his own hypocrisy, de la Fe lets Smiley out of the war (163). Similarly, Saturn/Plascencia's ex-girlfriend, Liz, asks him to remember that she "exist(s) beyond the pages of this book." She might one day have children, she says, and she doesn't "want them finding a book in which their mother is faithless and cruel and insults the hero" (138). Although he's not particularly nice about it, Saturn/Plascencia discharges Liz from his war just as de la Fe decommissions Smiley. Later, Saturn/Plascencia even reprieves his new girlfriend, Cami, of

---

15. This contradiction should remind us of the "antifoundationalist paradox" Stanley Fish identifies at the heart of theoretical discourse.

her bee stings and shark attacks. In fact, just a few pages after the book kills her off, she's resurrected and granted her own space "beyond the pages of this book" where, as we read within the pages of the book, she discovers *The People of Paper* at a used bookstore and reads about her textual death (227). Externalized and literalized in the bookstore, the ostensibly all-powerful text now lies wasted on the remainder pile.

Of course, because Cami's existence beyond the pages of the book (*hors-texte*) ultimately remains within the pages of the book (*dans-texte*) we're reading, we *could* read *The People of Paper* as paradigmatic metafiction, as an embodiment of Derrida's "Il n'y a pas de hors-texte." But that interpretation is too easy, and it also ignores the negative affective resonance such poststructural conceits carry in the novel's plot. Not only do de la Fe's and Saturn/Plascencia's textual tactics not work, they also annoy and alienate nearly everyone in the novel. De la Fe and Saturn/Plascencia are insensitive egomaniacs, and their closest comrades and colleagues generally disapprove of their poststructural approach to love, freedom, and power. Despite wearing its poststructuralism on its sleeve, then, *The People of Paper* highlights the politically misguided, narcissistic emptiness of that particular approach to value production. Yes, Cami discovers herself in the book in the book, but that discovery also occurs in the world—that is, in the real world as it's represented in the book. We shouldn't read Cami reading *The People of Paper* in a bookstore in *The People of Paper* as textual recursion; we should read it as an injection of literary realism. It's a realism that beats back and cuts through the metafiction, a literalized representation of reflexive metafiction, not a performance of it. The novel allegorizes theory's demand for reflexive thinking, but recognizing that such demands can be politically counterproductive now that theoretical forms have been disarticulated from political freedom, it ultimately concludes that we need not necessarily follow orders. Antifoundational reflexivity is not the only way to be free.

Emphasizing this point, *The People of Paper* consistently directs readers' attention to the space and time beyond the contours of the novel, to a world beyond the text. This occurs primarily through Baby Nostradamus, a mute infant whose thoughts remain opaque to Saturn/Plascencia throughout the novel. Blessed with a totalizing knowledge that "extended beyond the plot and details of this book, reaching not only into the future but beyond it, circling fully around, intersecting with the past and resting wherever he wished," Baby Nostradamus knows everything about de la Fe's war, everything about Saturn/Plascencia's war, and even everything about us (160). He knows, for example, "the different grips of the readers, how some cradled the open covers while others set the book on a table, licking their fingers before turning each page, saliva soaking into the margins" (166). Of course, as with the Cami example, we *could* describe Baby Nostradamus as yet another layer of textuality. He authors the authors; his book contains their books. And while that layering certainly exists, we should also once again listen to the novel's plot, because even as his capacious vision gives him "the power to undercut Saturn by prematurely disclosing information and sabotaging the whole of the novel," he never uses his textual superpowers to do so. Although he has the capacity to think reflexively, to interrogate and undermine all conditions of textual possibility, he is bound by the soothsayers' "Laws of Comportment" not to; despite the "epic proportions" of his thought (161), he never betrays "the codes of his profession" (167). Containing the totality of all textual possibility, Baby Nostradamus has more power than anyone in the novel, but he refuses to close the text off to the world and instead allows the world to proceed whichever way it wants. And *The People of Paper* eventually does so as well, concluding with de la Fe and his daughter walking "south and off the page, leaving no footprints that Saturn could track" (245). Having thoroughly deployed many of the key ideas behind theory's linguistic turn, the novel ultimately turns against language, sending its characters beyond the text and into a world where freedom is no longer a function of dead authors, signifying chains, or *différance*.

The Word as World

The People of Paper reclaims the world from textuality by diagnosing the unwelcome violence of a world swallowed up by words. Percival Everett's *Percival Everett by Virgil Russell* does so by insisting on the ontological equivalence of world and word. For Everett, the world doesn't collapse into the word; rather, the word is just more world. Neither swallows the other because they exist on the same plane of being. This idea—that the primary value of language derives from its being in the world rather than from its ability to refer to the world—rests at the heart of Everett's decades-long literary project. "Given the existence of the story," Everett explains, "the story is a fact and the elements of the story are in fact not fiction at all, not only within the context of the story but in the totality of reality." Seeing no gap between text and world, fiction and reality, content and form, Everett encourages us to "refocus our gaze from the transcendental connections of meaning(s) toward the obscure and indeterminate surface of fiction" ("Modality" 154). Everett has little interest in the referential relationship between word and world and the meaning, or lack thereof, that relationship produces. His writing does not reflexively query and erode the conditions of its own production; it simply is those conditions. The resulting fiction is equivalent to the tools, materials, and processes involved in building it. One of Everett's favorite tools happens to be theory, although he deploys it in a way that directly counters its drive to reflexively deconstruct meaning and value.

The cover of *Percival Everett by Virgil Russell* provides an apt example. There we find an Escheresque image of two hands, each writing part of the novel's title on a sheet of paper. The hands are across from each other, so one part of the title, *Percival Everett,* is upside down, while the other half, *by Virgil Russell,* is right side up. We might see this image, along with the inclusion of the author's name in the novel's title, as a typically reflexive, metafictional move: the image reveals the always-already written-ness of the world, including the textuality of the author himself. Folding in on itself, the text ungrounds readers, setting them adrift in a world of pure language—word has swallowed world. But that interpretation isn't quite right. Yes, the world is language, but that doesn't necessarily mean that there is no world. In fact, Everett learns the opposite lesson from this textualized worldview: the word is world. The novel's self-reflexive cover does not speak to language's inadequacy, indeterminacy, and failure to touch the world; rather, it depicts the creation of reality. Word and world are not separate spheres, struggling to connect; they do not define distinct ontological modes. Instead, just as a hammer and nails do not occupy an order of reality separate from the house that they are used to build, words for Everett do not occupy an order of reality separate from the world they construct. He thus deploys theory's troubling of the word-world relation only to supersede it and imagine novels not as linguistic approximations of the world, but as coextensive with it.

To reimagine the word-world relation in this way, *Percival Everett by Virgil Russell* tangles with analytic philosophy, particularly with the longstanding distinction that tradition draws between the sense and reference of language. As I'll explain in greater detail, Everett collapses the sense-reference distinction, which in turn allows him to produce a novel whose fictional surface exists as a fact in the world rather than as a linguistic reference to it or representation of it. But first, a quick primer on this key concept from analytic philosophy. The distinction between the sense and reference of language derives from Gottlob Frege's work, which argues that a word's meaning entails more than its referent—the object which it designates—and must also include its sense. To illustrate this, Frege observes that Cicero and Tully designate the same person; they have the same referent. And yet, the meaning of "Cicero is Tully" differs from the meaning of "Cicero is Cicero"; they have a different sense. Another, more famous example observes that both "morning star" and "evening star" refer to Venus, despite connoting very different senses. Everett signals his interest in this question as he titles the first half of his novel Hesperus (the name in Greek myth for the evening star) and the second half Phosphorous (the name in Greek myth for the morning star), suggesting that the two halves of the novel, perhaps like the two hands cowriting the book's title on its cover, refer to the same thing but in different ways, with different senses. Everett introduces this distinction into the novel, however, because he wants to overcome it. The novel consistently emphasizes the identity and sameness of the referent, not the discrepancies of sense. In this way, the novel demonstrates that referents and their multiple senses are all just coextensive parts of the same fabric called the world. Or as the novel's indeterminate narrative voice asks, "When do two things that are in fact the same thing converge and negate any notion of their ever having been anything but one thing? When does Cicero become Tully?" (170).

While a more theoretical impulse might lead one to dwell on the apparent irreducibility of identity that language introduces to being (Cicero will never become Tully because language won't permit it), Everett works from the opposite impulse, using language in a way that emphasizes the identity of Cicero and Tully, that insists on viewing the distinction between linguistic sense and reference as a superfluous distraction from the unified singularity of being. Conceived this way, language is no longer that which severs us from the world, or which swallows up the world, but is instead just another thing in the world. Cicero is Tully when language makes it so. The novel's narrator calls this "entification," which he describes as the process by which story becomes world, the way language becomes the thing that there is (62). Even though everything we "utter is a metaphor," metaphors are also "essential facts" (66–67). In this way, Everett's theory of language is Leibnizian, not Nietzschean. Language's inevitable lapse into metaphor is not a foundational lie against the world; it's the beginning of the world: "Metaphor did not derive out of an extension of some thought and so relied on nothing really for actuality, substance, or even tenor, but appeared, arrived complete, like one of Leibniz's monads and like a universe unto itself the metaphor was forever collapsing in on itself while giving the appearance of expansion" (130). Although language is always already metaphorical, there's no indeterminacy or slipperiness. It's not a lie, as Nietzsche insists in "On Truth and Lying." Rather, it's just what there is.

Crucially, Everett's determination to supersede the sense-reference distinction, his attempt to make two things the same thing in language, is not an indulgent exercise in literary experiment. Rather, the novel is motivated by Everett's desire to reconnect with his father, also named Percival Everett, who died in 2010. In fact, Everett dedicates the novel to his father, Percival

Leonard Everett, thereby literalizing in its opening pages the sense-reference problem: how can two names point to the same thing? Only the problem here is even more complicated because Everett wants the same name, Percival Everett, to point to the same thing even as the same name actually designates two distinct entities, father and son. To overcome the distance that the sense-reference distinction places between a thing and its meaning, between Everett and his father, Everett must not only show that the two names point to the same thing, he must also render himself and his father as the same thing. In other words, he faces not just a linguistic problem, but an ontological one. Ultimately, Everett's post-theory take on the indeterminacy of language provides him the means to effect that ontological union in novel form.

The literary suturing begins on the opening page, where a father tells his son, "I've written something for you. . . . Not to you, but for you. It's sort of something you would write, if you wrote. Here it is:" (3). After the colon, the characters stay the same—there is an "I" and someone the "I" refers to as "my father"—and a narrative commences about the son visiting his aging father in an assisted-living facility in Philadelphia. Until, that is, it's interrupted several pages later with the son telling his father, "You don't live in Philadelphia . . . we're both here in California." As the father explains, "It's called fiction, son. This is the story you would be writing if you were a fiction writer" (6). Of course, the referent of "this" is unclear. Which parts are written by the father as if he were the son writing a novel, and which are written by the son? It soon collapses into a game of "Pin the Tail on the Narrator" (6). The same problem arises elsewhere, in the novel's second section, "Phosphorous," which tells a relatively unified story about a group of elderly patients staging an insurrection against their mistreatment in an assisted-living facility. In the middle of that plot, however, the narrator acknowledges "the complete absence of clarity regarding one pressing and nagging matter, that being: just who the fuck is telling this story?" "Is it an old man or the old man's son." Assuring us that he "will clear up the matter forthwith, directly, tout de suite," he reports, "*I* am telling this story" (107).

As with the other novels treated here, such metafictional trickery does not spin readers outward into epistemological indeterminacy. This is not a lesson about the interpretive impossibility resulting from *différance*, about the way radically open structures produce permanently undecidable worlds. Because once again, despite the novel's explicit consideration of its own conditions of production ("These pages that I would have you write, if you wrote, or that you are writing because I wrote . . ." [45]), Everett doesn't allow that reflexivity to puncture a hole in the center of his text. He's not dropping poststructural bombs that rupture the possibility of meaning and value. Instead, he's using this classically poststructural premise—"Writing is that neutral, composite, oblique space where our subject slips away, the negative where all identity is lost, starting with the very identity of the body writing"—to produce the presence and wholeness of identity, the connection and union of bodies (Barthes, "Death" 1322). He uses this poststructural premise to obviate the separation and difference that the sense-reference distinction institutes. Once the poststructural premise of the novel collapses sense and reference, then Everett becomes free to produce a world in which he and his father are one: "Your old man posing as you in a voice that is at once yours and at once mine and at once neither" (29). Here the radical indeterminacy of the narrative voice allows each to occupy the position of narrator, thereby allowing each to become the other as well.

Like "two keys hopefully capable of opening the same lock," the novel writes the father and son increasingly closer together until they become indistinguishable. Eventually, it even seems plausible that both father and son are dead. Early in the novel, for example, the son says to the father, "Dad, you realize that I'm dead." And the father replies, "Yes, son, I do. But I wasn't aware that you knew it" (14). The exchange is reversed at the novel's conclusion, where the father tells the son, "I'm dead, son." And the son replies, "I know that, Dad. But I didn't know you knew it" (227). Thus, the narrator elsewhere reports, "I could be writing you could be writing me could be writing you. I am a comatose old man writing here now and again what my dead or living son might write if he wrote or I am a dead or living son writing what my dying father might write for me to have written" (216). The novel's linguistic loops make it simultaneously true that each has lost the other and that each is writing in an effort to heal that loss. Both father and son write both the life and the death of the other.

The novel's many competing plots use similar poststructural techniques to collapse the sense-reference distinction and achieve counter-poststructural ends—that is, to produce presence and unity rather than absence and difference. Textual evidence suggests, for example, that both father and son have brothers married to sexually attractive French women. Another instance of treacherous reference implies that both father and son were chased by the KKK while out driving with their respective fathers. Other plots narrated in the third person contain equally mutable characters, although even the third-person characters are frequently avatars of the father and/or the son (it's never clear which). One character named Murphy, for example, is a handyman, but then a horse trainer, living in Riverside. He later appears as a doctor living in Washington DC. But this isn't too surprising as everyone in the novel has multiple identities: one character, Gregory Lang, is married to Claire, but just pages later her name is Sylvia; a woman, Meg Caro, claiming to be Gregory's

THEORY, METAFICTION, AND CONSTRUCTIVISM • 97

daughter is twenty-two years old when he meets her, but weeks later she's twenty-seven; a nurse at the assisted-living center has at least three different names over the course of her plot; and a teenager working at a mall "key-osk" (they make keys) has three different names on the same page of text. Again, it might seem that language is getting the better of these people, that they are just people of paper whose worlds have been reduced to words. But the effect is precisely the opposite. Rather than proliferating difference, the novel moves toward sameness. The point is not that meaning and subjectivity are indeterminate, but that multiplicity is still just identity. I might have three names, multiple senses, but I'm still me. The distinction between sense and reference, Everett suggests, is a red herring. The many are one. Language makes it possible for everyone, not just Cicero, to be Tully. What theory views as a difference that spreads, Everett sees as a singularity that unifies. Free to ignore questions of sense *and* reference, Everett's work conjures a world where "all meaning must collapse under the weight of its own being" (59), a world in which being, not meaning, is the most relevant feature of language and the worlds it entifies.

Unreal Realism

As with Plascencia and Everett, Marcus's *Notable American Women* displays a keen awareness of itself as a textual artifact even as it refuses the recursivity such reflexivity so frequently begets. But Marcus doesn't just view word and world as coexisting on the same plane of being as we saw in Everett. He takes the additional step of using those words in the world as the building blocks of new worlds, or what I'll describe here as unreal realisms. In particular, he uses an array of theoretical concepts as the building blocks of a speculative world, treating theoretical concepts not as mandates for reflexivity but simply as objects in the world that can be used to construct new realisms. Here we find another approach to what I've been calling theoretical literalism. If these theoretical concepts were deployed reflexively within the text, then the text would absorb the world in a typically metafictional way. But when they are deployed literally, as the component parts of the text's diegetic world, they contribute to the literary production of an entirely new, but distinctly nonreflexive, reality. In this way, *Notable American Women* cannot be mistaken for contemporary realism, but it also bears little resemblance to earlier forms of experimental metafiction motivated by theory's mandated reflexivity.[16]

---

16. See Marcus's "Why Experimental Fiction Threatens to Destroy Publishing, Jonathan Franzen, and Life as We Know It" for a lengthy attack on contemporary realism in general and Jonathan Franzen in particular.

Marcus's novel details the various silencing technologies pursued by a cult of women who believe that human language and movement do violence to the weather. The Silentists move into Ben Marcus's house (Ben Marcus is not just the author, but also the protagonist and first-person narrator for much of the book), and *Notable American Women* chronicles his family's gradual conversion to increasingly hushed modes of being.[17] The Silentists' impulse to quiet derives from a poststructural understanding of language as simultaneously over- and underdetermined, an idea we also saw in Plascencia's novel where textuality proved both oppressive and liberating. The overdetermined materiality of signifiers has the power to physically injure and wound even as their underdetermination leaves them struggling to connect meaningfully to the world. The violent implications of a theoretically reflexive notion of language are clearly exemplified in Ben's comments on naming: "Spelling a person's name is the first step toward killing him. It takes him apart and empties him of meaning" (56). Here, the absence of referential value (underdetermination) only heightens the penetrating materiality of language (overdetermination); words are potent but hollow tools. This quasi-Lacanian take on language (elsewhere Ben reports, "To speak is to grieve" [94]) grounds the Silentists' commitment to quiet. Rather than repairing and reconnecting language to the world or fetishizing the structures of absence and deferral lying at its heart, they abandon it altogether.

In the novel's opening chapter, however, Ben's father, writing from an underground prison in the backyard of the Silentists' compound, ostensibly steers the novel away from silence and toward conventional literary realism. The father criticizes *Notable American Women* for "fractur[ing] a reality that must in every way be preserved" (7), and he yearns for Ben "to believe once again in [Ben's] power to exhibit frank statements about the world and its secret histories" (6). Even as he calls for a more realistic account of the Silentist invasion of the Marcus homestead, however, the father also deploys metafictional devices that wrest authorial control away from Ben. For example, the father persistently questions Ben's reliability, implying that Ben is biased, resentful (4), mediocre (11), and mildly retarded (10). Although they are launched in the service of realism and greater transparency, these attacks on Ben's authorship ultimately bring a metafictional reflexivity to the text. As readers parse Ben's authorship of a novel authored by Ben Marcus, a novel that then contains not just Ben's father's indictment of Ben's authorship, but also his father's own claim on that authorship, reality gets left far behind. At one

---

17. I will use "Ben Marcus" or "Marcus" to refer to the living author of *Notable American Women* and "Ben" to refer to the novel's protagonist and narrator.

point, for instance, the father claims primary authorship of *Notable American Women,* insisting to readers, in italics: "*It should never be forgotten that Benjamin Marcus is being commanded at this and all moments by the person* [the father] *whose words you are reading*" (9). And yet, "caution[ing] the careful and fair-minded reader to be ever vigilant against [Ben's] manipulations," the father earlier implies that Ben has absolute control over *Notable American Women*: "I fully expect even this statement to be omitted, given how it might contradict the heroic role he will no doubt claim for himself," the father reports (4). So did the father "command" Ben to write the father writing "this statement," or is Ben "manipulating" the father's manipulation of Ben's authorship? It's an undecidable question opened up by the metafictional reflexivity that the father introduces into the novel's opening pages. Like the "language poison" unleashed against the father in his subterranean cell, the father's metafictional tricks infect the novel itself with language's own tendency toward poisonous, reflexive self-destruction. The homology between theoretical reflexivity and freedom is in tatters.

But the father's early metafictional intrusions into the novel do not faze Ben. Once he assumes responsibility for the narrative, the novel moves in an entirely different direction—not toward realism or reflexive metafiction, but toward silence. Thus, a section titled "Blueprint" functions as a user manual for those ideal readers who share the novel's broader devotion to silence and stillness. Fully aware of the violent dangers that the text's language might pose for readers—apparently four readers have already died (80)—Ben suggests that anyone committed to "bringing a New Stillness upon their persons . . . should read no further, for even reading is an embarrassing spasm of the body" (46). Just as the father earlier encouraged readers to "forgo whatever follows in this book . . . and burn the thing to cinders with the greatest haste" (8), Ben here urges us to stop reading. (Elsewhere he describes various prophylaxes which, should we insist on reading, will buffer us from the deleterious powers of the word.) But Ben's call to cease reading differs markedly from his father's. The father wants us to ignore the text because he views it as unreliable and indeterminate, an affront against reality, but Ben simply hopes to prevent readers from injury or death.

Of course, we keep reading either way, but these competing interventions have very different effects on our reading experience. The father's intervention distances and alienates us from the text; it uses language's conditions of possibility—its simultaneous hollowness and potency—against the novel itself. But Ben's intervention protects us from the text, using those same threatening conditions of possibility to build a new world through and within the novel, a world built from theoretical concepts but safe from the dangers of theory's mandated reflexivity. Unlike the father's suggestions, Ben's recommendations are not intended reflexively. He doesn't use the indeterminacies of language to undermine the novel and sabotage the reading experience. The novel is not compelled to silence; it doesn't have to apply Silentist tenets to itself. Instead, it uses language's failure as the ground for an entirely new, speculative reality, an unreal realism that manages to convey the very emotions and feelings that the Silentists hush and repress. In this way, the novel countervails its conditions of possibility rather than succumbing to them.

Put differently, rather than considering and following through on theory's implications for the novel, *Notable American Women* literalizes and materializes the theoretical concepts for use as novelistic content. The novel isn't exactly an allegory of theoretical concepts, but more like one of Joseph Cornell's boxed assemblages: it concretizes theory's major concepts, constructing its reality out of them. Peering into the box, we find: dead authors ("I should still be alive in this book. I should not have died so young, or died at all, or ever been alive" [52]"); écriture féminine ("Finland proposes a separate language for women, becoming the first European nation to do so" [81]); archiwriting ("breathing itself was considered the first language" [62]); the pleasure of the text ("If you wish to fondle the author, I should take off my clothes for you and sit on a bed to the tune of a funeral march" [50]); the waning of affect ("If the head's hollow space (chub) is filled with materials like cloth . . . then less life can enter and, perhaps, fewer emotions will result" [116]); posthumanism ("At the time of this writing, the head probably cannot be omitted from the person pursuing the female life project" [121]); constructed subjectivity ("you had decreasing access to the physical territory we will refer to as 'me'" [239]); becoming animal ("There are so many animals in the world now, and the history of behavior has become so vast, that a woman should have no trouble finding a creature that corresponds to her emotion surplus" [129]); and signifying chains ("No one . . . was sure what to call her [Ben's sister]. . . . I have to admit that I'm not sure what name she began with" [95]). None of these concepts infects the novel, corroding it from the inside. Instead, they populate the novel, determining the conditions and parameters of the lives lived inside the text. Theory doesn't undermine but instead provides the material basis for an entirely new world altogether.

Notable American Women, in other words, transforms theory's eroding absences into substantive presences. We find an example of this in the novel's discussion of typographical errors and misspellings. Here Marcus plays with a classic trope of postmodern metafiction: intentionally including typos and misspellings in a text. Because we're all accustomed to reading books with unintentional errors, the inclusion of intentional errors makes it impossible to determine the foundational truth of the text. How can a reader distinguish between intentional and unintentional typos? Worse, if many of the mistakes are intentional, then a word spelled correctly might actually be a mistake. Maybe it was supposed to be a typo. For earlier authors like Barth, Pynchon, and Warhol, these reflexive tricks forced readers to acknowledge the fundamental indeterminacy of any text, the constitutive absence at the heart of language.[18] But for Marcus, they do the opposite; they result in perfectly legible texts. Whether something is other than what it's supposed to be is beside the point; it still is:

> If all the words of this book are misspelled, but accidentally spell other words correctly, and also accidentally fall into a grammatically coherent arrangement, where coherency is defined as whatever doesn't upset people, it means this book is legally another book. Likewise, if another book is comprised entirely of misspelled words that, through accident or design, happen to spell correctly and in the proper order the so-called words of this book, which in fact will be proven not to be words at all, but birdcalls, then that book might be regarded as a camouflage enterprise or double for this book, though it would be impossible to detect whether this were ever the case, in which case something is always a decoy for something else, and the word "camouflage" simply means "to have a family." (55)

This passage acknowledges the slippery impermanence and ultimate undecidability of language. It recognizes that chance and contingency can never be purged from the sign systems a novel comprises. And yet, indeterminacy is not the result. Some other thing is. This novel might not be this novel, but if it's not, then it's another novel. "Camouflage" might not mean "disguise," but that doesn't render its meaning undecidable. Instead, it means "to have a family." This happens throughout *Notable American Women*. Rather than playing with the *différance* within and between signifiers and signifieds, the narrative simply pegs language to a different reality. "Heart," for example, means "wind" (54); "to raise" means "to flay off skin and insert another body inside the pelt" (218); and intercourse is called "stitching" (131).

---

18. Thomas Pynchon does this in *The Crying of Lot 49*, John Barth in "Lost in the Funhouse," and Andy Warhol in *a*. See Paul Benzon's "Lost in Transcription" for an argument that links this technique to the wonderfully materialist insight that authors at the time wrote with typewriters. For a disturbing contemporary manifestation of the intentional typo and further evidence that metafictional formal innovations have been completely severed from any particular politics, see Annie Linskey, "Inside the Trump Tweet Machine," which reveals that Trump staffers intentionally added grammatical and spelling mistakes to Trump's tweets to make him appear more authentic.

The novel overflows with such redefinitions until it describes an entirely new (and remarkably bizarre) world devoted to producing and maintaining silence. Like good science fiction, that world consistently adheres to its own internal logic. Unlike science fiction, readers are not asked to determine what that world represents, allegorizes, or critiques. We are not required to find Silentist analogues in our own life-world. Instead, Marcus assembles the contents of that unreal reality to produce a certain feeling, to transmit a particularly affecting intensity that conveys the text's qualitative value to its readers, a value that is not representational or referential. Marcus builds a world that produces "the way it feels to be alive," and he demonstrates "the way language can be shaped into contours that surround and illuminate that feeling" (Marcus, "Experimental Fiction" 41). In this way, despite its formal innovations, the novel is remarkably conventional: it's about love, and the lack thereof, in a typical American family. But these ideas are not represented as much as they are produced as an effect of reading about the curious demands and structures of Silentism.

Committed to affective value production rather than representational meaning, *Notable American Women* is not particularly interested in whether words speak adequately about the world. For Marcus, language's inability to mean does not preclude its capacity to affect. Immersed in Silentism, the novel's characters model this affective form of value production for us. The Silentists, for example, encourage Ben to "drink the liquid that had been near [his] own copulation" as a way to increase future sexual potency. A "thought rag" absorbs the language spoken into it, and exchanging thought rags with others serves as "a shortcut to intimacy" (120). "Action butter" is "the residue a person leaves behind after performing certain tasks," and it "can then [be] used as a topical ointment to prevent that action in others" (124). And a "Storm Needle" is an antenna that picks up "person sounds" that travel through the air like radio waves (214). In all of these examples, value is transmitted physically, almost osmotically, not depicted representationally.[19] The value of a life is not to be described, explained, or spoken about; it's to be touched, felt, and absorbed. Building and conveying these gestural, expressive emotions from theory's repurposed concepts, Ben invites us to engage his text similarly: "It would be foolish to simplify the role of the skin in reading, thinking, and eating. . . . You are training your body to be a full-scale receiver of language, to feed on the noise of words as it does with so-called food" (77). If we agree to think of language as something that we eat, absorb, or transmit rather than

---

19. See Scott Lash's *Another Modernity* for an extended discussion of the difference between represented and transmitted meaning.

as a site of reference, signification, and interpretation, then we substantially defuse theory's ability to erode textual value. In turn, as we find in *Notable American Women*, theory literalized becomes available as a literary tool or device capable of building worlds and transmitting feelings.

Positive Negations

In his discussion of post-postmodernism, Jeffrey Nealon borrows from Deleuze's *Cinema 2* to make a distinction between what he calls the negative and positive powers of the false. According to Nealon, during the linguistic turn and the heyday of postmodernism, theory operated primarily according to the negative power of the false: "that which unmasks the exclusions or illegitimacy of the totalizing 'truth' by showing it to be beholden to multiple viewpoints" (158), and which, beholden to "the logic of the signifier, performs the relentless work of the negative, always and everywhere hollowing out the true (the signified)" (159). In place of these negations, Nealon suggests that the post-postmodern era—that is, the contemporary post-theory moment from which Plascencia, Everett, Marcus, and Foer all write—is marked by a positive power of the false, which "gives another account of the real altogether, one that's beyond the current regimes of true and false" (158). Like Everett's metaphors that aren't Nietzschean lies but "essential facts," this is "'a decision of nontruth' that nevertheless 'produces effects of truth' in an alternative fashion," a negation that "takes on a productive function of its own" (162).[20] In place of poststructuralism's mandated reflexivity, which introduces a negation that undoes and undermines, Nealon here describes a negation that recognizes the untruth of language but nevertheless builds a positive truth out of it. This positive truth is what I've been describing as theoretical literalism. In effect, the willingness to accept theory, and language itself, as positive facts rather than harbingers of absence and indeterminacy indicates a post-theory decision not to worry about the problems of meaning, textuality, and representation, not to belabor literature's conditions of possibility, and instead to explore new ways of producing literary value and significance.[21]

---

20. The interpellated citations in the first quotation are from Michel Foucault's "Lives of Infamous Men." *Essential Works of Foucault, Vol. II,* eds. N. Rose and Paul Rabinow, New Press, 2003, pp. 292–93.

21. Nealon offers readings of conceptual work from Bruce Andrews and Kenneth Goldsmith as examples of literature that's looking for new ways to conceive literary value. I would add the collection of texts I discuss here to his list.

To borrow Dames's felicitous phrasing once more, theory's concepts and its reflexive mandate are "no longer the key to all the world's things"; they no longer provide universally true insight into the meaning and value of the world we inhabit or the words we use. Instead, they become just more things in the world, added to the set of forms an author might use to construct his or her fiction. They become part of the *langue* of literary production, the distribution of the sensible, the set of concepts and forms that can serve as the building blocks of a text without having to be reflexively turned back against the text. This makes their value general rather than universal, again understanding the general to be the historically contingent field or domain of terms, concepts, and forms that one draws on to produce a singularity, and which, *a la* Dewey, is also always being constructed anew through its ongoing encounter with new singularities. The resulting configuration can be described as *generally* true within the context of the *langue* from which it draws, but because the *langue* makes no claim on universality and instead only comprises an arbitrary set of contingent historical phenomena, it can also never be more than generally true.

One of the most innovative takes on this generalized mode of value production has been Jonathan Safran Foer's *Tree of Codes,* a text Foer produced by negating large chunks of Bruno Schulz's *The Street of Crocodiles,* written and published in Polish in 1934. Foer reproduces the English translation of Schulz's text word for word, but a deliberate die-cutting process has deleted ninety percent of the words from the original text, leaving a streamlined *Tree of Codes* clinging to delicate pages that are mostly empty space. Creating a story by erasing the majority of an already-existing one, Foer would seem to be up to his old experimental stunts—ploys that have led many to dismiss him as an overly precious, ultimately hackneyed author deploying an outmoded and unwelcome bag of tricks. But while *Tree of Codes* is perhaps the biggest gimmick Foer has attempted yet, it also exemplifies contemporary literature's embrace of the positive power of the false over and against its negative capacities. As such, I offer Foer's work as a paradigmatic example of the post-theoretical impulse motivating a significant cross section of contemporary experimental writing.[22]

In Bruno Schulz's *The Street of Crocodiles,* one finds a power of the false that remains distinctly negative and undermining. It emerges most conspicuously in the protagonist and first-person narrator's father, whose compulsive

---

22. This technique of composing by deleting is not unique to Foer. He's just the most mainstream author doing it. Other examples include Jen Bervin's *Nets,* Yedda Morrison's *Darkness,* Daniel Snelson's *Radios,* Derek Beaulieu's *A, a novel,* and Holly Melgard's *The Making of the Americans.*

reflexivity only further obscures and alienates the man from his family. The father spends "days, even weeks," "plumbing the depths of his own entrails," motivated by his unique theory of matter: "Matter has been given infinite fertility, inexhaustible vitality. . . . The whole of matter pulsates with infinite possibilities that send dull shivers through it. Waiting for the life-giving breath of the spirit, it is endlessly in motion" (14). What's more, matter represents "a territory outside any law," and "all attempts at organizing matter are transient and temporary, easy to reverse and to dissolve" (31). Because of this infinite pulsation, the father views form as "an arbitrary tyranny imposed on a helpless block" (35), a betrayal of "the infinite diversity of forms which the multifarious matter could adopt" (39). In other words, he wants to deconstruct the static solidity of matter by revealing its antifoundational conditions of possibility, its indeterminate shiftiness. In pursuit of matter's hidden depths, the father grows distant from his family, losing himself in specks of dirt in the cracks of the floor, spending weeks at a time locked up with dozens of birds he's imported from around the globe. Echoing Federico de la Fe's self-presentation in *The People of Paper*, the boy describes his father as a "lonely hero who alone had waged war against the fathomless, elemental boredom that strangled the city" and as a defender of "the lost cause of poetry" (25). And yet, the father's deep inquiries into the grounding conditions of existence, his interrogation of matter's very conditions of possibility, leave him alienated from the world of human reality: "We did not count him as one of us anymore," the boy says. "What still remained of him—the small shroud of his body and the handful of nonsensical oddities—would finally disappear one day, as unremarked as the gray heap of rubbish swept into a corner" (17). Turns out that the reflexivity Barthes demands "even at the cost of destruction" actually requires a fair bit of destruction.

In Schulz's world, however, the alternative—*not* plumbing the indeterminate depths of matter—doesn't necessarily produce better outcomes. In the story, the titular Street of Crocodiles represents another instance of "the infinite diversity of forms" that fuels the father's self-defeating investigations. Describing the street's constitutive state of flux, the narrator explains: "Our language has no definitions which would weight, so to speak, the grade of reality, or define its suppleness. . . . Nothing ever succeeds there, nothing can ever reach a definite conclusion" (70). It is a place where "possibilities threaten" but always go unrealized, a domain where one can only "wander from shop sign to shop sign and make a thousand mistakes" (71). Unlike the father, however, the city's citizens refuse to dive in. They are "attracted to the tawdry charm" of the Street of Crocodiles, but no one wants "to expose this sham." Like Smiley, from *The People of Paper*, who is reluctant to steal the pages of Saturn's novel lest doing so result in his own death, no one dares penetrate this reality which, "as thin as paper," "betrays with all its cracks its imitative character" (68). Confronted with this poststructural wasteland, a world "cut out from last year's moldering newspapers," the father chooses to lose himself in the infinite depths behind the façade, while everyone else is content to live in a condition of "self-parody," too cheap "to afford anything better than a paper imitation" (72). Depressingly, these are the only terms of existence available within Schulz's work. Embrace the negating power of the false, escape the parodic façades of "reality," and disappear into infinite possibility, endless deferral, and perpetually fluid forms. Or, remain content with the superficial façades of self-parody, don't ask questions or think reflexively, and keep shopping.

These are the options, that is, if you accept a theoretical mode of value production in which the freeplay of a constitutive absence, the *différance* of language, ensures the "infinite fertility [and] inexhaustible vitality" of the world. But the absences in Foer's *Tree of Codes*, the holes created from die-cutting Schulz's text, are a different kind of absence. They are not negations that prove the indeterminacy of meaning but are instead negations that produce meaning. These are positive negations that delineate, demarcate, and frame. They demonstrate the positive power of the false, the way an absence can build rather than erode. Whereas the father in *The Street of Crocodiles* pursues an absence that only results in permanent instability, the absences in Foer's *Tree of Codes* result in stable forms. The father heeds theory's reflexive mandate; Foer does not. Foer's cutting away of Schulz's text doesn't reveal the groundlessness of its foundations; it sculpts an entirely new literary object out of the *langue* of a preexisting one.[23]

If the father in *The Street of Crocodiles* rants against form and hopes to reduce all matter to flow, Foer's carefully excised text performs the reverse operation, surgically circumscribing matter (i.e., Schulz's text) into form. The father sees such forms as tyrannical usurpations of the truth of matter, but Foer identifies an alternative truth to matter, a truth that has nothing to do with its inner meaning and value. Instead, Foer makes text matter by treating it as tangible material, as the composite components required to make something new. The narrative of *Tree of Codes* tells a story in which the radical indeterminacy that defines the world of Schulz's text has been mitigated into more concrete forms, and the text itself, excised from Schulz's, similarly avers that its value derives not from acts of indeterminate reference and represen-

---

23. For a reading that supports my sense of *Tree of Codes* as an ultimately stabilizing text, see N. Katherine Hayles's "Combining Close and Distant Reading." And see Matt Rager's "[_]Tree[_] of C[__]od[_]es" for a more effusively poststructural take.

tation but from a careful and deliberate set of material and tangible choices. *Tree of Codes* thus lays bare its conditions of production, but they remain committedly reductive rather than recursive. A bigger thing was reduced into a smaller thing, and if that procedure were repeated, it would result in something smaller, and so on. Those general conditions of possibility remain internal to the structure of the building process and never threaten to loop back onto and engulf the structure. The "paper imitation" (72) in *The Street of Crocodiles* that can only be countered with the self-defeating, negative power of the false becomes in Foer's text, through die-cutting's positive power of the false, "better than a paper imitation" (96).

"Better than a paper imitation" is pretty good when it comes to literature. It suggests a set of positive developments for contemporary experimental fiction, which, as the examples above indicate, has abandoned the deconstructive project it pursued in theory's heyday in favor of a more broadly constructive project today. But when it comes to political concerns and questions, how far exactly will forms and ideas that are better than paper imitations get us? It makes sense that the politics connected to these generalized forms of value production will be rather weak. After all, they are partly the result of the failure of much stronger political claims based on the now defunct homology between theoretical reflexivity and liberatory politics. If those kinds of strong political claims are no longer available to us because of the unavoidable vacillation of the relationship between theory's conceptual forms and radical politics, then what type of politics is available to theoretically literal texts produced in the wake of that relationship's disarticulation?

If we listen to the works discussed above, we don't find many good answers. *The People of Paper* implies that there's little to be done about totalizing forms of oppression besides walk away. *Percival Everett by Virgil Russell* argues that things should be allowed to be what they are and shouldn't be forced to be otherwise. *Notable American Women* endorses a quietism at cross-purposes with all forms of political activity. Taken too far, the subtraction that produces *Tree of Codes* leads to zero. Of course, we should also avoid reducing complicated works of experimental literature to digestible and actionable political messages. The one conclusion I do feel comfortable drawing from these texts, which broadly endorse a conception of value grounded in the general but not universal truth of theoretical concepts, is that any politics we might imagine in the wake of the collapse of the form-politics homology will be completely ad hoc. It cannot be motivated by sweeping utopian visions, enduring ideological commitments, or a confident sense of justice and right. Instead, it will be a politics of the contingent historical phenomenon, the singular, perhaps even the idiosyncratic. The terms and conditions, as well as the results and outcomes, will be specific to the moment. They will be general but not universal. And that, I think, is where politics emerges in the novels discussed above—not necessarily in the particular configurations of the world that they provide, but in their common recognition that the worlds they describe are just one of a finite but still very large number of possible worlds available to us, depending on the way we decide to configure and compose them on an ad hoc basis.

CHAPTER 3

Revolution, Historical Fiction, and Gesture

During the 2016 Democratic primary, Bernie Sanders described his movement as a "political revolution." The precise nature of that revolution? Reforming Democratic Party leadership, convincing "hundreds of thousands of people to become childcare workers and teachers," and developing "great business people who can produce and distribute the products and services we need in a way that respects their employees and the environment" (Sanders). Just months later, committed Trumpsters, fearing a Hillary Clinton victory, anticipated "another Revolutionary War" and promised to expel Clinton from office "by any means necessary" (Parker and Corasaniti).

But what, exactly, does "revolution" mean when the left-wing of the Democratic party and the Trump wing of the Republican party are its equal champions? Obviously very little, and certainly nothing too revolutionary. But maybe we should be heartened that these folks are at least managing to use the word in its properly political context. These days, more often than not, the language of revolution belongs to the world of capital, not politics. One foundational moment in capital's claim on revolution might be located in Nike's infamous appropriation of the Beatles' *White Album* song, "Revolution 1," to introduce its Nike Air shoes in 1987.[1] More than two decades later,

---

1. I call this appropriation "infamous" because it spawned a series of lawsuits challenging the song's commercial use (Hilburn). Nike's use of the Beatles' song is particularly brilliant/cynical not just because it deploys a song about revolution for its own profit-maximizing ends

Apple hewed to the same logic when it introduced its iPad as a "revolution [that's] only just begun."[2] More recently, a Pepsi commercial enlisted model Kendall Jenner to lead what Stephen Colbert satirized as an "attractive lives matter" protest that culminates in a standoff with the police. Peace, and excessive amounts of self-congratulatory cheering, break out when a cute police officer accepts Jenner's proffered Pepsi.[3] Little surprise, then, that a pyramid-scheme-y company offering seminars and webinars promising to maximize its customers' residual incomes is named Global Revolution.[4] Or that Revolution Analytics, a software company devoted to open source formats, was so revolutionary that it sold itself to Microsoft in 2015. Then there's Revolution Capital, an oxymoron (and also a global private investment firm) of the highest order, along with Revolution Ventures, a venture capital group investing in "technology-enabled businesses that disrupt existing, multi-billion-dollar industries."[5] That'll show 'em.

Of course, countries ruled by dictatorial strongmen remain susceptible to real political revolution, and its frequent aftermath, civil war. Events in Sudan, Tunisia, Egypt, Syria, Yemen, Hong Kong, and Iran over the past decade suggest as much. And more localized protests still occasionally exhibit a revolutionary flare, as we've seen after police shootings of black men in Ferguson, Missouri; Charlotte, North Carolina; and Baton Rouge, Louisiana. And yet, as most leading theorists loosely working within the Marxist tradition indicate, we live today after the end of revolution. Characterizing "the old radical Left" as the "sympathetic living dead," Slavoj Žižek notes, for example, that revolutionary commitment has disappeared "from our political and ideological reality" (*Trouble* 210). Micah White, one of the founders of Occupy Wall Street, asserts that "revolutionary theory on the left and right has been at a dead end" for years now (126). Michael Hardt and Antonio Negri ground their influential trilogy—*Empire, Multitude,* and *Commonwealth*—on the claim that "some of the basic traditional models of political activism, class struggle, and

---

but also because the song is actually quite skeptical of revolution, implying that feeling good is more important than political change: "If you go carrying pictures of Chairman Mao / You ain't going to make it with anyone anyhow." You don't actually have to revolt, the song tells us, because everything is "going to be all right, all right, all right, all right. . . ." You can watch the advertisement here: https://vimeo.com/89811766.

2. Watch the "What is iPad?" commercial here: https://www.youtube.com/watch?v=MKZrqiBtUZo, and learn more about the revolution that has only just begun in Luke Dormehl's *The Apple Revolution,* one edition of which has the iconic raised fist of solidarity holding a mouse on the cover.

3. See https://www.youtube.com/watch?v=uwvAgDCOdU4.

4. See teamrevolution.com.

5. Join the revolution here: http://www.revolution.com/entity/ventures/.

revolutionary organization have today become outdated and useless" (*Multitude* 68). Such obsolescence can be blamed on any number of developments. Hardt and Negri note the globalization of the economy, the dominance of post-Fordist, immaterial labor, and the decline of sovereignty as an organizing political principle, all of which diffuse and disperse the object of revolution. The sociologist Todd Gitlin observes that students, once the "motors of change" but now encumbered with debt, don't have time to protest anymore, and even if they did, actual political rebellion has become "uncool" in an age that commodifies rebellious opposition and replaces "moral seriousness" with "sarcasm" (xii–xiii). We should also add to this list a general disenchantment and cynicism born of the twentieth century's long history of failed revolutionary activity: the Stalinist betrayals of the Bolshevik Revolution;[6] the tactical compromises that dissipated the revolutionary momentum of May '68 in Paris; the fracturing of the 1960s radical left in the US over the question of violence;[7] and the cozy relationship between free-market capitalism and political freedom that fueled revolutionary activity in many Soviet Bloc nations in the 1980s and early 1990s. With the end of history and triumph of liberal democracy in the 1990s, revolution was liberated from the political sphere, easily arrogated by Madison Avenue and sold to the highest corporate bidder, as we've seen most recently with the cadre of corporate giants lining up behind Black Lives Matter.[8]

And yet, despite the demise of revolutionary possibility at the end of the twentieth century, twenty-first-century fiction writers have taken up the theme of revolution and revolutionary protest in force. Some focus on large-scale revolutions of political power (the Russian Revolution of 1917, the 1945 August Revolution in Vietnam and the ensuing Vietnam War, the Cuban Revolution of 1959, or the 1979 Sandinista Revolution in Nicaragua) while others investigate more circumscribed revolutionary acts (the Unabomber's exploding packages, the Symbionese Liberation Army's kidnapping and conversion of Patty Hearst, the Weather Underground's bombing campaign, or the Italian Red Brigades' Autonomist movement in the late 1970s). Regardless of the specific nature of the revolution, however, all of these texts—Susan Choi's *American Woman* (2003) and *A Person of Interest* (2008), Christopher

---

6. Although, see Sean McMeekin's *The Russian Revolution*, which suggests that Lenin and the Bolsheviks were betraying the 1917 revolution before it even began.

7. Žižek argues that the Left's recourse to violence did not lead to its failure. Rather, the Left had already failed, and the recourse to violence was merely "a symptom of this failure, its effect and not its cause" (*Trouble* 210).

8. A more detailed genealogy of revolutionary activity in the twentieth century can be found in Hardt and Negri's *Multitude*, pages 69–93. And see Cedric Johnson for a critique of Black Lives Matter's corporatism.

Sorrentino's *Trance* (2005), Dana Spiotta's *Eat the Document* (2006), Hari Kun-zru's *My Revolutions* (2007), Peter Carey's *His Illegal Self* (2008), Rachel Kush-ner's *Telex from Cuba* (2008) and *The Flamethrowers* (2013), Jonathan Lethem's *Dissident Gardens* (2013), and Viet Nguyen's *The Sympathizer* (2015)—explore revolutions and revolutionary activity of the past. Why, I wonder, have so many twenty-first-century authors written historical novels about the violent revolutionary politics of the twentieth century? Are these texts symptoms of or responses to the impasses of twenty-first-century leftist thought? Are they nostalgic for a revolutionary possibility now foreclosed by the totalizing grasp of global capital? Are they, in a more Lukácsian vein, returning historical con-sciousness to a contemporary moment that still hasn't quite figured out "how to think historically in the first place"? (Jameson, *Postmodernism* ix). Or per-haps it's just too difficult to write about politics unfolding in the present?[9]

This chapter essays two different but complementary arguments about the proliferation of historical revolutions in contemporary fiction written after the apparent end of revolution. First, I'm interested in what these novels might indicate about the status and possibilities of contemporary leftist thought, in a US context, in the wake of revolution. As in the previous chapters on art and theory, I will argue that the demise of revolution can be viewed, in part, as the result of a vacillating relationship between form and politics, specifi-cally the unstable relationship between the form of revolutionary activity and the political goal or outcome such activity aims to achieve. When the form of revolutionary activity can no longer be correlated in any predictive or sta-ble way to its political result, revolution becomes a much dicier proposition. Ends-based forms of revolutionary activity that rely on the transcendent, pro-spective vision of leaders, institutions, and roadmaps, for example, risk rein-scribing the very hierarchical structures of oppression they seek to overthrow. Conversely, means-based forms that locate change in the immanent processes

---

9. In the United States, Occupy Wall Street and its related uprisings have yet to emerge as a primary concern for contemporary fiction. Ben Lerner lets an Occupier use his shower in *10:04* (2014), which inspires plenty of meditative navel-gazing about whether and how the privileged can be political. And Jonathan Lethem's *Dissident Gardens* ends with the grandson of a Communist organizer having sex with an Occupier in an airport bathroom. But based on my admittedly limited research, the only novel actually about Occupy is the not-quite-readable *Trading Dreams* by J. L. Morin (2012). Poetry has been much more engaged with the revolu-tionary movements arising out of the 2008 recession, thanks in part to the work Jasper Bernes, Joshua Clover, and Juliana Spahr are doing at Commune Editions. Spahr's *An Army of Lovers*, an experimental prose work coauthored with David Buuck, is another apt example.

Beyond my skill set and the purview of this chapter, the Arab Spring has left more of a mark on fiction, at least among Middle Eastern authors. Ursula Lindsey's "The Novel after the Arab Spring" and Nahrain Al-Mousawi's "Literature after the Arab Spring" detail those developments.

of revolutionary activity risk perpetuating the liquid logic of homogenized
equivalence that fuels late capitalism. Consequently, debates about the *form*
of revolution—and as we'll see, most of the conversations about the possibility of revolutionary activity today remain deeply preoccupied with its form—
founder on the ambivalent vacillation of the form-politics homology. The
novels discussed here reiterate, wrestle with, and occasionally supersede the
obsolescence of such homological thought, struggling to find new ways to
think about and beyond the end of revolution. As all of the historical novels
discussed here treat revolutions past, the new ways of thinking they identify
don't emerge from the texts' thematic representations of revolution as much
as they do from the formal features of their presentation. In particular, these
historical fictions broach the question of revolutionary form by staging the
formal problem of their own literary realism and the politics it may (or may
not) achieve. They use their own forms of realism to think through the formal impasses that beset the various revolutionary activities that their content
comprises.

Thus, this chapter's second argument, reciprocal to the first, contends that
these texts' various treatments of revolution can also tell us something about
the status of contemporary fiction in general and the contemporary historical novel in particular. What exactly does revolution do for these novels and
why are they so invested in this theme? In brief, to the extent that an ambiva-
lently vacillating form-politics relation has compromised revolution's purchase
on our contemporary moment, the theme of revolution affords authors the
opportunity to explore how the contemporary historical novel might negotiate
its own political purchase on and standing in a world where the relationship
between literary form and politics has proven to be similarly unstable and
unreliable. Taking these two arguments together, this chapter enlists contemporary historical fiction to think beyond the end of revolution, and it relies
on these novels' treatment of revolution to consider the political status of historical fiction today.

In each of the novels discussed here—Jonathan Lethem's *Dissident Gardens*, Dana Spiotta's *Eat the Document*, and Rachel Kushner's *Telex from Cuba*
and *The Flamethrowers*—we find various attempts to correlate revolutionary
form with specific political values, but those correlations are always skewing
and signifying in unintended ways. This leads to a crisis in the possibility
of revolutionary activity, which in the novels plays out as a broader crisis of
historical fiction itself. Of course, according to Lukács, the historical novel
had already lost its ability to provide "the concrete possibilities for men to
comprehend their own existence as something historically conditioned" (*Historical* 24) by the late nineteenth century when "the severance of the present

from history creates an historical novel which drops to the level of light enter-
tainment" (183). Writing at the beginning of the twenty-first century, Fredric
Jameson corroborates Lukács's diagnosis, but finds some political potential
for the historical novel in science fiction, a genre which, by asking large-scale
questions about the present's future, might dialectically integrate individuals
into a broader collective and help us see ourselves in and as History.

My aim here is not to hold my archive of contemporary historical novels
to the strict standards of this Marxist tradition, but instead to explore the ways
in which these texts view history as a resource to generate new modes of relating to the past, new forms of generality that move beyond Lukács's and Jameson's dialectical demands. Each of these novels struggles to determine the best
way to stage the present's encounter with a revolutionary past, but they don't
all necessarily approach that struggle through generality. I will use *Dissident
Gardens,* for example, to diagnose and map out the conceptual parameters and
limitations of the contemporary historical novel. *Telex from Cuba* and *Eat the
Document* explore whether history might provide modes of affective connection that could ground an alternative politics in sympathy (*Telex*) and irreducible human complexity (*Eat*). Then the second half of the chapter turns to *The
Flamethrowers* to introduce Kushner's attempt to supersede the form-politics
homology and its contemporary vacillations through more general forms. In
particular, I will argue that Kushner develops a theory of gesture—which,
along with the generic, case study, and the constructivism of theoretical literalism, stands as a fourth example of an emergent logic of generality—that
functions in Kushner's novel as both a distinctly postrevolutionary approach
to revolutionary activity and as a literary mode that productively intervenes
in the impasses of the contemporary historical novel.

Revolutionary Forms

Attempting to characterize the nature of revolution today, Thomas Nail distinguishes twentieth-century revolution—the statist, Party-led overthrow and
seizure of power that aims to establish radically new social, economic, and
political institutions—from twenty-first century revolution, which instead
favors intersectional analyses of power, prefiguration, directly participatory
democracy, and decentralized horizontalism (375). Even as the possibility of a
revolution built around "the capture of the state, the political representation of
the party, the centrality of the proletariat, or the leadership of the vanguard"
has died, Nail observes that "today we are witnessing the return of revolution," although "it seems to be taking none of the traditional forms" (375).

Those who practice this twenty-first-century form of revolution, who reduce ends to means and emphasize new modes of being and becoming, pursue this path not out of mere personal preference but because of perceived historical necessity. These immanent forms emerge in direct response to late capitalism's apparently total subsumption of contemporary politics, society, and culture, an economization of life that makes it difficult to locate any terrain from which one might launch an external revolution against its totality. Without an outside, revolution has no choice but to proceed immanently.

As recently as the 1960s, the Italian autonomists developed revolutionary tactics that relied on spaces and temporalities external to capital. Through work slowdowns, work-to-rule strikes, and ad hoc wage and price setting, they cordoned off spaces and actions autonomous to capital's control of labor. But as the mode of capitalist production in the West became increasingly immaterial, shifting from the industrialized manufacture of durable commodities to the deindustrialized production of intangible services, communications, and affects, workerist autonomy evaporated. Even the soul, Franco Berardi suggests, has been put to work. The immaterial things that once existed outside and beyond capitalist labor—love, care, creativity, the social—have now become its primary methods and objects.[10] This is what Hardt and Negri, via Foucault, Deleuze, and Guattari, name the "biopolitical production" of contemporary capitalism, which they suggest takes at least three distinct forms: "the communicative labor of industrial production that has newly become linked in informational networks, the interactive labor of symbolic analysis and problem solving, and the labor of the production and manipulation of affects" (*Empire* 30). Focusing in particular on affect, Hardt and Negri emphasize that this shift to immaterial labor is still quite physical and bodily to the extent that late capitalism touches us ontologically, devoting itself to the production and reproduction of being (47). Life used to be separable from work, but now that work has taken life as its primary object of value, they are perfectly conflated.

For Hardt and Negri, this is not cause for excessive alarm. Instead, they suggest that the very features of biopolitical production and economic totality that make it impossible to separate work from life also provide the groundwork for new forms of revolutionary resistance. Life's immanence to capital simply means that our revolutionary forms of resistance must be immanent

---

10. See Franco Berardi's *The Soul at Work*. As Jason Smith writes in the preface to Berardi's book, "The sphere of desire, the field of the imaginary and the affective, whose affirmation as the fundamental field of the political once led to a collective abandonment of the sphere of work, [has] been transformed into the privileged force in the contemporary order of work, the privileged moment in the production of value" (13).

as well. Consequently, they detail a program for twenty-first-century revolution—revolution after the end of revolution—that is networked rather than dialectical, immanent rather than utopian, and ontological rather than epistemological and ideological. If the battle is to be waged over forms of life, then political antagonism will play out through modes of being and becoming, not through dialectical forms of political antagonism grounded in a particular ideology, class inequality, or system of beliefs.

Hardt and Negri name the primary force in this battle the multitude, which they describe as "the living alternative that grows within Empire," "an open and expansive network in which all differences can be expressed freely and equally" (*Multitude* xiii–xiv). Stuck in "a world that knows no outside," inextricably subsumed into a "set of social structures, with no possibility of transcending them" (*Empire* 413), today's "revolutionary movement resides on the same horizon of temporality with capitalist control" (*Commonwealth* 242–43). Consequently, the multitude remains immanent to Empire, functioning as an ongoing, self-constituting force of resistance within our total subsumption by global capital. This means that revolutionary action under the current global dispensation must move further into capital rather than oppose it, with the hope that accepting and doubling down on its totalization will produce new forms of being that might reconfigure that totalization even though they will never transcend it. Hardt and Negri name this process of being and becoming that is also potentially a revolutionary act, *posse*, that is, "power as a verb, as activity" (407). *Posse* is the constituent power, the self-constituting power, by which the multitude brings itself into being. "Through the production of subjectivity," Hardt and Negri contend, "the multitude is itself author of its perpetual becoming other, an uninterrupted process of collective self-transformation" (173).

Occupy Wall Street, Tahrir Square, the Indignados Movement in Madrid, the Indignant Citizens Movement in Athens, the occupation of the capitol in Madison, Wisconsin: these twenty-first-century protests exemplify immanently self-constituting revolution.[11] Although they were protesting income inequality in New York City, political dictatorship in Cairo, austerity in Madrid and Athens, and union busting in Madison, all of these revolutionary movements were organized horizontally, refused ideological categorization, and rejected the representational features of representative democracy in

---

11. See Hardt and Negri's *Declaration*, which exuberantly embraces these revolutionary movements as material evidence of the real-world deployment of the ideas they introduced in *Empire, Multitude,* and *Commonwealth.*

favor of a radical democratic practice that treats every single person as equal.[12] These are revolutionary movements that make "social change . . . *immanent to the process* unfolding in the encampments" (Scholl 319). They believe that "revolutionary potential lies beyond vanguards and political parties; that decentralized, diverse and autonomous organization is key to social change; and [that] radical democracy sits at the heart of radical politics today" (Curran 227).[13] They subscribe to the Zapatista motto, *Preguntando caminamos,* (Asking, we walk), which involves rejecting the current dispensation, walking away from it without necessarily knowing where you want to go. Instead, as they walk and ask, ask and walk, "they are creating new ways of being . . . new possibilities, still to be determined" (Sitrin and Azzellini 6). Such immanent revolutions also embrace the Zapatistas' attempt to change the world without taking power,[14] to imagine revolution as a noninstrumental mode of being, shorn of programmatic politics and ideological positioning. Or, as Michael Taussig gushes in his own enthusiastic missive from his visit to Occupy Wall Street, "Revolution is different now" (32). Revolution has freed itself from the dialectic of history and is now fueled by the knitting needles of older women in Zuccotti Park making clothes for winter, by the stationary bikes the Occupiers pedal to run their generators, by the façades of Wall Street buildings repurposed as giant video screens for those occupying the park. This is "politics as aesthetics," "politics as affective intensity" (40), politics as "a new form of being" (34). For W. J. T. Mitchell, it's also a revolutionary politics that "renounces the demand that it make specific, practical demands, while opening a space in which innumerable demands can be articulated" (103).[15]

Maybe. But as Slavoj Žižek has suggested, this process-based approach to revolution remains so enthralled to horizontal, nonrepresentational, imma-

---

12. They also all located the telos of protest in the ongoingness of occupation itself, although this is more true tactically than it is strategically, and it's more true for some of the occupations than others. The revolutionaries in Cairo, for example, clearly aimed to oust Hosni Mubarak while the Occupiers in Zuccotti Park had no unifying goal beyond prolonging and expanding the occupation.

13. Curran names this approach "post-ideological anarchism."

14. John Holloway borrows this idea for the title of his book on postideological revolution, *Change the World without Taking Power.* Also see his *Crack Capitalism* for an expansion of his thinking that remains firmly rooted in Zapatista principles.

15. It's interesting to compare Taussig's and Mitchell's observations to the postmortem that Micah White, one of Occupy Wall Street's main organizers, offers in *The End of Protest.* White is more inclined to see Occupy as a failure precisely to the extent that it was unable to achieve the very specific, concrete goals he had ascribed to occupation: "It was obvious we had lost: the bankers weren't going to be arrested and the influence of money on democracy wasn't going to be halted" (33).

nent becoming that it might be inviting the enemy in through the back door. "Is this 'molecular' spontaneous self-organization really the most efficient new form of 'resistance'?" Žižek asks. "Is it not that the opposite side, especially capital, already acts more and more as what Deleuzian theory calls the post-Oedipal multitude?" (*Trouble* 182).[16] For Žižek, "non-representative direct self-organization" is a "myth," "the deepest illusion that is most difficult to renounce" precisely because it's so perfectly conducive to the continued functioning of global capital (206).[17] Instead, signaling his distrust of immanently self-constituting multitudes, Žižek suggests that we reclaim the economic from its post-Fordist diffuseness and insist on the continued possibility of a revolutionary politics that takes communism as "the ultimate horizon of our emancipatory struggles" (214).[18] For Žižek, this requires a "Master figure" positioned outside revolution, a transcendent leader who binds the collective together with a unified vision, tactics, and strategy (184).[19] This binding affords the revolution a necessary moment of representational reflection; it can see

16. Žižek makes a similar argument in "The Ideology of the Empire and Its Traps" where he extends this critique to Foucault, Deleuze, and Guattari, the "ultimate philosophers of resistance" whose work merely reinscribes "the ideology of the newly emerging ruling class" (261). Jodi Dean's *Crowds and Party* is premised on a similar critique. Also see Jean Baudrillard's *Forget Foucault* and Franco Berardi's discussion of Baudrillard's take on Foucault in the third and fourth chapters of *The Soul at Work*. Daniel Zamora's description of Foucault as a closet neoliberal offers another example of this argument ("Can We Criticize Foucault?").

17. Unsurprisingly, the language of capitalism quickly infected Occupy. In London, for example, Occupiers highlighted Friedrich von Hayek's idea "that distributed intelligence in a voluntary cooperative is a hallmark of real economy." They even seemed to take pride in their ability to out-capital capitalism, observing that Occupy "work[s] more like a market than the corporate boardroom of lobbyist-loaded politics" (Dewhurst et al.). Todd Gitlin makes a similar move in *Occupy Nation*, arguing that "Occupy is a different kind of entrepreneurship, a creative and cooperative endeavor, and it profits America by making human vitality grow" (xvi).

18. Crucially, Žižek does not imagine this horizon as the endpoint of an ineluctable teleology or dialectical utopianism, but rather as "a space of ideas within which we move" (244). Offering a similar take on communism today, Alain Badiou's "The Communist Hypothesis" describes communism as a "set of intellectual representations" or "intellectual patterns" (35). See Jodi Dean's *Žižek's Politics* for an extended treatment of the political implications of Žižek's work. Dean's *The Communist Horizon* departs from Badiou and Žižek by imagining communism as an empty, but nevertheless indispensable, universal: "The horizon is Real in the sense of *impossible*—we can never reach it—and in the sense of *actual* (Jacques Lacan's notion of the Real includes both these senses)" (2). (Conversely, Žižek says in *Trouble* that the Communist horizon is "not . . . an inaccessible ideal" [244].) Dean's Lacanian vision is more in line with the way Butler, Laclau, and Žižek discuss universality in *Contingency, Hegemony, Universality* (see chapter 1, note 35).

19. Jodi Dean's *Crowds and Party* theorizes the party in much the same way, describing it as a "transferential object" (242) and as "the apparatus through which we compel ourselves to do what we must" (210).

itself and what it's fighting for. Of course, Hardt and Negri would worry that this representational moment threatens to overdetermine, ossify, and possibly compromise the revolution with its hierarchical imposition. But Žižek eludes those concerns by offering a "Master figure" who, far from being fascistic or oppressive, functions more like a psychoanalyst onto whom a patient transfers a set of feelings so that the patient can reflect on and gain insight into those feelings. Žižek claims that after listening to a Master leader (he unironically offers Steve Jobs as an example), "people all of a sudden realize what they always-already knew they wanted—listening to the Master clarifies to them their own position, enables them to recognize themselves, their own inner-most need, in the project proposed to them" (190).

As I've suggested, the disagreement here can be understood as a debate over the proper role of representation in revolution. What representational form, if any, should revolution take? Hardt and Negri assert that the "proper form" of "revolutionary political militancy today" is "not representational but constituent activity" (*Empire* 413). Thus, their vision of revolutionary politics "is given substance only when we shift our focus from the question of form and order to the regimes and practices of production" (217). In place of a "van-guard that would seek to lead or *represent* the masses," they offer "the network of the laboring subjectivities that cooperate and communicate" (*Common-wealth* 246, my emphasis). Read closely, the immanentists' relation to form looks paradoxical. They say we should "shift our focus from the question of form" while also maintaining that there is a "proper form" for revolution to take today. The result of this contradiction is a weak, negative, and ultimately tautologous theory of form. The immanentists seem to reject formal concerns to the extent that they renounce all externally imposed forms in favor of revo-lution's self-constitution. But immanent self-constitution is itself a form, just a very weak one that conceives revolution's form as tautologous to, because emerging sui generis from, horizontally organized, radically democratic activ-ity itself.[20] Most importantly for my argument here, however, I want to empha-size that the immanentists' weak, tautologous theory of form still adheres to the form-politics homology. Their commitment to horizontal relations and rhizomatic networks leaves revolutionary form quite diffuse, but they clearly

---

20. This tautological theory of revolutionary form also makes their theory of revolution unimpeachable. If you reduce the multitude's revolutionary form to the multitude's practice, process, and production, then its form can never be wrong because its truth conditions only require it to be itself in its ongoing process of becoming. It will always be revolutionary just by virtue of its being.

believe that a specific political effectivity follows directly from their preferred revolutionary form.[21]

Of course, those horizontal relations and rhizomatic networks are precisely the forms that the likes of Žižek and Jodi Dean view as a "celebration of autonomous individuality" derived from "capitalist ideology" (Dean, *Crowds and Party* 4, 29).[22] They acknowledge the potential terror of verticality and consolidated power but insist nonetheless that revolution requires representation if it hopes to be intelligible and effective. "For the crowd to become the people [i.e., a political subjectivity], representation is necessary," Dean writes, adding, "There is no politics until a meaning is announced and a struggle over this meaning begins" (125).[23] Although they remain flexible about the representational *content* that the Master or the Party reflects on behalf of the revolution, dialectical representationalists like Žižek and Dean also rely on a form-politics homology that ascribes specific political outcomes to particular representational forms. Their homologous logic emerges not only in their argument against the immanentists, which contends that forms homologous to capital are inevitably complicit with it, but also in their own commitment to dialectical forms, which they present as indispensable for achieving specific political outcomes. Taken together, then, we find two different accounts of

---

21. To be sure, Hardt and Negri acknowledge that they must "engage directly with the question of organization because that is the terrain on which the progressive, liberatory, anti-systemic character of the multitude will have to be verified and consolidated in its own durable institutions" (*Commonwealth* 177), but in book after book, they never do so. They talk about love and poverty; they insist that the revolutionary multitude must be governed; they champion the value of democratic decision making. But as soon as revolutionary activity begins to take concrete forms of political organization, governance, and institutions, they immediately collapse those forms by insisting that they "always remain contingent and aleatory—floating structures . . . on the clashing waves of global society" (373). Hardt and Negri seem to be terminally allergic to all representational forms.

22. See Joshua Clover's *Riot. Strike. Riot* for another Marxist critique of "the issueless democratic urge" that motivated Occupy Wall Street's attempt to make "deliberation . . . an end in and of itself" (178).

23. Ernesto Laclau's critique of Hardt and Negri's *Empire* implies a similar demand for representation: "Perhaps the ultimate incoherence of [*Empire*] . . . is that it proposes fragments of a perfectly acceptable political program, while its conditions of implementation are denied by the central theoretical and strategic categories [i.e., immanence and self-constituting power] on which its analysis is based" ("Immanence" 30).

Just to be fair to Dean, it's important to note that her theory of the party's representational capacities is nuanced, complex, and in many ways acknowledges that Hardt and Negri's description of post-Fordist capital is correct. Thus, Dean's party doesn't tell the people what to think or do; it has no ideology or program. Instead, it's an "affective infrastructure" (*Crowds* 209) that "generates and mobilizes" the crowd's "dynamics of feeling" (210) in a political direction, thereby transforming the diffuse and indeterminate crowd into the politically subjectivized people.

revolution after the end of revolution: one, an antirepresentational approach championing revolution's immanent self-constitution; the other, a dialectical approach that requires an externalized, transcendent representational moment that lends revolution direction and meaning. Both ground themselves in a form-politics homology that views specific political ends flowing directly from specific revolutionary forms. To the extent that each sees the other as an exemplary symptom of the very thing it seeks to revolt against, however, those grounding form-politics homologies prove unstable. Specific revolutionary forms cannot be theorized as predictive guarantors of particular political outcomes.

I turn now to the forms of contemporary fiction about revolution as a way to think through and beyond these revolutionary models that remain stymied by vacillating homology. As we'll see, the representational impasses that befuddle revolutionary theory also emerge when contemporary historical fiction turns its attention to revolutions of the past. My hunch, however, is that literature might eventually do a better job thinking past these representational impasses than theory alone has done.

Failure to Represent

Jonathan Lethem's *Dissident Gardens* provides a sweeping vision of twentieth- and twenty-first-century revolutionary activity, tracing three generations of political activists in a single Jewish family from New York City, the Zimmers. Despite its comprehensive grasp on leftist political activity in the United States, however, the novel remains remarkably nonpolitical, struggling at every turn to represent revolution in a politically effective way. At most, we might say that *Dissident Gardens,* with its detailed chronicling of the rise and fall of the radical left, effectively chronicles a revolutionary historical trajectory that culminates in its own political impotence. Or, it's a historical novel about revolution that reveals the contemporary historical novel's own conditions of revolutionary impossibility.

The Zimmer family matriarch, Rose, is an active member of the Communist Party of the United States of America (CPUSA) in the middle of the twentieth century. Her daughter, Miriam, a child of the 1960s with strong hippie tendencies, views revolutionary politics much more expansively than her Communist mother. And then there's Miriam's son, Sergius, who is raised by Quakers after his parents are killed fighting for the Sandinistas in Nicaragua. Sergius eventually connects with a young woman, Lydia, actively involved in the Occupy movement. Filling out the novel's political platform are Rose's husband, Albert Zimmer, a CPUSA member who abandons his family when the Party relocates him to East Germany where he becomes an obedient appa- ratchik; Miriam's husband, Tommy Gogan, a composer of mediocre protest songs; Miriam's cousin, Lenny, a socially awkward misfit who ends up the most doctrinaire Marxist of them all; and Cicero Lookins, an African Ameri- can college professor who teaches affect and queer theory in Maine.

Dissident Gardens suggests that the history of leftist revolutionary thought from the 1930s to the 2010s follows a trajectory of increasing diffuseness. At every step, revolutionary politics loses its specificity, diluted by the personal, the social, and the emotional.[24] Rose and Albert's marriage, initially conceived as "a highly dialectical situation" (134), collapses under "their stupid guilt at their wasted lives" (16). Their daughter Miriam's "cloud politics," "unmoored in theory or party" (156), are freed from the strictures of dialectical history but also problematically nebulous: she lives in a commune and pursues largely symbolic acts of protest. Miriam's son, Sergius, champions Occupy as the new face of revolution in the twenty-first century, but he has no clear sense of what that means. It's just "a way of being," a more experienced Occupier struggles to explain, "just living differently" (360). As far as Cicero is concerned, how- ever, Occupy exemplifies leftist minstrelsy—privileged white kids living on the street, pretending to be destitute (220). Consequently, he juxtaposes such political imposture to the pure "transmission of affect," which, he insists to his class, "is as political as it gets" (221). But Lethem's satirical treatment of Cicero's jargon-laden, alienating pedagogy implies that we probably shouldn't put too much stock in that either. In each case, the fuzziness of personal inter- actions, social relations, and emotional response replaces the specificity of political antagonism and revolutionary conflict.[25] The desire to expand the field of revolutionary possibility, the belief that liberty and equality cannot be secured through political or economic revolution alone and instead require

---

24. In *Dissident Gardens*, Communism's betrayals aren't just personal, they're also politi- cal on a grand scale. When, in 1956, Khrushchev acknowledges Stalin's genocidal atrocities, the Communist "illusion" is destroyed for good, and "true Communism . . . float[s] free of history" (94). But even before that, with the forging of the Hitler-Stalin pact in 1939, the Soviet Union effectively destroyed the Popular Front—an idea that encouraged communist solidarity with anti-Fascist parties in other nations regardless of those parties' communist bona fides—and made it impossible for millions of communist Jews around the world to support the Party (144–45).

25. See Eric Hobsbawm's "Revolution and Sex": "Perhaps today in the west where, 'alien- ation' rather than poverty is the crucial motive force of rebellion, no movement which does not also attack the system of personal relations and private satisfactions can be revolutionary. But, taken by themselves, cultural revolt and cultural dissidence are symptoms, not revolutionary forces. Politically they are not very important" (219).

an overhaul of social relations, cultural norms, and ways of being, ultimately undermines the field of revolutionary possibility.[26]

As Lethem makes clear, form plays a key role in this process. Each successive generation believes that it has discovered the proper form through which to represent and bring forth the revolution. Each relies on a homology between form and politics to guarantee the effectiveness of *their* distinct take on revolution, but the homology never proves as secure as they would like, and their revolutions suffer the consequences.

First, Rose and Albert's doctrinaire Marxism, their insistence on a historical consciousness achieved through dialectical materialism, evokes Georg Lukács's thinking about the historical novel, which "has to demonstrate by artistic means that historical circumstances and characters existed in precisely such and such a way" (43). Novels that provide "this artistic demonstration of historical reality," that materially represent "the broad living basis of historical events in their intricacy and complexity" (43), provide the means by which individuals dialectically develop a collectivized historical consciousness. When Rose and Albert translate their marriage into dialectical terms; when Rose insists to Miriam that her "present world . . . is in fact a product of history" (37); when Lenny critiques a Greenwich-Village folksinger's "lack of historical grasp" (91); and when Albert condemns Americans for being "a deeply . . . ahistorical people" (226), each champions this particular approach to representing the world. They all demand a dialectically materialist realism, grounded in the actually existing economic conditions of a given historical moment, that can forge a necessary connection between life and political economy.

As Rose suggests to Cousin Lenny, however, achieving a clear vision of that necessary connection between life and political economy is hard to pull off. The historical novel all too easily slips into clunky, overdetermined "allegory" (257), amounting to little more than an elaborate game of "dress-up" (259). This is certainly the game that apparatchik Albert plays in East Germany where he claims to be a permanent student of dialectical history (226) but is actually making a religious fetish out of the decline of his aristocratic German family. For his daughter Miriam, Albert's work reads "like some Greek fable about being descended from gods, and then falling into the moral

---

26. This is a trend which, according to Hannah Arendt, we can trace back to the eighteenth century when the French Revolution diluted the political specificity of the American Revolution by introducing what Arendt calls "the social question," which includes concerns about poverty, social inequality, and other forms of immiseration. This is one reason, according to Arendt, that the American Revolution succeeded while the French Revolution failed. The Americans didn't confuse politics with the social order while the French conflated the two and became unable to achieve enduring revolutionary political change (59–114).

world." "From my perspective," she writes, "all the Dresden stuff that consumes you now, all that ruined culture, the stained glass and parapets, it looks from this distance like you're a monk in the Church of Dead Europe" (239). Lethem makes the literary point—that Albert's aesthetic forms are those of myth, fable, and allegory and therefore do not achieve the properly Marxist historical consciousness he pursues—by placing Albert's family home right next door to the Buddenbrooks House. This is the home of the Buddenbrooks family, chronicled in Thomas Mann's eponymous novel, which Lukács champions as a prime example of what the socially realist historical novel might look like in the twentieth century ("In Search"). By comparison, the family "allegory" Albert chronicles is, at best, historical-novel-adjacent.

In addition to this tendency toward caricatured allegory, the committed Communist's aesthetic forms struggle to accept the representational logic of images, signs, and symbols into their repertoire. According to Miriam, social realism isn't just uninterested in symbolic representation; its existence actually depends on a shortsighted rejection of it. The novel makes this point via an argument Miriam has with her father, Albert, about Picasso's "Guernica" and the real-life horrors that is represents. After Albert mentions to Miriam in a letter that the horrors of Guernica have been "exaggerated and distorted" by "Western propaganda" and don't compare to the violence suffered by Dresden's citizens during World War II, Miriam sends every ensuing missive to her father on a "Guernica" postcard. For Albert, "the depiction of a horse in oil paint consists of not an account from the historical record but rather a poetical interpretation," and therefore fails politically (234). But for Miriam, the fact that Albert must "discredit Guernica to make [his] case" for historical materialism is enough reason to consign his brand of materialist realism to the dustbin of history (240). Albert views the dissembling of artists, the supposed "politics" of Tommy's protest music, and the "Madison Avenue-style" "images and symbols" that bewitch Miriam's thinking as evidence of the younger generation's ideological mystification. But just as the older generation's orthodox Communism gives way to the cultural revolutions of the 1960s, so too does the social realism of the *Buddenbrooks*-esque historical novel step aside for a representational mode defined by signs and symbols.

Miriam thus embraces "the power of signs" (72), privileging symbolic forms of protest over and against the rigid script of her Communist parents and cousin. She expresses her solidarity with Cesar Chavez's United Farm Workers boycotts, for example, by liberating lettuce and grapes from the produce section of the grocery store and moving them to the freezer, where they'll surely be ruined (109–10). She organizes peace marches and sings protest songs. And after she and twelve other women are arrested at a Washington DC march, they remove the baloney from the sandwiches they're given in prison and produce "meat graffiti," slapping it on the wall, "political speech formed of animal product and binders, salt and enzymes" (113). In this image, however, we also see the critique of a politics predicated on symbolic representation. It is, quite literally, a bunch of baloney—as are her husband Tommy's protest folksongs, trading as they do on romanticized images of an American purity and integrity rooted in the rural soil. As Cousin Lenny puts it, Tommy's music, "seeking solidarity with the *folk*," "is the gasping cartoon the Popular Front left in its sorry wake" (89); it's a "walking advertisement for eternal innocence with a hayseed in its teeth" (90).

In the same way that the historical novel can't evade allegory, here Miriam and Tommy's symbolic politics can't escape the naiveté of caricature. They view symbolic representation as the appropriate form for the political diffuseness of their historical moment, but they struggle to control its significance and effectivity. Tommy, for example, writes a song cycle about the destitute denizens of the Bowery, naming each song after a man he meets on the street: "The songs *are* the men," Tommy tells his producer. "There's meant to be no distance between the two." "The point is to leave my own voice aside, to bear witness instead" (179). But as one devastating review asserts, the result is "a nauseous amalgam of keening country-blues ingratiation and arch poetry, larded through with platitudinous pity toward its subject matter" (186). As the older generation of Marxists predicted, once you enter the world of aestheticized signs and symbols, your politics loses its materialist ground and becomes susceptible to interpretive models beyond your control. You think your folksongs mean one thing, but there's no necessary reason they don't actually mean something else. Miriam and Tommy try to adapt formally to the changing nature of politics in the 1960s, but the imprecision of politics, its cultural diffuseness, infects their symbolic forms, leaving those forms just as politically suspect as the earlier generation's historical realism proved to be. Once again, the form-politics homology fails to hold.

This takes us to the third formal mode that Lethem pegs to the multigenerational trajectory of twentieth- and twenty-first-century revolutionary politics: performance. Much as Miriam and Tommy (incorrectly) view their turn to symbolism as a formal solution to Rose and Albert's historical realism and its tendency toward allegory, Cicero (incorrectly) views the bodily truths of affective intensity as a productive counter to the ideologically saturated world that Miriam and Tommy inhabit. Cicero's biopolitics of affect, desire, and the body, influenced by his reading of Deleuze and Guattari (49), replace Miriam's symbolic forms with more immanent forms of being, becoming, and performing. As a professor, for example, Cicero assigns readings to his students, but rather than conveying and processing information about the texts, he "hijack[s]" class and "unfurl[s] pedagogy" in a way that will "make something occur" (196). He hopes to produce pedagogical encounters that will "plummet [students] into that abyss of the inexpressible where the truth lies, where the action is." He "hammer[s] their bodies with his language," sending them "limp[ing] out the door crippled by the onslaught of him" (197). Cicero champions "the passage of exiled sentiment from one subject's body to another's" (221), but his actions ultimately prove to be little more than idiosyncratic displays of narcissistic individualism and solipsistic self-importance. As Cicero eventually realizes of his misguided and ineffective performative pedagogy: "[Students] shouldn't be called to indulge such self-importances, and he'd been in error to set himself as a permitting example. Cicero's gripes meant nothing to anyone but himself. . . . [He] might as well have torn open his clothes and displayed his belly and dick" (216). As with the previous two generations of revolutionaries, the form that seems most conducive to the contemporary moment doesn't register as intended. The form-politics homology motivating their actions never plays out as planned.

Taken together, *Dissident Gardens* provides three different political moments (midcentury orthodox Communism, the cultural protests of the 1960s and 1970s, and the queer and Occupy revolts of the twenty-first century) and aligns them with three aesthetic forms (the social realism of the historical novel, symbolic representation, and immanent performance). But in each case, those formal modes fail to bring any significant coherence to the revolutionary politics of the day. The novel's characters want to establish a necessary relationship between the form and content of their revolutions, but each new form ends up signifying in ways beyond their control. Their reliance on the form-politics homology negates the political revolution they hope to achieve.

But should the same be said of Lethem and *Dissident Gardens*? Not entirely. After all, as a novel about the historical disarticulation of representational form from revolutionary content, *Dissident Gardens* is a contemporary historical novel fully aware of its own inability to produce "the concrete possibilities for men to comprehend their own existence as something historically conditioned." The novel produces a consciousness of history—things used to be one way; then they changed; then they changed again—but it doesn't produce historical consciousness. Of course, that was never Lethem's aim in the first place. We shouldn't indict the novel for being just another instantiation of the political failures it describes. Instead, we should read it as a historical novel about the increasing impossibility of the historical novel, as an apt diagnosis of a crisis in contemporary revolutionary thought born of an ever-vacillating form-politics homology. In this way, we might say that *Dissident Gardens* is symptomatically successful to the extent that it reveals that the failure to "comprehend . . . existence as something historically conditioned" is itself the defining feature of our contemporary historical condition.

Historical Fiction Today

If Lethem is correct, then what other ways might historical fiction approach the past? Not necessarily in an attempt to achieve a properly Marxist historical consciousness, but to at least produce an encounter with history that is more than merely relativistic. Unsurprisingly, contemporary historical novels frequently address this question through narrative, particularly through the relationships their narrators have to the history they narrate and the different forms of realism that emerge from those narrative relationships to history.

In *Antinomies of Realism,* Fredric Jameson provides some helpful language for conceptualizing the different realisms that emerge from a narrator's particular relationship to history. There, he distinguishes between realism's "narrative impulse" and its "descriptive impulse," a distinction he further maps onto the difference between the past-present-future temporality of the *récit,* or tale, and the pure present of affect (8). Jameson contends that realism "comes into being in the symbiosis" of these two impulses, and authors can blend them in different ways to produce different realisms. In today's realist novel, however, Jameson no longer sees "symbiosis" and instead finds the total triumph of affect over narration, pure present-ness over chronology. Jameson names this contemporary literary mode "realism after realism," the defining feature of which is the "swollen third person"—a third-person narrative that nevertheless feels fully first person. Rather than narrating the events, actions, and effects that proceed from the narrative subject's encounter with the world, the swollen third person evades "the truly ontological obstacles of objects and otherness" to instead narrate pure affect: "a stream of perceptions, thoughts, desires, which are neither telling nor showing, but a performance that purports to offer both" (185).[27] Nothing really happens in books anymore, Jame-

---

27. Jameson's description of "realism after realism" echoes what James Wood describes as "hysterical realism" in his essay "Human, All Too Inhuman." Hysterical realism is one of the four different ways that Paul Dawson characterizes the resurgence of omniscience in contemporary fiction ("Return of Omniscience"). Also see David Shields's *Reality Hunger* for an argument committed to realism's continued capacity to innovate and challenge the status quo.

son complains. Instead, we're only offered the narrator's speculative thinking and feeling about, and on behalf of, the world and its characters.[28]

According to Jameson, this purely affective realist mode poses a particular challenge to the contemporary historical novel. Without the past-present-future temporality of the *récit,* historical fiction today struggles to capture historical change over time, and the subject-object dialectic that typically motivates narrative action collapses into a morass of personal mushiness. Or, to use the language from the above discussion of revolutionary forms, the swollen third person is, *à la* Hardt and Negri, a kind of self-constituting immanence that makes no effort to access an extrinsic, transcendent position from which to discern the meaningfully determinant differences that others (e.g., Dean, Žižek, and now Jameson) view as imperative for revolutionary political consciousness.[29] Operating fully within the Lukácsian-Marxist tradition, Jameson views the collapse of narrative's subject-object dialectic into self-constituting immanence as the primary reason that historical novels today fail to produce historical consciousness in their readers. Hardt and Negri, however, whose work aims to supersede dialectical Marxism, might find political promise in the affective, presentist immanence that symptomatizes the contemporary historical novel for Jameson. Reversing the homology that Jameson establishes between "realism after realism" and political impotence, we might imagine them suggesting that what Jameson sees as the contemporary historical novel's abdication of politics is actually better understood as a form of political realism that recognizes the impossibility of transcending today's capitalist horizon. This reversal in turn opens up the possibility of a contemporary historical novel that generates its political vision on the basis of, not in spite of, its affective presentism.

Rachel Kushner's *Telex from Cuba* doesn't go that far, but it does deploy two competing narrative modes in an attempt to explore different ways that the present might access and understand its history. Kushner's historical novel

---

28. Ben Parker's *LARB* review of Jameson's *Antinomies* offers Tao Lin's *Taipei* as a paradigmatic example. I'd add Ben Lerner's *10:04* to the list.

29. I'm not just shoe-horning this language of immanence and transcendence into Jameson's conceptualization of contemporary realism and the historical novel. Elsewhere in *Antinomies* he uses this exact language to describe the four different modes of realism (transcendent transcendence, transcendent immanence, immanent immanence, and Jameson's preferred mode, immanent transcendence) that emerge from different configurations of realism's narrative (transcendent) and descriptive (immanent) impulses. See, for example, section 4 of "The Experiments of Time: Providence and Realism" in *Antinomies.*

Jameson's sense that contemporary realism has entirely abandoned transcendence in favor of pure immanence clearly echoes Hardt and Negri's account of a post-Fordist, biopolitical contemporary, but Jameson does not share their optimism about the political potential of such self-constituting immanence.

transports readers to revolutionary Cuba in the 1950s, focusing in particular on the ousting of US-based corporate interests such as the United Fruit Company and the Nicaro Nickel Company, which, through cozy relationships with the Batista government, effectively controlled vast portions of prerevolutionary Cuban territory and wielded significant political influence.[30] The novel thus tells the story of Castro's rising revolutionary tide, primarily from the perspective of the US citizens it eventually washed away. In particular, we receive the story from a third-person narration focalized through Everly Lederer, a young girl whose father works for the Nicaro Nickel Company, and from the first-person narration of KC Stites, a young boy whose father oversees the United Fruit Company's Cuban operations. Both narratives ask whether and how these children, now fully grown, might understand the ways in which they, their families, and the United States, are profoundly implicated in Cuban revolutionary history. As we'll see, the different narrative modes attached to Everly and KC produce notably distinct answers to those questions.

Early in the novel we learn that the young Everly has consciously decided not to record her life as it unfolds. This is in direct opposition to her sister, Stevie, who vigilantly "document[s] her life as it happened." But for Everly, "Documenting life as it happened seemed like a way of not experiencing it. As if posing for photographs, or focusing on what to save and call a souvenir, made the present instantly the past. You had to choose one or the other was Everly's feeling. Try to shape a moment into a memory you could save and look at later, or have the moment as it was happening, but you couldn't have both" (43). Because she never paused or posed, because she chose immanence, Everly can't narrate. Instead, a swollen third-person omniscience narrates for her, immersing readers in Everly's immanent flow of affect and subjective perception, and making it impossible to determine if she fully understands her place in Cuban history or not.

KC doesn't have a coherent theory for living like Everly does, but he does have a set of documents—the "immaculate records" his mother kept of their lives in Cuba (307)—that facilitate his retrospective, first-person narration. This access to an extensively documented past makes KC's retrospective, first-person narration of his Cuban boyhood possible. (We learn at novel's end that he's narrating from Tampa, Florida, in 2004.) It also gives his narrative a doubled historical vision that allows adult KC to simultaneously narrate and reflect on his younger self: "You might call it racist, especially nowadays, but it was reasonable to assume that anybody black . . . was trouble" (24).

---

30. The novel's historical content begins with Batista's 1952 overthrow of Cuban president Prío and ends with Castro's overthrow of Batista in 1959.

Despite this ability to track historical change over time (what's racist now wasn't necessarily then), the adult KC, like Everly, never recognizes his place in the Cuban revolution. He admits, "The fact is we went down there and we took" (315), but he absolutely refuses to implicate his family in Cuban history. He defends, for example, his mother's "sympathy" for the locals even though, as KC's older brother—one of two Anglo boys who join Castro's revolutionaries—contends, "without any sympathy for what caused their circumstances," their mother's sympathy is "not real sympathy but sentimentality" (315). In adulthood, then, KC can see the faint outline of a connection between the colonial US presence in Cuba and that country's violent history, but because he sees no intentional violence and lots of amorphous sympathy, he ultimately views his experience in Cuba as incidental to that history.

On the one hand, then, Everly's immanence makes it impossible to know whether she achieves historical consciousness, integrating her individual life with the "collective fabric" of revolutionary Cuban history (292). On the other, the more transcendent perspective KC achieves through his mother's documentation makes it possible to locate his "I" in history, but it doesn't necessarily guarantee that any meaningful connection to history will be made. *Telex* suggests, therefore, that the way you live your life affects the forms you have available to narrate your life; and the form you choose to narrate your life affects your ability to conceive your life historically. The first person holds out some possibility, but the dialectical perspective KC achieves via his mother's mediating documents collapses into the mushy sentimentality of personal relationships and human kindness.

The swollen third person narrating Everly's pure immanence doesn't do the trick either, although at the very end of the novel readers receive some information that puts her affective and overly romanticized encounter with Cuba in a slightly different light. Unlike KC, who has no interest in returning to Cuba because he "understand[s] that the town is terribly run-down" and doesn't "want to see that" (316), Everly and her sisters return in 1999, track down their former Haitian worker Willy, and now go back every year to visit him and his wife. While KC finds this perplexing and can't even remember Willy's name, referring to him only as "the houseboy," Everly apparently sends Willy money every month "as if he were practically a blood relative" (316). I say 'apparently' because all of this information about Everly's present-day commitment to Cuba and Willy arrives third-hand. KC learns of Everly's comings and goings from an old widow, Mrs. Crim, with whom Everly visited after one of her trips. So Everly might very well have outgrown her romanticized relationship to Cuba; she might even imagine her monthly payments as a form of reparations acknowledging that the violence her family brought to Cuba was more than incidental; she could actually be a communist sympathizer and not a merely sentimental sympathizer as KC suggests. But we'll never know for sure because she, and her narrative, are all immanence. To the extent that it's Everly and not KC who manages to sustain a meaningful relationship to her Cuban past as an adult, however, it might not matter that we'll never know whether Everly is "a sympathizer to communism" or, like KC's mother, "just a sympathizer period" (316). Perhaps KC's brother is wrong to call their mother's sympathy for the exploited Cuban workers mere "sentimentality" just because she fails to evince "any sympathy for what caused their circumstances" (315). Maybe Everly's return indicates that sympathy can be a potent force in the world, and maybe the only reason Everly can have such substantive relationships in the present is because she chose as a child to live immanently, "as [life] was happening" (43).[31]

History's Affect

That's a lot of maybes and perhaps, but such epistemological indeterminacy is the price one pays for being, and remaining, in the immanent thickness of things. And yet, to the extent that *Telex* is also quite critical of its characters' inability to understand and accept their complicity with Cuba's violent exploitation at the hands of US capital interest, I'd say that Kushner isn't quite ready to pay that price in full. Better to say that she's making a down payment on the possibility that the sympathies born of immersive living shouldn't be dismissed out of hand just because they fail to achieve a particular political consciousness or effect, but in *Telex,* her first novel, she's not entirely sold on that idea either.

Dana Spiotta's *Eat the Document,* a novel interested in affective attachments and the modes of being that follow from them, is also invested in that possibility. More specifically, Spiotta's novel quite deliberately explores the political forms that emerge when revolutionary history is absorbed into a present moment totally subsumed by capital, asking whether the immanence of that subsumption can be the basis for anything other than soul-sucking complicity. The specific historical revolutionary event confronting the novel's present, which stretches from 1998 to 2000, concerns the accidental death of a housekeeper in a political bombing from 1972. That's when two of the novel's central characters, Mary and Bobby, planted a bomb in the house of a corpo-

---

31. Beyond the scope of this chapter, anyone interested in thinking about the political potency of sympathy will find Viet Nguyen's *The Sympathizer* indispensable.

rate executive whose company produced napalm. When they realize they've effectively murdered an innocent bystander, they separate and go underground, transforming themselves into Louise, a suburban mom, and Nash, a fixture at a Seattle independent bookstore catering to radicals and anarchists. Readers know Louise and Nash's history from the beginning, but Jason, Louise's teenage son, and Miranda, Nash's young acolyte, do not. They embody the present that, over the course of the novel, comes to know the truth of an older generation's revolutionary history. Whether that history has any significant purchase on the present, and precisely what political form that significance might take, are precisely what Spiotta's novel examines.

One key scene that stages these questions quite explicitly occurs in "a large, trendy clothing store called Suburban Guerrilla" (255)[32] where Miranda and her boyfriend Josh find, among other things, a "Paris 68" wall calendar with pictures of "Situationist graffito," a Subcomandante Marcos shower curtain, factory-produced patches that say "D.I.Y.," and a deck of "Movement Rebels, Outlaws and Fugitives playing cards" for only $19.95 (257–59). Miranda finds these commodities completely appalling, symptomatic of corporate capitalism's total absorption of revolutionary history. For her, history commodified is history evacuated of revolutionary potential. Josh, on the other hand, finds these products exhilarating, indicative of capitalism's ability to achieve the very democratic leveling the left has craved for decades. "All can be and will be commodified," he pronounces (258).

Josh and Miranda's form-politics debate in Suburban Guerilla recapitulates a disagreement between the historical Mary and Bobby that eventually leads to their decision to bomb the corporate executive's house. Mary, arguing that years of protest and demonstration have changed nothing, wants direct opposition through "tangible, unequivocal action" (188). The men who make napalm think nothing of their victims' humanity so why should she think about theirs? "It is a moral duty to do something, however imperfect," she tells Bobby (228). But Bobby isn't so sure. He feels more comfortable making protest films that he imagines as "polemical propaganda pieces" (225). But his cohort of revolutionaries, including Mary, argue that his films show the complexities and complications of reality in a way that doesn't inspire the proper outrage and action. In one film, for example, Bobby confronts the inventor of napalm with the infamous image of Phan Thi Kim Phuc, the naked, nine-year-old Vietnamese girl running down a street, skin burning from napalm. Instead of directly condemning the man, however, Bobby's film zooms in on

---

32. Spiotta's description leads one to suspect that Suburban Guerilla satirizes Urban Outfitters.

his "weary, defeated face" for several minutes before turning its attention to the quotidian artifacts of his home: "the wreath surrounding the door knocker. The woven welcome mat. . . . Some garden gloves" (226). Mary condemns Bobby for allowing the man's "humanity" to come through in the film, and she insists that the film, far from revealing the complexities of human existence, is pure "sentimentality."

More than twenty years later, similar tensions continue to rend the revolutionary left as they meet and plan various actions at Nash's bookstore. Nash allows the store to be used as a clearinghouse for a seemingly endless array of protest groups, and the young Miranda eventually grows disillusioned, concluding that "his groups [have] no intention of executing" any of their ideas (130). Their "actions [are] the discussion and planning of actions"; Nash's "conceptual direct-action" groups are, as far as Miranda is concerned, "just another kind of lie" (134). While Miranda, like Mary two decades earlier, wants to "save the world, or enlighten people or change [things]," Nash insists that they nourish their own humanity in the face of capitalist totality. Their actions are "for their benefit," Nash explains, "not to educate or humiliate the public, even the most evil of corporate bureaucrats" (131).

In each of these instances—at Suburban Guerilla, in Bobby's films, and at Nash's activist meetings—we find a version of the immanentist position, articulated most clearly by Hardt and Negri, committed to operating within the capitalist horizon. Josh leans into the commodity form. Bobby and Nash decline outright critique and opposition in favor of something more aesthetic and artful, even beautiful (145). Meanwhile, Miranda and Mary, thinking beyond those immanent modes, insist on meaningful difference, heightened contradictions, ideological conflict and commitment. But where exactly do Spiotta and her novel stand in this debate? Published by Scribner, an imprint of Simon & Schuster, which is itself a subsidiary of CBS Corporation, it's hard not to see Spiotta and *Eat the Document* leaning into capital too. Although she implicitly raises the possibility that her novel is no better than a Subcomandante Marcos shower curtain, Spiotta doesn't abandon the possibility that some form of meaningful political knowledge might arise from the commodified historical novel, from a historical novel that treats revolutionary history as nostalgia and style. At the same time, however, she also acknowledges that the meaningful political knowledge produced from the commodification of revolutionary history might not count to some as all that political, or even meaningful. This doubleness is most apparent in the novel's temporal form.

Oscillating between revolutionary past and quotidian present, the novel's plot attempts a dialectical production of historical consciousness befitting a properly Lukácsian historical novel. Framing each section of the novel with

dates, Spiotta stages the present's gradual recognition of history and its connection to it. The first six sections of the text, for example, alternate between
the 1970s and 1980s on the one hand and the late 1990s on the other. As the
sections advance, the historical portions span more time (Part 1 focuses on
1972, Part 3 treats 1972–73, and Part 5 spans 1973–80), while the present portions move more slowly through Fall and Winter of 1998 and then Spring 1999
until, in Part 7, the past and the present finally unite in a section that stretches
from 1982 to 1999. Having dialectically synthesized past and present, Part 8
then moves forward to the year 2000. This organization allows readers to dialectically recontextualize present-day Louise and Nash as the revolutionaries
Mary and Bobby, and vice versa. Curiously, however, once Part 8 delivers the
dialectical synthesis of past and present, Part 9 abandons the historical dialectic and proceeds with no dates at all, as if the present has been connected
to history only to ignore history once again—as if history has been detached
from its original context and recontextualized in the present only to be commodified and sold as *Eat the Document,* a historical novel written after the end
of history. Notably, this dateless final section, removed from time, delivers the
novel's historical ur-scene of revolutionary violence: Mary planting a deadly
bomb in the chemical executive's home. But the payoff this scene delivers is
just that: a payoff, a delivery of goods, detached from history, that effectively
transforms the scene from political act into commodity—more Subcomandante shower curtain than substantive revolutionary act.

Similarly, Jason and Miranda learn the truth of history—namely, that Louise and Nash are actually the revolutionaries Mary and Bobby—through forms
that are entirely detached from revolutionary historical consciousness. Jason
recognizes his mother's face in one of those art films Bobby made in the 1970s
that emphasizes the human complexity rather than the ideological evil of corporate executives. And Miranda identifies Nash on one of those "Movement
Rebels, Outlaws and Fugitives playing cards" that Josh purchases at Suburban
Guerilla with his "gold corporate American Express card." Why would Spiotta
reveal the truth of history to Jason and Miranda through the very forms (art
film and Suburban Guerilla commodity) that others in the novel have explicitly denounced as counterrevolutionary? Because, I would suggest, she sees
a certain kind of value in them anyway, a value grounded in the irreducible
complexity of our affective relationships to the world and to each other. As
Bobby says in defense of his films, "When I am behind the camera, I feel a
desire to understand and empathize. To undercut my own points. The truth
is, that's when it becomes interesting" (227).

The same can be said of Nash's own face, which Miranda finds curiously inscrutable: "He would undermine his own expressions by only half-

committing his face to them. His frowns were belied by amused eyes; his grins pushed the edge of smirk by a narrowing boredom in his brow. It could be noted, this tendency. And read as unsettling, or intriguing. Miranda, anyway, noticed" (61). The same could also be said of Spiotta and *Eat the Document*, a historical novel that formally develops a dialectical relationship between past and present only to undermine the lessons the dialectic might teach in favor of more affective truths about the personal, even sentimental, attachments that fuel history just as much as systemic, structural inequalities do. This is unsettling. It's also intriguing. At the very least, we should notice the way Spiotta uses history as a resource for the production of an affective realism that refuses to be dismissed as reactionary complicity. It's a mode that Nash sees in the young activists who meet at the bookstore, although, in the same way that Miranda struggles to read Nash's affect, he struggles to interpret and assign specific political value to it, not because he belongs to an older generation of revolutionaries, but because it is, by its very nature, resistant to interpretation and the assigning of meaning. The best he can do is observe that they experience "everything [as] both earnest and ironic at the same time" (28). Miranda, for example, writes on her shoes, a "strange form of self-expression . . . half-motivated by declaring your difference to the world . . . and half motivated by a desperate enslavement to what other people thought of you" (41). And her friend, Sissy, has a "whip-thin look" that Nash simply can't "read": "Was it cultural capitulation or rebellion against being a body in general? Against needing to consume at all?" (38). According to Nash, all of these cases represent "either a total dodge or some attempt at a new way to be" (28). To be sure, these new ways of being will not be legible in conventionally political ways, but Spiotta's novel asks readers to at least consider the possibility that they also aren't a total dodge—that history might function as a source of affective material by which the present develops modes of being that simply can't be homologously pegged to a particular political orientation.

Gesture's Generality

Thus far, we've seen the same forms that define the theoretical debate about the possibility of revolution after the end of revolution—that is, the antinomous forms of transcendence and immanence—emerge in contemporary historical fiction's attempt to narrate and represent revolutionary history. In the same way that the vacillation of the form-politics homology leaves the political effects of a given revolutionary form unmoored and undecidable, contemporary historical fiction struggles to determine which narrative forms best access history, and whether that access manages to be political in any substantial way. *Telex* and *Eat the Document* have signaled contemporary historical fiction's distinct interest in the nonideological, affective potential of revolutionary history, although anyone who remains invested in the Lukácsian/Jamesonian project of making history appear in and for the present would surely find that approach lacking.

Rachel Kushner's *The Flamethrowers* has learned the lessons of these other texts' struggles and tasks itself with identifying a new take on revolutionary history along with a new realist mode for the contemporary historical novel. Gesture plays a crucial role in both of these projects, and I will argue that Kushner's gestural forms succeed to the extent that they escape the antinomy of transcendence and immanence that has defined these other works. Gesture's production of value, Kushner's novel suggests, avoids that antinomy. Gesture's value is neither representational nor ontological, transcendent nor immanent, but is instead drawn from a pre-existing set of commonly shared movements, actions, and behaviors—a generalized *langue* of life.[33] Given this distinct mode of value production, it would be incorrect to see gesture as a mere synthesis or balance of immanence and transcendence. Gesture's logic, a logic of generality, is separate from theirs. Moreover, as my reading of *The Flamethrowers* will explain, a certain amount of political possibility materializes from Kushner's gestural approach to revolution and the historical novel, although, as we've already seen in *Telex* and *Eat the Document*, it remains "a politics independent of a defined and knowable political goal" (Rodriguez, *Sexual Futures* 5).[34]

---

33. A vast body of scholarship on gesture has been produced across many disciplines, including linguistics, communication, theater, film, performance studies, anthropology, semiotics, dance, and phenomenology. It's important to appreciate, then, that the theory of gesture I distill from Kushner is at odds with a great deal of other work on gesture, if only because there are so many divergent treatments of the concept. However, if, broadly speaking, theories of gesture tend either to emphasize gestures' phenomenological particularity by treating them as "*events, singular performances that . . . are never performed twice in exactly the same way*" or to emphasize their semiotic codedness by treating them as "iterable" actions manifesting "a deeper affinity with mechanical apparati," then my reading of Kushner's take on gesture as generality aligns more with the latter than the former (xxiv). This description of dichotomous theories of gesture comes from Carrie Noland's "Introduction" to the excellent *Migrations of Gesture*, a collection that takes gesture as the means for conceiving the phenomenological and the semiotic as complementary rather than mutually exclusive. Noland extends her thinking about gesture in *Agency and Embodiment*. See Erin Manning's *The Minor Gesture* for work that emphasizes gesture's phenomenological particularity.

34. Many theories of gesture imply a distinctly nonideological politics. See, for example, Vilém Flusser's *Gestures*, particularly the appendix, and Lauren Berlant's *The Female Complaint*, which treats gesture as a mark of one's "attachment to the pre- and postpolitical" (165).

In Kushner's novel, an aspiring land artist, nicknamed Reno after her Nevada hometown, moves to New York City and begins a long-term romance with Sandro Valera, a minimalist sculptor and scion of the Valeras, a well-connected Italian family that grew rich selling motorcycles and rubber tires to Mussolini during the war. The novel has three distinct settings: the Bonneville Salt Flats in Utah, where Reno implements a poorly conceived land-art project but sets the female land-speed record while she's at it; New York City, where she falls in with a group of idiosyncratic artists and quasi-revolutionaries; and Italy, where Reno accompanies Sandro on a trip to visit his stultifying and inhospitable family near the Swiss border before she breaks with Sandro and travels to Rome, where she spends several weeks among the revolutionary Red Brigades of Italy's Autonomist movement. The novel also chronicles two distinct historical moments. Some chapters follow the life of Sandro's father, T. P. Valera, including his early exuberance for Futurist aesthetics, his time in World War I, the growth of his industrial empire, and his influence on and complicity with midcentury Fascist politics in Italy. Intercalated with those omnisciently narrated historical chapters are those that Reno retrospectively narrates in the first person.[35] These chapters stretch from 1975, when Reno moves to New York and meets Sandro, to the summer of 1977, where the novel ends (chronologically, not narratively) with the New York City blackout that prompted widespread violence and looting.

As in *Telex, The Flamethrowers* approaches the antinomy of transcendence and immanence as an antinomy between representation and being, an antinomy the novel metaphorizes as a conflict between waiting and velocity. (Waiting aligns with representation and transcendence because it entails standing apart from things, being outside of events. Velocity aligns with being and immanence because it entails a full immersion in things, a seamless coinciding with events.) Upon moving to New York as an aspiring artist, for example, Reno initially theorizes waiting as a potentially productive life strategy. Looking down from her apartment window, transcendent, on a group of chauffeurs waiting on the street, Reno realizes "that [she], too, had it in [her] to wait. To expect change to come from outside, to concentrate on the task of meeting it, waiting to meet it, rather than going out and finding it" (88). And for much of her time in the city, with "the stream of New York . . . mov[ing] around her," she waits, convinced that "something would happen" (49).[36]

---

35. The retrospection of her narration makes Reno's chapters historical as well, although we never learn from when or where she's narrating.

36. In "The Contemporary Novel and Postdemocratic Form," Rachel Greenwald Smith reads Reno's waiting as an "anything goes" form of neoliberalism that leaves itself dangerously

Set in contradistinction to Reno's transcendent position outside events, a young T. P. Valera discovers the potent immanence of velocity. Sitting at a café in Rome in 1912, he witnesses a gang of motorcyclists "streaming down the Corso," sending a "seditious crackle through the air, those headlights, promising that something would happen" (40–41). The stream doesn't flow around these young men; they are the stream. They aren't waiting for something to happen; they are the happening. Valera immediately joins the flow, learning from the group's leader, Lonzi, that they want "speed and change" as quickly as possible (73). Echoing an Italian Futurism that adumbrates Italian Fascism (as well as Hardt and Negri's notion of self-constituting immanence), Lonzi teaches that "the only thing worth loving was what was to come, and since what was to come was unforeseeable . . . the future had to be lived now, in the now, as intensity" (74). Sometimes, Reno's life in New York manages a similarly immanent velocity. After meeting a wild group of artists in a bar, for example, she reports, "I was in the stream that had moved around me since I'd arrived. It had moved around me and not let me in and suddenly here I was, at this table, plunged into a world, everything moving swiftly but not passing me by." But her full immersion comes at a cost, requiring her to sacrifice vision, knowledge, and understanding: "I was with the current, part of it, regardless of whether I understood the codes, the shorthand, of the people around me" (65).

An early scene in the novel, at the Bonneville Salt Flats in Utah, suggests the limitations of both waiting and velocity. Watching drivers speeding to break the land-speed record, Reno observes that the vehicles move so fast that there's nothing to see. Thus, Reno admits, "We weren't there to see. We were waiting on news of some kind of event, one that could pierce this blank and impassive and giant place. What else could do that but a stupendous wipeout? We were waiting on death" (26). This indictment of waiting's passive violence similarly indicts velocity, which not only produces "nothing to see," but also ends in death. Almost everyone in the novel who moves in straight lines at high speeds crashes. As everything goes "liquid and blurry," they lose all perspective on the world and end up badly battered and bruised (26). The "acute case of the present tense" that immanent velocity achieves certainly undoes the passivity of transcendent waiting, but it also threatens to undo the self entirely (30).

Reno's boyfriend, Sandro, offers a different approach, a way to be in the stream without the loss of perspective and understanding caused by total deli-

---

susceptible to authoritarianism. I argue, however, that Reno ultimately figures out how to do more than just wait. She learns how to gesture.

quescence: "You had to maintain your hold on [reality] by vigilantly keeping watch over whatever slight and intangible thing gave your life its meaning." Like a sinker that keeps a bobber standing upright in water, these objects—"a movie, a lover. Friends. Complicities. . . . Art"—allow individuals to "weigh[t] themselves" and avoid dissolution (364). Neither outside the stream nor dissolved in its flow, Sandro imagines a way of moving amid motion. Crucially, Sandro's position is not a compromise between waiting and velocity. He's not suggesting that we sometimes wait, sometimes flow, or that we oscillate between them. And the weight he recommends is not a mediating object facilitating the dialectical synthesis of waiting and velocity. Rather, as I'll examine at length once the discussion turns fully to the nature of gesture, Sandro is describing an entirely distinct mode of being general that departs from waiting and velocity altogether.

An ancient Greek sculpture that Sandro and Reno view at the Met provides an early model. The bas-relief sculpture captures the profile of a young girl holding a dove to her lips, gesturing for a kiss. The entirety of the sculpture remains firmly ensconced in the marble stone from which it emerges, except for the area around the dove's head and the girl's mouth. There, "a pocket of real air" circulates behind the dove's head, making it "the only part of the relief that's three-dimensional." The rest of the bas-relief is two dimensional. "Its flatness holds her away from us," Sandro marvels. "She doesn't share our space. She's from another world, lost forever. Only that promise of the kiss shares our space." This union of the second and third dimension makes the sculpture "real and false at once," suggesting a realism that is transcendent and immanent, that represents and is, simultaneously (106).[37]

Reno finds herself inhabiting this same curious mode when working as a China girl, which is the name given to the woman whose image appears in the leader portion of films. (Lab technicians would use China girl images as a reference point for skin color. Adjusting the color to make their skin look realistic would ensure the accuracy of the film's overall coloring). Originally conceived, the job positions Reno in strictly two-dimensional space. As her employers explain, her image doesn't even index her, only her skin tone. "You're not supposed to evoke real life," they instruct, "Just the hermetic world of a smiling woman holding the color chart" (140). Conversely, once the image is run through the projector, she is fully absorbed into filmic flow, her image

---

37. Sandro's father, committed to speed and change, juxtaposes the three-dimensional volume of immanent velocity to "the ancient Egyptians, who depicted everything flat, in two dimensions, because volume was terrifying unknowability. Yes, it *was* terrifying, Valera agreed with the Egyptians, and that was why he wanted it" (128). Here, the bas-relief sculpture offers both two- and three-dimensionality.

passing "too quickly" to be seen (86). Thus, she is either isolated from the stream or dissolved into it, visible but dead or alive but invisible. Reno identifies a way out of the impasse, however, when she learns that some projectionists and film technicians go back over the China-girl frames "more closely." In fact, "pieces of the film leader were collected and traded like baseball cards," with "plainer-looking China girls . . . traded just as heavily" since "their ordinariness was part of their appeal: real but unreachable women who left no sense of who they were" (86–87). These "real but unreachable women" are of course modern echoes of the Greek bas-relief, which, like China-girl Reno, functions as both representation and reality, index and thing, all at once. Perhaps inspired by the Greek girl's "promise of [a] kiss," Reno inhabits this distinct mode of being by gesturing differently during her China-girl photo sessions: "I smiled in a tentative but friendly way, as if some vaguely intimate possibility might exist between me and whoever caught a glimpse of me on film, just the slightest possibility" (140).

Throughout the novel, Kushner associates this new mode of being—simultaneously static and flowing, representational and real, two- and three-dimensional, transcendent and immanent—with gesture. When Reno's new friends, Nadine and Thurman, shoot each other in the crotch with a gun loaded with blanks, Reno describes this as "a stupid and ridiculous gesture" (69). While stopped at a gas station on her way to the Salt Flats, Reno watches a man spray gasoline on a woman and throw lit matches at her, "little sparks—threats, or promises—that died out limply." As Reno understands the scene, the man isn't actually trying to light the woman on fire. Rather, according to Reno, "certain acts, even as they are real, are also merely gestures. He was saying, 'What if I did?' And she was saying, 'Go ahead'" (14). The Greek bas-relief's "promise of [a] kiss" and Reno's China-girl smile that intimates the "slightest possibility" are similarly gestural promises, and gesture also defines Reno's first sexual encounter in New York—with Ronnie, not Sandro—which begins in the backseat of a car when Ronnie places his hand on her leg. "I read the gesture of his hand on my leg as exactly that," Reno reports. "A man's hand on a woman's leg" (62). With this interpretation which is not one, we see how gestures have a certain value (they can be "read"), but not a representational value. They don't refer or index; they are not signs pointing to the world; they don't "mean" in quite the same way language does.[38] Instead, the key feature

---

38. As Carrie Noland explains, gestures "counte[r] the signifying potential of the conventional sign" ("Introduction" xiii) and cause "a suspension of the interpretive regime" (xiv). This idea supports Julia Kristeva's thinking about gesture as a "productivity . . . anterior to *representation* as a phenomenon of significance in the circuit of communication" (267). Cru-

of Reno's reading is the move she makes from *Ronnie's* hand on *her* leg to *a man's* hand on *a woman's* leg. The value of the gesture is its transformation of Ronnie and Reno into a man and a woman. The gesture opens onto forms of generality as it produces value through its relation to common, preexisting forms, not through its representational or ontological capacity.[39]

A conversation Reno has with her employer, Marvin, about stock footage nicely captures some of the implications of this gestural mode of being. At a previous job, Marvin was tasked with gathering stock footage of "people dying violent deaths" for a director making a documentary (321). Marvin grew fascinated by the fact that real people had to die for these film clips to exist, and yet, by definition, as stock footage, it didn't matter who had died. At one point, he realizes that one of the clips might depict the execution of a Valera, one of Sandro's relatives, and he returns to the film vault to do more research. The employee at the vault, however, is perplexed by Marvin's request for that particular clip. "If you love stock footage so much," he asks Marvin, "won't any piece of it do?" (322–23). Eventually, Marvin acknowledges that the employee is correct. An actual person had to die for the footage to exist, but the historical specificity of that death has been replaced by a more general form. The death itself doesn't matter. Marvin emphasizes his point by drawing an analogy to Reno's own work as a China girl: "You're a reference file for Caucasian skin tones," he tells her. "It doesn't matter that you exist. For the technician or projectionist, you're an index for the existence of woman, flesh, flesh tones. . . .

---

cially, however, Kristeva distances herself from those who, beginning with Condillac in the eighteenth century, view gesture as the origin of language. For Kristeva, gesture's anteriority to representation isn't chronological; it's not "diachronically anterior," she explains (271). Instead, it's a "synchronic anteriority," "a spatial and not a temporal anteriority," that allows gesture to "englobe" instances of signification and representation (269). In "Notes on Gesture," Giorgio Agamben argues that the gesture "has nothing to say" and is "always a gesture of not being able to figure something out in language" (59). Relatedly, in *Stage Fright* Martin Puchner demonstrates that twentieth-century playwrights have used gesture to make textuality more theatrical, but also to make theatricality more textual. Thus, he positions gesture "right at the border between literature and theater" (28) and observes that it has historically occupied "the gray area between nature and culture, between pure expression and conventional articulation, between the unsayable and the sayable" (43). I read this in-between-ness, as well as Noland's description of gesture's "suspension of the interpretive regime," Kristeva's vision of gesture "englobing" signification, and Agamben's nonlinguistic conception of gesture, as related attempts to capture a general mode of value production distinct from and unavailable to verbal and written language.

39. Although she does not necessarily endorse this behavior and views it as sentimental "fantasy," Lauren Berlant suggests in *The Female Complaint* that "gestures" are an ideal way for a woman to "achieve [a] condition of generality," "a vague or simpler version of herself" (7). Of course, a theme of this chapter (and, to be sure, a theme of much of Berlant's own work) is that such sentimental fantasy might also be put to different, more effective uses.

You, as *you*, have nothing to do with it" (322).[40] As in the back seat of the car with Ronnie, Reno is not Reno. She is just a woman standing in for womanness in general. In the novel's many gestural interactions, characters behave like stock footage—what Marvin calls "life in quotes" (322)—repeating generic movements and actions that produce value, not by indexing some historically specific reality, but by drawing on a *langue* of common behaviors, actions, looks, and movements. Thus Kristeva theorizes gesture as an "*impersonal mode*," a domain in which "the individual cannot constitute himself" (272).[41]

A Gestural Revolution

Thus far, my discussion of gesture has focused primarily on the personal becoming impersonal. But the gestural is not just a way to sidestep the antinomy of transcendence and immanence in the context of individual being and human interaction. It might also help us think differently about revolution, which, as this chapter has thoroughly detailed, struggles with the same antinomy. To pivot to those other concerns, please bear with a brief theoretical digression.

In a slim little essay, "Notes on Gesture," Giorgio Agamben links gesture with cinema. For Agamben, the rise of cinema allows us to break "the mythical rigidity of the image" and replace it with a form in which there are "only gestures" (55). Cinema liberates "the image into gesture," just like those ancient Greek legends "in which statues break the ties holding them and begin to move," or like the bas-relief sculpture of the young girl in which the second dimension gestures its way into the third (56). Agamben develops this idea out of Deleuze's description of cinema as *coupes mobiles*, "images themselves in movement," which, like Sandro in the stream, move in time without being dissolved into it.[42] For Deleuze, we misunderstand cinema when we simply juxtapose its immanent flux and flow to the static two-dimensionality

---

40. Smith's "Contemporary Novel" reads this conversation between Marvin and Reno as more evidence of Reno's dangerous passivity. The notion that these women don't matter is admittedly disturbing, but as we saw with Heti and Kraus in chapter 1, Reno here seems legitimately comfortable with her absorption into the general. Suspicious of agency and subjectivity, these female authors are all exploring the productive potential of not mattering.

41. More dramatically, she writes, "Gesture is the epitome of an incessant production of death," by which she means, of course, that gesture dissolves subjectivity, not that it actually kills you (272).

42. Lauren Berlant's description of gesture's temporality as "a thick moment of ongoingness, a situation that can absorb many genres without having one itself" echoes Deleuze's understanding of gesture's distinct form of movement (*Cruel* 200).

of photography. Instead, cinema is an entirely different mode, distinct from the dichotomies of movement and stasis, velocity and waiting. Agamben conceives gesture in a similar way, as the "sphere of a pure and endless mediality," as an entirely distinct condition that is neither representation nor being, transcendence nor immanence (59).[43] For Agamben, gesture's pure mediality describes a condition of in-between-ness, a "being-means," that must be conceived as its own distinct mode of being. It's not a synthesis, compromise, equilibrium, or simultaneity of two other modes. It is its own distinct form, a form of generality with its own distinct mode of value production.[44]

For Agamben, this gestural mode of being is potentially political because it "allows the emergence of the being-in-a-medium of human beings," which in turn "opens the ethical dimension for them" (58). Later, he contends: "Politics is the sphere of . . . the absolute and complete gesturality of human beings" (60).[45] The gesture, in other words, offers humans a way to be together, a way to establish a collectivity, that relies on neither the self-constituting immanence of the multitude nor the transcendent vision of a party (Dean) or "Master figure" (Žižek). Politics as "complete gesturality" is always already collective, but not in any particularly ideological way. Gesture's generality opens onto a shared, common space, but the gestural content of that space can also be configured and deployed in any number of different ways. Emphasizing that gesture is "neither ends- nor means-oriented," that is, neither transcendent nor immanent, Lauren Berlant echoes Agamben's thinking about the pol-

---

43. For more on Agamben's thinking about mediality, see Asbjørn Grønstad and Henrik Gustafsson's *Cinema and Agamben*.

44. To capture gesture's distinction, Agamben is good about using neither/nor language. (Gesture is neither immanence nor transcendence.) Kushner, however, tends to use the language of simultaneity, which makes it harder to properly conceive gesture as more than just a synthesis of two already existing modalities. Nevertheless, it seems to me that when Kushner highlights simultaneous modes of existence (the simultaneous two- and three-dimensionality of the bas-relief sculpture, for example, or the simultaneous stasis and velocity of the China girl), it's always in an effort to conceive and articulate a new mode beyond the already available ones.

45. For an extended consideration of the possibilities and limitations of Agamben's gestural politics, see Lucia Ruprecht's "Introduction: Towards an Ethics of Gesture." Agamben's thinking about the politics of gesture emphasizes what I describe above, in footnote 33, as gesture's semiotic codedness—that is, its generality. Those theories of gesture that instead emphasize its phenomenological singularity attribute a different political valence to gesture. For example, Erin Manning's *Minor Gesture* argues that gesture's "punctual reorienting of the event . . . invents new modes of life-living. It moves through the event, creating a pulse, opening the way for new tendencies to emerge, and in the resonances that are awakened, potential for difference looms" (8). Although I read Kushner as being more interested in the commons made available through gesture's generality, there is no reason that these two approaches can't work together according to the reciprocal intercourse of the singular-general relationship I describe via Dewey in the introduction.

itics of gesture and describes gesture as "a sign of being in the world, in the middle of the world, a sign of sociality" (*Cruel* 198). More specifically, Berlant contends that gesture "makes time, holding the present open to attention and unpredicted exchange." But it is also "only a potential event, the initiation of something present that could accrue density," or not (199). The political value of the gesture, in other words, does not derive from its meaning or signification, but rather from "the layered accumulation of affect" that accrues to it (Stimson 76). Its formal power lies in neither particularity nor universality but in generality, in a "simple, formal iterability" that gathers mass precisely to the extent that its formal simplicity can be generalized beyond itself to the larger social body (71).[46]

In *The Flamethrowers,* gesture appears as this kind of political tool when Reno finds herself in Rome, caught up in the revolutionary fervor of the Autonomist Red Brigade protests against the state. During one mass demonstration, the people coming together in the plaza form "a vast shifting texture, a sea of heads filling the square," and they produce "sound swells [that roll] across the immense piazza like great sluggish ocean waves" (274–75). Once again, Reno finds herself negotiating her proper relation to the stream: should she stand outside it, lose herself in it, or something else entirely? "How do we find each other?" she wonders, "people lost in the vast thickets of the world. People lost among people, since there wasn't anything else. *The world was people*" (277). Like Agamben's notion of gesture as pure mediality, Kushner is here imagining politics as "the being-in-a-medium of human beings," which is different from entirely dissolving oneself in the medium. If the stream is other people, what relations should we have to them and what tools do we have to establish those relations? Reno's first, transcendent attempt to answer those questions involves filming the protests with her Bolex Pro handheld camera, but her position behind the camera leaves her isolated. The stream flows all around her, but she's never really connected to it.[47] Abandoning the

---

46. Lesley Stern's "Ghosting" provides a remarkably similar description of the way gesture produces value in film:

> The force of the first scene derives most obviously from the gestural impulse, though it is only when this gesture is repeated, in the second scene, that it comes into focus, precisely through the force of repetition, *as a gesture*. And in the moment of its repetition, it reconfigures the earlier iteration. The repetition reflects on the origin, recasting both its semantic and affective valency. It is only when this gesture migrates and returns in "another" body that the generalized misery comes into focus as grief. . . . This gesture . . . does not 'mean' grief . . . , but through narrative accrual, temporal accumulation, and gestural repetition, the somatic is imbued with or overlayed by the semantic. (203)

47. We shouldn't be surprised at Reno's filmic failure. Elsewhere in the novel, we receive a long meditation on the development of Italian realist cinema in the mid-twentieth century. The

camera while running from the police, however, Reno establishes a new and different relationship to the people. Part of the stream but not dissolved into it, she joins "a network of people who acted in concert against the government, against the factories, against everything that was against them" (285–86). The problem of finding each other, of connecting, of grounding collectivity in the union of individuals, ceases to be a problem once you become general, once you become just another person among the people in the world. Like Sheila realizing that she's no different from the other 99,999 copies of the human book being sold in *How Should a Person Be,* Reno's "people" erases individual particularity in favor of generic generality.

Notably, all of the people's concerted actions during the protest are gestures. Someone fixes the traffic lights to remain red for a whole afternoon; others eat at restaurants without paying; a pirate radio show announces how much people should pay for rent and electricity (285). The actions Reno films before losing her camera are similarly gestural: a boy picks up a discarded cigarette and asks the woman who threw it on the ground for a light; a young pregnant girl with a "guileless smile" squirts a stream of milk from her breast onto the face of a man filming her; a group of young protestors improvise a rain dance; students remove the paving stones from the streets; others, with "painted faces," pass out fur coats they've liberated from a high-end clothing store; a mass of white balloons floats from a department store into the sky; a young girl, "her pretty face a pictograph of sadness, but a lovely, strange, and playful sadness," begins singing to an appreciative crowd (276–82). Later, Reno imagines these as "comical, taunting gesture[s]" that exude a "playfulness" and "lighthearted" "attitude about life" (317–18).

Now, I don't mean to suggest that such gestural acts are the answer to all of revolution's impasses. In fact, the relationship between these gestures and a specific political vision or ideology remains opaque. Think about the typical questions asked of any protest movement or act of resistance: "What do you hope to achieve by doing this? What significance do your actions have? What do they mean?" The transcendent political movement will respond by explaining the links in the chain between its particular actions and the utopian vision it hopes to achieve. Its arguments and actions signify, gain meaning and value, because they will lead us to a better world. The immanent political movement will respond by explaining that it prefers to live, enact, and embody the

---

cinematic history begins with the unrealistic *telefoni bianchi* produced by Cinecittà before the war, moves forward to the neorealism of the war's immediate aftermath, and then concludes by considering the direct cinema movement of the 1960s. *The Flamethrowers* indicts each of these realisms for different reasons, but taken together, it's clear that Kushner doesn't think that increased cinematic immanence—immersing the camera into the flow of life—brings viewers any closer to historical truth.

utopia for which it fights. It has no goals beyond its very being. Its actions signify, gain meaning and value, because they *are* a better world. A gestural movement, however, would offer an entirely different answer. That's because gestures produce value by drawing on a preexisting generality, not by asserting their representational or ontological truth. The political significance of a gesture, then, is not that it points to utopia, or that it embodies utopia, but that it engages a generality to which we all have access by virtue of being people in the world. Or, "understanding" a gesture requires us to inhabit an entirely different mode of being, a mode of being general. And inhabiting that general mode has political potential even if it's not inherently political. We can't draw a formal homology between generalized forms and a specific politics. Generality is not an inherently liberating or oppressive form, and that's precisely the point. Gesture has no politics of its own, but as a set of shared and common actions, practices, movements, and behaviors, it offers new configurations of the political, new ways to imagine revolution for those dissatisfied with the vacillations of homological thought. Some of the gestures that the Roman revolutionaries deploy—looting, striking, singing—draw on, and also reinvent, the general forms of revolutions past. Others, however—the squirting of breast milk, rain dancing, balloon liberation—expand the field of generality, contributing new generalities from which future revolutionaries might draw. Such acts are what Juana Rodriguez has described as "activist gestures," "prior forms" that "are never-ending and open to interpretation within collectively produced frames of reference, which are themselves potential sites of activist intervention" (76). Like Chris Kraus deploying the case study to expand the general field of female subjectivity in chapter 1, these gestures expand the potential forms of revolutionary activity. They make revolution people.[48]

Historical Fiction as Gestural Realism

The Flamethrowers' commitment to gesture as the best "technique for inhabiting the world" bears directly on its search for the best techniques for producing compelling historical fiction today (364). This connection between the novel's themes and forms becomes apparent in a scene that also clarifies its

---

48. This is, I think, what Vilém Flusser means when he explains the political urgency behind his call for a comprehensive theory of gestures: "We are probably in a revolutionary situation," he writes. "This, our feeling of being in a revolution, manifests itself as, among other things, a sense of having to reorient ourselves to be able to act at all, as a sense of needing to develop new kinds of theories. The suggestion of a general theory of gestures came from such feelings: of gestures, because they concern the concrete phenomenon of our active being-in-the-world, and of revolution, because a revolution is always, in the end, about freedom" (176).

title. Near the novel's conclusion, we learn of Sandro's boyhood affection for some paper dolls that represent the various Italian military units that fought in World War I. Each unit sports different uniforms and accessories, with Sandro's favorite being the flamethrowers, "both brutal and ancient and at the same time horribly modern" (360). Sandro's two-dimensional cardboard cutouts have enough specificity—unique helmets, weapons, badges, and even hand-drawn wristwatches—to capture his historical imagination. But Sandro's father, who actually rode in a motorcycle brigade during the war, insists on adding "inglorious details" (359). The flamethrower regiments, he explains, were not fearsome "harbinger[s] of death" but were actually "a hopeless lot," burdened with heavy equipment that left them easy targets for the enemy (360). Because the assault teams were never accompanied by medics, the father additionally insists that Sandro not place the flamethrower dolls on stretchers. Pushing the father's realist demands even further, Sandro's older brother Roberto pours gasoline on the dolls, incinerating them to nothing. Here we find the problem of how to be in the world, relative to the flowing stream, recast as a question of form. What form, exactly, should our representations of history take? Does the realist spectrum, stretching from Sandro's two-dimensionality to his brother's performative flamethrowing, afford the optimal options for answering that question? Can realism be more than a thin, two-dimensional representation without burning up in the fire of full, performative being? These are not just questions Sandro must answer, but Kushner as well. How might *The Flamethrowers* be more than a mere representation of the fire of revolutionary history? What will make this historical novel successful? How should history's forms be conceived? Are details enough? Can historical fiction be on fire with history without burning itself up?

I think so. Like Sandro and his stream, Kushner's *Flamethrowers* identifies a literary mode that can be in the flow without becoming pure flow, that burns "with," without burning up (365). I call this literary mode gestural realism—a supersession of the transcendence-immanence antinomy on the level of realist literary form, an intervention in the formal impasses, diagnosed by Jameson, in the contemporary historical novel. To be clear, gestural realism doesn't exactly solve the crisis of the contemporary historical novel as Jameson sees it. Gestural realism isn't going to help historical fiction represent "the broad living basis of historical events in their intricacy and complexity" so that readers might discern the dominant modes of socioeconomic production that shape their individual existence. Rather, it changes the project of historical fiction by changing its approach to history. In place of Lukács's and Jameson's notion of history as the broad social and economic forces that define our lives, Kushner's gestural realism offers history, particularly twentieth-century revolutionary history, as stock footage. She replaces the project of representing history to incite individual recognition of the historicity of the present with a transformation of individuals into gestural manifestations of history's general revolutionary forms (e.g., the gun, the protest, the strike, the riot). Gestural realism is in turn the narrative mode best equipped to articulate and apprehend this generalized approach to the individual's relationship to history. Of course, someone working in the Lukács-Jameson mold could easily dismiss this as just another failure to narrate history. I'd suggest instead, however, that we view gestural realism as a narrative mode well-suited to a contemporary moment that finds literary form disarticulated from any consistent politics.

The key vehicle of Kushner's gestural realism, the sinker that weights Reno's narration and holds her upright in the stream of New York City, is her Valera motorcycle. Like the many guns in the novel that are "imaginary, symbolic, or real, all at once," Reno's motorcycle is another example of gesture's distinct mode of being (169). The owner of a hotel she stays at on her way to Utah, for example, thinks he must be dreaming: "I never met a girl who rides Italian motorcycles," he tells her. "It's like you aren't real" (18). To be sure, Reno and her motorcycle are the stuff of (this man's) dreams, but they are also quite real. She enlists the motorcycle all the time. But even as she enlists it, because it's a Valera motorcycle, it's also symbolic, connecting her romantically to Sandro and historically to his father and Italy's Fascist past.[49] In this way, we can understand the motorcycle itself as a gesture—"imaginary, symbolic, [and] real, all at once"—that Reno rides through the streets of New York City.[50]

Unlike her record-setting motorcycle ride in the Utah Salt Flats that makes everything blurry and ends in a crash, riding in New York gives Reno "the sense of being in, but not of, the city, moving through it with real velocity." Like the "real but unreachable women" working as China girls, or the bas-relief girl whose "flatness holds her away from us," Reno, while riding her motorcycle, is "separate, gliding, untouchable." "It was only a motorcycle," she says, "but it felt like a mode of being" (297). What kind of mode of being, you ask? A mode of being general: "I was a girl on a motorcycle," she explains (344). Here, the motorcycle transforms Reno from her particular self into a more general form (just like when Ronnie's hand on her leg turns them into the more general, man and woman). She is just a girl, or, to paraphrase Marvin's description of her work as a China girl, Reno as Reno has nothing to do with it. Rather than struggling to situate individuals in history in some

49. For an excellent discussion of Reno's motorcycle and an analysis of the text that comes to somewhat different conclusions about its status as a historical novel, see Andrew Strombeck's "The Post-Fordist Motorcycle."

50. Rodriguez evocatively suggests in *Sexual Futures* that "gestures are where the literal and figurative copulate" (4).

politically meaningful way, individuals don't matter in this historical novel. Kushner doesn't aim to produce historical consciousness; she aims to render individuals and the history they inhabit as generality. Inhabiting this general mode of being, Reno rides through the city, narrating it gesturally.

One particular ride coincides with an important historical event in New York City, a blackout in the summer of 1977 that led to widespread looting, vandalism, and arson. While riding through the city, Reno narrates history generally, as an array of stock footage: "women were pulling shopping carts out of Mays, multiple carts tied together and crammed with merchandise"; "people pulling boxes and boxes of Jox tennis shoes out onto the sidewalk" (348); "[a] group of people wheeled racks out of Says *Who?*"; "two men backed through the broken window of an Orange Julius" (349). Narrating the looting from her own gestural mode of being "a woman on a motorcycle," Reno offers a generalized view of the city's "streaming" and "flowing" people—that is, of history as general stock footage. Reno's particular relationship to the history unfolding before her is not at issue when she operates in this gestural mode.[51] The political valence of the gestures she witnesses are similarly neutral. For example, while continuing her generalized narrative, Reno observes that "people said it was despicable that looters would turn on their own, and target struggling and honest neighborhood businesses." But such political critique, she suggests, is the wrong way to think about these events. As with the Red Brigade protests in Rome, we shouldn't ask if they're effective, what they mean, or what politics they entail. "To expect [the people] to identify particular stores as enemies and others as friends was a confusion," Reno says—a misunderstanding of what and how gestures mean. For Reno, looting carries no political valence. It is simply "a declaration" that "the system is in 'off' mode," and "in 'off' mode" everything reverts back to a general state ("no private property, no difference between Burger King and Alvin's Television Repair"), ripe for reconfiguration (349). In these culminating passages, Reno gesturally narrates history as gesture from the seat of a motorcycle that itself functions as gesture.

Of course, not all narrative in *The Flamethrowers* is structured in this way, but I do think it makes sense to imagine Reno's first-person narration as gestural—"separate, gliding, untouchable"—moving among a world of similarly gestural actions and events. Her first-person narration, in other words, effectively keeps her in but not dissolved into the stream of people that is her

---

51. Notably, when she parks her motorcycle and begins walking around the city, her individual relationship to historical events changes. She sees a man she knows, Burdmoore, encouraging a group of masked youth to burn down the city, and this personal particularity puts a hiccup in her otherwise gestural narration (350–53).

world. Take, for example, her narration of a morning spent with Sandro at his family's home in Italy:

> Chesil Jones was already down at the pool when Sandro and I arrived. He was lying on the stones next to the edge, nude except for a hand towel that was folded into a small square and balanced over his privates, his eyes closed as though he were encased in a tomb of sunlight. Sandro flashed me a look of amusement and tugged me toward the open pavilion next to the pool, a raised platform with couches, he picked me up and tossed me into a pile of throws on the couch. When I giggled a bit too loudly, the old novelist sat up and glanced at us, squinting against the sun and holding his inadequate towel over his crotch like a tiny curtain. He began gathering his things. Leaving the young to their privacy, I felt him think. (237)

Here Reno locates and describes the actions of other people poolside even as she includes herself in those events. She also resists speculating about the interiority of the other characters. Any feelings they might be having are instead communicated through gestures (Sandro's "flashed . . . look of amusement," the novelist's glance and squint). Even the novelist's idea that he should give the young some privacy is something that Reno *feels* him think, so we're not inside the novelist's head as much as we are privy to a gestural interaction between him and Reno. As first-person narrator, Reno isn't the movie camera recording the film. She's the point of view making the film that is also part of the film. She is a recorder of moving images that is itself also a moving image, and this keeps her from being either passively distant from or entirely dissolved into the stream of ongoing present-ness in which the moving images swim.

This is all quite different from the novel's historical chapters, which narrate Valera's enchantment with Italian Futurism and his later complicity with Italian Fascism. These chapters are narrated by an unidentified, third-person omniscient narrator who constantly delves into Valera's complicated emotional interiority:

> Valera longed for a French girl named Marie, closing his eyes to close the physical gap between their two bodies, as he pretended his own hand was Marie's lips, mouth, and tongue. Dark-eyed, pale-skinned Marie, who lived at the convent next door. . . . Every morning the girls were taken into the convent courtyard by the nuns, and Valera would strain at the kitchen window to see them doing their knee bends and stretches. On occasion the sun angled in such a way that it penetrated the girls' thin white cotton blouses,

and he was able to glimpse the shape of Marie's breasts, which were round and large. They were not suspended in any kind of undergarment, like the complicated muslin-and-elastic holsters his mother wore, and he wondered if brassieres were only for married women. When he looked in the mirror he felt unfree, a hopeless entwinement of longings and guilt. His private pleasures were wrecked by the specter of guilt, even with the door locked, the covers pulled up: a fortress of privacy breached by his mother's voice, calling his name. He figured he'd stored up a lifetime of lust and that upon its first release he would unburden himself in one violent salvo and then settle into a more manageable state. He imagined that physical proximity would instruct him in many things—first of all, the real distance between people. (33–34)

Weirdly, we actually gain more access to Valera's interiority via this third-person narrator than we do to Reno's interiority via her first-person narration. And notice here not only the emotional interiority—the way the narrator knows the content of Valera's masturbatory fantasies, his "hopeless entwinement of longings and guilt"—but also the dilated temporality born from it. For example, Valera isn't pretending that his hand is Marie's mouth at a certain moment in time; he watches the girls do their exercises "every morning"; and even Marie's breasts, which "were not suspended in any kind of undergarment," aren't undergarmentless in any particular instance. Valera doesn't look in the mirror and feel unfree. Rather, *when* he looks in the mirror he feels unfree, but when exactly is that? We don't really know, at least not in the same way that we know when Sandro throws Reno on the couch.

The omniscient narration of Valera's chapters, in other words, which Jameson would identify as an instance of the swollen third person, dissolves Valera into a vague morass of blurry history. It's all affect and no objective historical truth. Reno's gestural narration, however, comes much closer to that "realism without affect" that Jameson believes might return the subject to the stream of history's unfolding (187). But Kushner's means of accessing history is also a little different. Jameson's vision for successful historical fiction remains hopefully Lukácsian. For him, no one compares to the eighteenth- and nineteenth-century realist masters, whose narratives "carefully thread [their] way through the objective, [their] subject-centers brushing against this or that, luminously and momentarily transforming each passing thing into a flare of perception" (*Antinomies* 185). For Jameson, the splayed-out, omniscient interiority that plagues today's historical novels narrated in the swollen third person undoes this subject-object dialectic—a historical dialectic, which, when properly executed, should produce a politically distinct historical consciousness. Kushner shares Jameson's concern about narrators who are "always telling you what things mean, [who] can see the humor in every situation, or the cruelty, the absurdity." In *The Flamethrowers*, however, she deliberately engineers a first-person narrator who is generally unknowing: "I'm trying to replicate an experience that seems true to me," Kushner explains, "which is to understand some things and be bewildered by others" (Barron).[52] Consequently, Reno's narration provides something akin to the "flares of perception" Jameson desires, but they aren't flares of insight or political recognition. They are, instead, the flares of gesture. Their payoff isn't knowledge or understanding; it's access to generality. In part, that's because "the objective" that Reno carefully narrates her way through isn't the broad sweep of history. Rather, it comprises streams and streams of "people lost among people, since there wasn't anything else. *The world was people*" (277). These are the kinds of flares one finds when there isn't a clear politics to be had.

The Flamethrowers thus reimagines history, the contemporary historical novel, and the possible forms available to revolutionary thought today. It considers history as gesture, as simultaneously two- and three-dimensional, withdrawn from us, but also reaching out to us, perhaps for a kiss. In turn, it reevaluates the work it might do as historical fiction. Recognizing that the forms available for apprehending history (i.e., transcendence and immanence) no longer translate in any politically reliable way, *The Flamethrowers* approaches history gesturally, reminding us of the common *langue* we share with a world made of people in general. Finally, it offers that gestural mode as an alternative, nonrepresentational way to think about contemporary forms of revolution, indicating that gesture's ability to avoid the antinomy of transcendence and immanence might be worth the price of abandoning any predetermined, homologous politics.

---

52. For an extended meditation on the novel's competing narrative voices, see Matthew Hart and Alexander Rocca's interview with Kushner in *Contemporary Literature*. There, Kushner describes Reno's narration as "neutral" (201) and suggests that her apparent passivity is really just "how people actually are" (204).

CODA

Mark Bradford and the Generality of Abstraction

> It is the process of abstraction itself—that is, the removal of understanding outward from any particular experience to a general, all-purpose explanation or figure or type—that can paradoxically serve as a locus of affective or embodied engagement.
>
> —Blake Stimson, "Gesture and Abstraction"

This book has detailed the forms of generality that emerge in a cross section of contemporary US fiction that explores the conceptual and political viability of art, theory, and revolution after their supposed ends. Those perceived ends, I've argued, were partly the result of a vacillating form-politics homology that prevented a secure alignment between the conceptual forms of art, theory, and revolution on the one hand, and leftist politics on the other. Replacing the dominant conceptual forms of art (autonomy and heteronomy), theory (reflexivity), and revolution (immanence and transcendence) with variations on the singular-general relationship, the fiction writers compiled here develop generalized forms of value production irreducible to homological thought. Starting from the assumption that there is no necessary relationship between form and politics, their turn to generality signals a more limited, ad hoc approach to value, political or otherwise. I have followed these authors' lead in thinking through the alternative political mode generality affords—a historically contingent politics of ongoing access to and reconfiguration of general but not universal truths—but I have also tried to be modest in my claims on its behalf.

Beyond the political, however, it's also worth noting some of the other distinct ideas that follow from these authors' engagement with the singular-general relationship:

- a rejection of mutually exclusive thinking in all its forms
- an impersonal, generic notion of individual subjectivity that refuses to entertain the problematic relationship between particularity and universality
- a flexible conceptualization of genre as a domain of generality that's always changing vis-à-vis its encounters with singularity
- a relational mode of value production that replaces the meaning derived from reference and representation with that achieved through the reciprocal intercourse between singulars and generals
- a functionalist, pragmatic treatment of previously hypostatized concepts like reflexivity and negativity
- a mode of being that engages the world gesturally instead of through the inside/outside logic of immanence and transcendence
- an array of literary forms—Heti's textualized theater/theatricalized text; Kraus's case study; the theoretical literalism of Plascencia, Everett, Marcus, and Foer; Kushner's gestural realism—that draw in various ways on the singular-general relationship to provide a new sense of literary form's value

Not every author discussed here manages all of these innovations. And the field of contemporary fiction is so vast that it would be absurd to see this shared turn to generality as anything more than a trend within a cross section of twenty-first-century literature. Nevertheless, as the above list indicates, replacing the form-politics relationship with the singular-general relationship has extensive and profound conceptual implications.

By way of conclusion, and to shift media from the literary to the visual arts, I'd like to discuss one other form of generality that I haven't touched on explicitly yet, and that's abstraction. At first, it might seem like generality and abstraction are synonymous, but I'd suggest that abstraction is just one of several different ways to generalize, one of several different forms that generality might take. Given the baseline representational responsibilities of fiction writers, it makes sense that we should turn instead to the visual arts for more accessible examples of abstract aesthetic form. After all, even though we often describe novels as abstract, that usually means that they're conceptually dense and discursive, not, as in the visual arts, that they don't resemble any known object in the world. It's the rare book that can be abstract in the way a Norman Lewis or Frank Bowling painting is. Thus, to think more deliberately about generality as abstraction, I want to turn briefly to the visual art of Mark Bradford, a contemporary African American painter from Los Angeles who has been producing large-scale abstract art since the turn of the twenty-first century.[1] Bradford's work, which consistently gestures toward the history of racial injustice and violence, will also help us think one last time about the political implications of generality.

First, Bradford's abstract paintings aren't what we typically imagine when we think of paintings. He refers to them as paintings and even describes himself as a painter, but he rarely uses paint in his work. From a distance and at a glance, his pieces certainly look like paintings. They are rectangular, two-dimensional, and hang on the walls of art museums just like paintings do. But when you get up close and see their thick texture, you realize that you're looking at layers and layers of distressed paper, not paint. To produce his work, Bradford builds up large canvases with ten or fifteen layers of paper—white, black, colored, newsprint, billboards, photographs, album covers, maps, posters—much of it found on the streets of Los Angeles. As he works, he scissors some into smaller pieces, shellacs some layers, adds bleach or paint from Home Depot, and frequently embeds other elements like string, caulk, glue, wood, cord, or rope. Thus, in lieu of "the raw, limitless potentiality of oil, clay, wood, bronze, graphite, or any 'fine art' materials," Bradford uses "materials and systems that have a form and a life that antedate him and his work." His materials are "functionally specific" and "socially bounded," arriving with a "built-in-history" (Bedford, "Against Abstraction" 11). But this accretion of materials, this configuration of a general field (or what we might think of as the work's *langue*), is only half of Bradford's artistic process. Because once the work has been sufficiently built up, Bradford attacks his multilayered assemblage with power sanders and other tools, gouging and tearing away the layers, ripping up the cords or rope buried underneath, until a complex abstraction emerges. Instead of making something out of nothing, in other words, Bradford produces singular artworks born from preexisting fields of generality.

Linking this process to the many years he spent working as a stylist in his mother's hair salon, Bradford says, "I work with what you bring me" (Shiff 75). We might view this as a deliberately heteronomous move on Bradford's part. Using the paper detritus of his city as the foundational material for his art establishes a meaningful connection between his work and the world. But that work-world relation that drives the aesthetic regime's preoccupation with formal autonomy and heteronomy is not Bradford's immediate concern. Instead, as "the student of materiality rather than its master," his work remains "open to processes that have as yet no criteria for success or failure" (76). His aesthetic mode, in other words, is akin to what Dewey calls the logic of inquiry:

---

1. Bradford also makes sculptures, videos, and text-based art, but the bulk of his work is large-scale abstraction. For a fantastic survey of abstraction in African American visual art, see Sarah Lewis's "African American Abstraction."

the ongoing process by which the pursuit of knowledge "originates" the general (but not universal) forms of understanding that make knowledge knowable (5). Elsewhere, Bradford describes this art-as-inquiry method as a form of "call and response," as the process of "creating a condition and responding to it" (May 77). Bradford's work asks, What do we learn about the social when we configure and then disfigure it abstractly? What relations, structures, or generalized conditions of being come into view when the world is treated generally, as an abstraction that can be reshaped, decreated, gouged with an industrial sander?

For Bradford, this engagement with an antecedent set of general materials is one of the reasons he understands his work to be political. Intentionally maintaining his studio space in South Los Angeles, deliberately taking his raw materials from the surrounding streets, the "you" in "what you bring me" is always "the local culture and its systems of exchange," "the social economy of the street" (Shiff 77). In this way, Bradford explicitly differentiates himself from the history of abstract painting in the US, which he reads as completely "sanitized" of politics. Instead, Bradford aligns himself with a tradition of European abstraction (Asger Jorn, Wols, the CoBrA group), which, he says, has more of a "worker's feel" (May 80).[2] At the same time, however, Bradford never claims to know or understand "the local culture," and in this way, he also differentiates himself from more overtly political black art that might resist total abstraction for fear of attenuating its politics. (I'm thinking here of work by artists like Kara Walker, Glenn Ligon, and Gary Simmons, which abstracts its material, but not to the point of complete, nonrepresentational abstraction.) For Bradford, however, the racialized content on which his work draws has no predetermined meaning, political or otherwise. It forms the basis of his aesthetic inquiry, but its worldly significance and value aren't imported, prepackaged into the art. Unpacking his relationship to blackness, for example, he explains, "When I started making work, I felt like there was no space. It was almost like everyone knew more than me about blackness, so I thought what I need to do is abstract it in order to find space" (84). Bradford's aim is neither to include the world in his art nor to connect his art with the world but rather to use aesthetic abstraction as a generalized mode of inquiry into the relations that shape the world. And because Bradford's materials are "entirely contingent upon—in fact, produced by—the logic of the economies that structure his working environment," there's no telling where

---

2. Bradford makes his political commitments even more explicit through a community art and outreach space, Art + Practice, that he cofounded with Eileen Norton and Allan DiCastro in his South Central Los Angeles neighborhood of Leimert Park. The organization focuses in particular on providing social services to local foster youth.

those inquiries will lead. For Stephen Best, this contingency is precisely what makes Bradford's visual art so generative for black politics. Suggesting that Bradford's work manifests "a 'style' of freedom" that "literary critics are not yet willing to entertain," he champions Bradford's "freedom from constraining conceptions of blackness as authenticity, tradition, and legitimacy; of history as inheritance, memory, and social reproduction; of diaspora as kinship, belonging, and dissemination" (22–23). These are things that politically committed scholars think they already know about blackness, but for Best, Bradford helps us (re)think otherwise.

Christopher Bedford has dubbed Bradford's art "social abstraction," which he defines as "a mode of abstraction" that retains "a literal, material relationship to the social contexts that were [Bradford's] subject" ("Patterns" 100). Bradford has embraced the description, using it in interviews to explain his work, and defining abstraction for him as "a conceptual framework that I use to interrogate my surroundings and my relationship to them."[3] This approach to abstraction proves to be an absolutely necessary feature of the work. Describing South Central Los Angeles as "the most formalized, described, figurative known place in the world," Bradford explains that his abstracting processes break free of that overdetermination and allow him to capture the more generalized socioeconomic conditions of the racialized bodies living there (Smee 78).[4] Abstraction for Bradford is the only way to produce new conceptualizations of the racialized urban spaces from which his work draws. But social abstraction's generality doesn't just allow Bradford to think beyond the media's overdetermined representations of his social milieu, it also allows him to tackle a degree of complexity in that social milieu that would otherwise be overlooked. Describing the fact that his neighborhood includes "a Korean nail salon, a black wig store, and a Mexican taqueria" as "abstract," Bradford suggests that existing reality "is too complicated for existing categories, for a system of classification that separates things that actually interact" (K. Siegel 114–15). Consequently, to capture the complexity of that interaction, his call-and-response logic of inquiry prompts him to abstract his materials, producing a visual field that generalizes the spatial configurations structuring his world. And he doesn't just do this for black social space. For example, the three "Sample" paintings from his *Scorched Earth* series, which tackle the AIDS epidemic among black gay men, do the same for queer community;

---

3. Bradford's "Black Venus," from 2005, is both my favorite piece of his and, to my mind, *the* paradigmatic example of his "social abstraction."

4. Bradford does not use the word "figurative" the way a literary scholar would, to mean the opposite of literal. Rather, for the visual arts, "figurative" names work that includes figures—identifiable representational elements. Used in this way, it's the opposite of abstraction.

and works like "Black Wall Street" and *Pickett's Charge,* which I'll discuss at length in a moment, offer a similar take on the history of racial violence in the United States.

Bradford is, as Rancière might put it, using the generalizing power of abstraction to distribute and redistribute the sensible. Or as Bradford himself puts it: "It was revolutionary for me that you could put two things together based on your desire for them to be together" (Shiff 80). But this together-ness, in Bradford's work, is always abstract. His art isn't representing, severing itself from, or becoming the world. Its value is not a function of its relative autonomy and/or heteronomy. Instead, its value is a function of the relation its singular parts bear to each other and to the totality of the abstract general-ity, which itself comprises the materiality of social and/or historical space. In addition to sidestepping the homological logic of autonomy and heteronomy, then, Bradford's process and materials also resist dialectical conceptions of value. "You're not mixing black and white paint to get a third thing," Brad-ford explains. "It's simply one paper on top of another paper, and part of it's eroded and bleeding through the other. They're singular yet in tandem with each other" (Eliel 63). The result is a purely relational conception of value in which there is no incommensurability, no mutual exclusivity. "There are no contradictions for me," Bradford insists (Walker 96). Thus, even as he's rip-ping and tearing his materials apart, the abstraction's generality is bringing and holding everything together. Drawing on the full contranymic power of the word, we might say that Bradford *cleaves* his materials, relating them to each other by ripping them apart, and vice versa. The process of *décollage,* like the positive power of the false I discussed in chapter 2, pursues an ad hoc constructivism, not a theoretically motivated deconstruction.[5]

All of Bradford's violent ripping and tearing is also in conversation with a longstanding critical tradition that emphasizes the individualized gestural potency of Abstract Expressionists like Jackson Pollock, Franz Kline, and Lee Krasner. In that tradition, the unique gesture of a brushstroke or a paint splat-ter supposedly reveals "a primal form or spirit emerging from the recesses of the psyche" (Storr 42), "some inborn genius, some inescapable touch of per-sonal style" (Shiff 78). As Christopher Bedford argues, however, "Bradford's subjectivity is one among many at play in the surface of his paintings," and the way in which Bradford produces social abstraction through "premeditated

---

5. Bradford, another example of an artist-critic, was trained at Cal Arts in the late 1990s and readily acknowledges his "very theoretical education" (Eliel 59–61.) Much like Plascencia, Everett, Marcus, and Foer, however, Bradford doesn't use his theoretical knowledge in theo-retical ways. Instead, Bradford notes, "I'm not a theorist, but I know what I'm talking about" (Aquin 78).

accident" undermines Abstract Expressionism's emphasis on "the autographic mark as the essential conduit for subjective expression" ("Patterns" 102–3). Instead, as we saw in Heti and Kraus, Bradford's decreations make his work impersonal, affecting but not emotional. Bradford is not in his art, and his art is not about him. Or as Stephen Best explains, Bradford pursues an aesthetics of "self-divestiture" that generates "a more muted, contingent, relativistic selfhood" (23). Bradford's gestures, in other words, are not highly individualized acts of unique selfhood but are instead more general, or what we saw Agamben describe in chapter 3 as the "pure mediality" of gesture. Thus, Richard Shiff argues that "Bradford is as much formed by materials as he is the one who forms these same materials into art. He is a maker being made, a human work in progress. His present remains unfixed and fluid, defined not by the essence of his individual being . . . but by his ordinary movement" (Shiff 78).[6] Like Reno moving through space on her motorcycle, Bradford, decreating his generalities, ripping cord from his canvases, encounters the world as an impersonal gesture of pure mediality.

In *Pickett's Charge,* a more recent work commissioned by the Hirshhorn Museum in Washington DC, Bradford brings these techniques and processes to bear on the deeper material history of slavery in the United States. Taking inspiration from the violent racial history of the nation's capital and the surrounding region, Bradford produced an eight-paneled "painting" that was installed, floor to ceiling, on the walls of the Hirshhorn's perfectly circular inner gallery. Basing the project on Paul Philippoteaux's nineteenth-century painting of Pickett's Charge, which was installed in the cyclorama at the Battle of Gettysburg visitor's center,[7] Bradford includes versions of that painting (two soldiers from Philippoteaux's painting remain quite discernible) among the decreated materials of his own work (see fig. 1).

In this way, much like the historical novelists discussed in chapter 3, Bradford's work interrogates the possibility of thinking history in the present. Instead of trying to make the truth of history knowable, however, Bradford's work highlights the possibilities of a more gestural relationship to racial

---

6. In an interview with Hamza Walker, Bradford states that he intentionally "removes the emotion from the gesture" (97).

7. Pickett's Charge is often referred to as "the high-water mark of the Confederacy" because it's widely seen as the best chance the Confederacy had to win the war.

In a cyclorama, a viewer stands in the middle of a 360-degree room that has a painted visual scene on the walls with added diorama material between the walls and the viewer. The idea is to produce maximal, immersive depth for the viewer. In the Gettysburg cyclorama, Philippoteaux's painting allowed the viewer to stand in the middle of the room with the Battle of Gettysburg happening all around her. The Hirshhorn Gallery is also circular, but shaped like a donut, which means that it's impossible to stand in the middle of Bradford's 360-degree work.

FIGURE 1. *Pickett's Charge* (Two Men). 2017. Mixed media on canvas. 365.8 × 1524 cm / 144 × 600 in. Installation view, "Mark Bradford. Pickett's Charge," Hirshhorn Museum and Sculpture Garden, Washington DC, 2017. Photo: Cathy Carver.

violence and the Civil War fought in its defense. First, Bradford generalizes history by abstracting it into thick layers of paper with long lengths of parallel cords embedded horizontally underneath. (In *Pickett's Charge*, Bradford deploys cord more consistently and regularly than he does in any previous work, laying it across the entirety of nearly every panel at regular intervals.) Spanning almost 400 linear feet across all eight panels, the cords—many of which have been ripped out, leaving behind loosely hanging strips of layered paper—penetrate the synchronic layering of paper with a violently diachronic motion (see fig. 2).

We could read this, as Evelyn Hankins does in her catalog essay on the piece, as an abstract representation of "the relentless march of time and how the linear narratives offered to us are . . . colored by different memories or subjectivities, specifically those whose position of authority empowers them to recount history" (18). The circular staging of the piece also reminds us, in the Age of Trump when the work was installed, that this linear history of racial violence in the United States is also circular—that the struggle to imagine the past in the present isn't a struggle at all since it's always already here. Even more important than the work's potent merging of history's synchronic layers and diachronic motion, however, are the violent gestures that cleave them together and apart. Thus, while the cords certainly conjure the linear motion of history, Bradford also explains in an interview with Stéphane Aquin that he embedded them there only so he could rip them out in "one gesture that interrupts [the] narrative" of American greatness. "The string for me is the

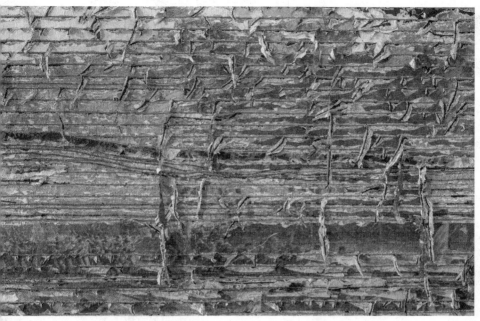

FIGURE 2. *Pickett's Charge* (Witness Tree) (detail). 2017. Mixed media on canvas. 365.8 × 1524 cm / 144 × 600 in. Photo: Joshua White / JWPictures.

violence," Bradford continues. "The tearing of the actual painting by pulling and tattering it becomes a way for the violence to come through, to reveal the underlying violence in the grand narrative" (74). Cutting through history's immanent flow, the violent gestures of *Pickett's Charge* aren't synchronic snapshots of, say, the scarring on an enslaved person's back. Instead, as gestures, they point to enslavement as the ongoing modality of history, to racial violence as history's enduring medium. The moment of violent ripping is an act of gestural abstraction that generalizes the artwork's meaning and value, effectively highlighting the structure of violence rather than any given instance of it. It's a moment of abstraction that, as Blake Stimson says in the above epigraph, can "paradoxically serve as a locus of affective or embodied engagement" (69). Consequently, *Pickett's Charge* isn't a representation, index, or allegory of historical racial violence as much as it's an exploration, an inquiry, into the general forms of relation produced out of a violent racial history that continues to define the parameters of contemporary knowing and being.

In this way, Bradford's abstractions communicate, oftentimes quite gesturally, the general conditions of knowledge at the present time. "All I do is give the local community access to contemporary ideas," Bradford tells Aquin. "That's it. Not art, but contemporary ideas" (75). In the spirit of nonmutual exclusivity that grounds Bradford's contemporary ideas *and* the contemporary ideas of those authors who, as I've demonstrated throughout *Art, Theory, Revolution,* are reorienting US fiction toward other forms of generality, I'd like to conclude by emphasizing that the arguments and methods pursued here should not be seen as precluding other arguments and methods. I do not offer my descriptively analytical approach to reading in exclusive opposition to any other mode of reading. I do not intend the ideas developed here about generality to supersede or replace other conceptual forms like identity, universality, or the dialectic. The ideas in this book, and in the books this book is about, do not purport to be the best, or the most ideologically pure and politically potent, ideas. Rather, they are the ideas that have originated in and developed over the course of a very specific intellectual inquiry into the political purchase of form in the twenty-first century. This might make those ideas appear circular, or even evanescent. But unless you believe that our ideas come to us from somewhere beyond whatever it is we're all doing here, there's no other way for ideas to be.

WORKS CITED

Adorno, Theodor. *Aesthetic Theory*. Trans. Robert Hullot-Kentor, University of Minnesota Press, 1997.

Agamben, Giorgio. "Notes on Gesture." *Means without End: Notes on Politics*, University of Minnesota Press, 2000, pp. 49–62.

Al-Mousawi, Nahrain. "Literature after the Arab Spring." *Middle East Institute*, February 5, 2016.

Anderson, Linda. *Autobiography: An Introduction*. Routledge, 2001.

Aquin, Stéphane. "The World Is on Fire: An Interview with Mark Bradford." *Mark Bradford: Pickett's Charge*, eds. Evelyn Hankins and Stéphane Aquin, Yale University Press, 2018, pp. 71–90.

Arendt, Hannah. *On Revolution*. Penguin Books, 1990.

Aristotle. "On Interpretation." Trans. E. M. Edghill. http://classics.mit.edu/Aristotle/interpretation.1.1.html.

Ashley, Kathleen, et. al. *Autobiography & Postmodernism*. University of Massachusetts Press, 1994.

Auster, Paul. *City of Glass*. Penguin Books, 1987.

———. "Unpublished Interview with Paul Auster." http://www.bluecricket.com/auster/links/secret.html.

Badiou, Alain. "The Communist Hypothesis." *New Left Review*, vol. 49, Jan–Feb 2008, pp. 29–42.

Barron, Jesse. "Insurrection: An Interview with Rachel Kushner." *Paris Review*, April 3, 2013.

Barthes, Roland. "The Death of the Author." *The Norton Anthology of Theory and Criticism*. Eds. Vincent Leitch et al. 2nd ed., Norton, 2010, pp. 1322–26.

———. "Interview: A Conversation with Roland Barthes." *The Grain of the Voice: Interviews 1962–1980*, trans. Linda Coverdale, Northwestern University Press, 2009, pp. 128–49.

Baudrillard, Jean. *Forget Foucault*. Semiotext(e), 1987.

Beaulieu, Derek. *A, a novel*. Jean Boîte Éditions, 2017.

Bedford, Christopher. "Against Abstraction." *Mark Bradford*, ed. Christopher Bedford, Wexner Center for the Arts, 2010, pp. 7–29.

———. "Patterns of Intention." *Mark Bradford: Through Darkest America by Truck and Tank*, White Cube, 2013, pp. 97–103.

Benjamin, Walter. "The Work of Art in the Age of Mechanical Reproduction." *Illuminations*, Schocken Books, 1968, pp. 217–52.

Benzon, Paul. "Lost in Transcription: Postwar Typewriting Culture, Andy Warhol's Bad Book, and the Standardization of Error." *PMLA*, vol. 125, no. 1, 2010, pp. 92–106.

Berardi, Franco. *The Soul at Work: From Alienation to Autonomy*. Semiotext(e), 2009.

Berlant, Lauren. *Cruel Optimism*. Duke University Press, 2011.

———. *The Female Complaint: The Unfinished Business of Sentimentality in American Culture*. Duke University Press, 2008.

———. "On the Case." *Critical Inquiry*, vol. 33, Summer 2007, pp. 663–72.

Bervin, Jen. *Nets*. Ugly Duckling Presse, 2004.

Best, Stephen. *None Like Us: Blackness, Belonging, Aesthetic Life*. Duke University Press, 2018.

Birns, Nicholas. *Theory after Theory*. Broadview Press, 2010.

Bishop, Claire. *Artificial Hells: Participatory Art and the Politics of Spectatorship*. Verso, 2012.

Bogel, Fredric. *New Formalist Criticism: Theory and Practice*. Palgrave, 2011.

Bourriaud, Nicolas. *Relational Aesthetics*. Les Presse Du Reel, 1998.

Bové, Paul. *In the Wake of Theory*. Wesleyan University Press, 1992.

Brown, Nicholas. *Autonomy: The Social Ontology of Art Under Capitalism*. Duke University Press, 2019.

Buchmann, Sabeth. "The (Re)Animation of Medium Specificity in Contemporary Art." *Contemporary Art: 1989 to the Present*, eds. Alexander Dumbadze and Suzanne Hudson, Wiley-Blackwell, 2013, pp. 107–16.

Bürger, Peter. *Theory of the Avant Garde*. University of Minnesota Press, 1984.

Butler, Judith. *Frames of War*. Verso, 2009.

Butler, Judith, Ernesto Laclau, and Slavoj Žižek. *Contingency, Hegemony, Universality: Contemporary Dialogues on the Left*. Verso, 2000.

Buurma, Rachel, and Laura Heffernan. "Notation after 'The Reality Effect': Remaking Reference with Roland Barthes and Sheila Heti." *Representations*, vol. 125, Winter 2014, pp. 80–102.

Campanioni, Chris. *Death of Art*. C&R Press, 2016.

Carroll, Noël, ed. *Theories of Art Today*. University of Wisconsin Press, 2000.

Censer, Jack. *Debating Modern Revolution: The Evolution of Revolutionary Ideas*. Bloomsbury, 2016.

Chow, Rey. "The Interruption of Referentiality: Poststructuralism and the Conundrum of Critical Multiculturalism." *South Atlantic Quarterly*, vol. 101, no.1, 2002, pp. 171–86.

Christian, Barbara. "The Race for Theory." *Cultural Critique*, vol. 6, 1987, pp. 51–63.

Clover, Joshua. *Riot. Strike. Riot: The New Era of Uprisings*. Verso, 2016.

Cook, Michael. "The Death of Theory." *Salvo*, August 12, 2005.

Couser, Thomas G., and Joseph Fichtelberg, eds. *True Relations: Essays on Autobiography and the Postmodern*, Greenwood Press, 1998.

Curran, Giorel. *21st Century Dissent: Anarchism, Anti-Globalization and Environmentalism.* Palgrave, 2006.

Currie, Mark. "Introduction." *Metafiction,* ed. Mark Currie. Routledge, 1995, pp. 1–18.

Dames, Nicholas. "Theory and the Novel." *n+1,* vol. 14, 2012, pp. 157–69.

Danto, Arthur. *After the End of Art.* Princeton University Press, 1997.

———. *Beyond the Brillo Box: The Visual Arts in Post-Historical Perspective.* Farrar, Straus, Giroux, 1992.

———. "The End of Art." *The Death of Art,* ed. Berel Lang, Haven, 1984, pp. 5–35.

Davis, Ben. "What Arthur Danto Means to Me." October 30, 2013. http://www.benadavis.com/archives/?category=Artinfo.

Davis, Colin. *After Poststructuralism: Reading, Stories and Theory.* Routledge, 2004.

Dawson, Paul. "The Return of Omniscience in Contemporary Fiction." *Narrative,* vol. 17, no. 2, May 2009, pp. 143–61.

Dean, Jodi. *The Communist Horizon.* Verso, 2012.

———. *Crowds and Party.* Verso, 2016.

———. *Žižek's Politics.* Routledge, 2006.

DeKoven, Marianne. "The Politics of Modernist Form." *New Literary History,* vol. 23, no. 3, 1992, pp. 675–90.

Deleuze, Gilles, and Felix Guattari. *What Is Philosophy?* Trans. Hugh Tomlinson and Graham Burchell, Columbia University Press, 1994.

de Man, Paul. "Autobiography as De-facement." *MLN,* vol. 94, December 1979, pp. 919–30.

Deranty, Jean-Philippe. "Regimes of the Arts." *Jacques Rancière: Key Concepts,* ed. Jean Philippe Deranty, Acumen, 2010, pp. 116–32.

Derrida, Jacques. *Of Grammatology.* Johns Hopkins University Press, 1998.

———. "Structure, Sign, and Play in the Discourse of the Human Sciences." *Writing and Difference,* trans. Alan Bass, University of Chicago Press, 1978, pp. 278–94.

de Saussure, Ferdinand. "Course in General Linguistics." *The Norton Anthology of Theory and Criticism,* eds. Vincent Leitch et al. 2nd ed., Norton, 2010, pp. 850–66.

Dewey, John. *Logic: The Theory of Inquiry.* Henry Holt and Company, 1938.

Dewhurst, David, Peter Dombi, and Naomi Colvin. "How Hayek Helped Us to Find Capitalism's Flaws." *Financial Times,* January 25, 2012.

Dix, Hywel, ed. *Autofiction in English.* Palgrave, 2018.

Docherty, Thomas. *After Theory: Postmodernism/Postmarxism.* Routledge, 1990.

Dormehl, Luke. *The Apple Revolution: Steve Jobs, the Counter Culture, and How the Crazy Ones Took Over the World.* Virgin, 2012.

Drucker, Johanna. *Sweet Dreams: Contemporary Art and Complicity.* University of Chicago Press, 2005.

Dubey, Madhu. "Post-Postmodern Realism?" *Twentieth-Century Literature,* vol. 57, nos. 3 & 4, 2011, pp. 364–71.

Eagleton, Terry. *After Theory.* Basic Books, 2003.

Elias, Amy, et al. "Postmodern, Postwar, Contemporary: A Dialogue on the Field." *Postmodern/Postwar—and After: Rethinking American Literature,* University of Iowa Press, 2019, pp. 27–56.

Eliel, Carol. "Dynamism and Quiet Whispers: Conversations with Mark Bradford." *Mark Bradford,* ed. Christopher Bedford, Wexner Center for the Arts, 2010, pp. 57–74.

Elliott, Jane, and Derek Attridge. "Introduction: Theory's Nine Lives." *Theory After "Theory*," eds. Jane Elliott and Derek Attridge, Routledge, 2011, pp. 1–15.

Eugenides, Jeffrey. *The Marriage Plot*. Picador, 2011.

———. *The Virgin Suicides*. Picador, 1993.

Everett, Percival. *Erasure*. Hyperion, 2001.

———. "A Modality." *symplokē*, vol. 12, nos. 1 & 2, 2004, pp. 152–54.

———. *Percival Everett by Virgil Russell*. Graywolf Press, 2013.

Felman, Shoshana, and Dori Laub. *Testimony: Crises of Witnessing in Literature, Psychoanalysis and History*. Routledge, 1991.

Felperin, Howard. *Beyond Deconstruction: The Uses and Abuses of Literary Theory*. Clarendon Press, 1985.

Fisher-Lichte, Erika. "The Avant-Garde and the Semiotics of the Antitextual Gesture." *Contours of the Theatrical Avant-Garde*, ed. James Harding, University of Michigan Press, 2000, pp. 79–95.

Flusser, Vilém. *Gestures*. Trans. Nancy Ann Roth, University of Minnesota Press, 2014.

Foer, Jonathan Safran. *Tree of Codes*. Visual Editions, 2010.

Fournier, Lauren. *Autotheory as Feminist Practice in Art, Writing, and Criticism*. MIT Press, 2021.

Fowles, John. *The French Lieutenant's Woman*. Signet, 1969.

Fried, Michael. "Art and Objecthood." *Art in Theory 1900–1990*, eds. Charles Harrison and Paul Wood, Blackwell, 1992, pp. 822–34.

Gass, William. *Fiction and Figures of Life*. Knopf, 1970.

Ghitis, Frida. *The End of Revolution*. Algora Publishing, 2001.

Gillick, Liam, and Maria Lind. "Participation." *Contemporary Art: 1989 to the Present*, eds. Alexander Dumbadze and Suzanne Hudson, Wiley-Blackwell, 2013, pp. 204–13.

Gilmore, Leigh. "American Neoconfessional: Memoir, Self-Help, and Redemption on Oprah's Couch." *Biography*, vol. 33, no. 4, Fall 2010, pp. 657–79.

———. *Autobiographics: A Feminist Theory of Women's Self-Representation*. Cornell University Press, 1994.

Gitlin, Todd. *Occupy Nation: The Roots, the Spirit, and the Promise of Occupy Wall Street*. Harper Collins, 2012.

Greenberg, Clement. "Modernist Painting." *Art in Theory 1900–1990*, eds. Charles Harrison and Paul Wood, Blackwell, 1992, pp. 754–60.

Grønstad, Asbjørn, and Henrik Gustafsson. *Cinema and Agamben: Ethics, Biopolitics and the Moving Image*. Bloomsbury, 2014.

Gusdorf, Georges. "Conditions and Limits of Autobiography." *The Routledge Auto/biography Studies Reader*, eds. Ricia Chansky and Emily Hipchen, Routledge, 2016, pp. 24–33.

Hankins, Evelyn. "Mark Bradford: Into the Fray." *Mark Bradford: Pickett's Charge*, Yale University Press, 2018, pp. 1–70.

Hardt, Michael, and Antonino Negri. *Commonwealth*. Harvard University Press, 2009.

———. *Declaration*. Argo Navis, 2012.

———. *Empire*. Harvard University Press, 2000.

———. *Multitude*. Penguin, 2004.

Harris, Wendell, ed. *Beyond Poststructuralism: The Speculations of Theory and the Experience of Reading*. Pennsylvania State University Press, 1996.

Hart, Matthew, and Alexander Rocca. "An Interview with Rachel Kushner." *Contemporary Literature,* vol. 56, no. 2, Summer 2015, pp. 192–215.

Hayles, N. Katherine. "Combining Close and Distant Reading: Jonathan Safran Foer's *Tree of Codes* and the Aesthetic of Bookishness." *PMLA,* vol. 128, no. 1, 2013, pp. 226–31.

Hebdige, Dick. *Subculture: The Meaning of Style.* London: Routledge, 1979.

Hegel, G. F. W. *Aesthetics. Lectures on Fine Art.* Trans. T. M. Knox, 2 vols. Clarendon Press, 1975.

Heti, Sheila. *How Should a Person Be?* Picador, 2012.

———. "An Interview with Chris Kraus." *Believer,* vol. 101, September 1, 2013, https://www.believermag.com/issues/201309/?read=interview_kraus.

Hilburn, Robert. "Beatles Sue Nike Over Use of Song." *Los Angeles Times,* July 29, 1987.

Hoberek, Andrew. "Literary Genre Fiction." *American Literature in Transition, 2000–2010,* ed. Rachel Greenwald Smith, Cambridge University Press, 2018, pp. 61–75.

Hobsbawm, Eric. "Revolution and Sex." *Revolutionaries: Contemporary Essays,* Weidenfeld and Nicolson, 1973, pp. 216–19.

Holloway, John. *Change the World without Taking Power.* Pluto Press, 2002.

———. *Crack Capitalism.* Pluto Press, 2010.

Horkheimer, Max, and Theodor Adorno. "The Culture Industry: Enlightenment as Mass Deception." *Dialectic of Enlightenment,* Stanford University Press, 2002, pp. 94–136.

Howard, Jennifer. "The Fragmentation of Literary Theory." *Chronicle of Higher Education,* December 16, 2005.

Huehls, Mitchum. "Historical Fiction after the End of History." *American Literature in Transition, 2000–2010,* ed. Rachel Greenwald Smith, Cambridge University Press, 2017, pp. 138–51.

———. "The Post-Theory Theory Novel." *Contemporary Literature,* vol. 56, no. 2, 2015, pp. 280–310.

Hulatt, Owen, ed. *Aesthetic and Artistic Autonomy.* Bloomsbury Academic, 2013.

Hutcheon, Linda. *Narcissistic Narrative: The Metafictional Paradox.* Wilfrid Laurier Press, 1980.

———. *A Poetics of Postmodernism: History, Theory, Fiction.* Routledge, 1988.

———. "The Politics of Postmodernism." *Cultural Critique,* vol. 5, Winter 1986–87, pp. 179–202.

Jackson, Shannon. "What Is the 'Social' in Social Practice: Comparing Experiments in Performance." *The Cambridge Companion to Performance Studies,* ed. Tracy Davis, Cambridge University Press, 2008, pp. 136–50.

"Jacques Derrida." *The Norton Anthology of Theory and Criticism,* ed. Vincent Leitch et al. 2nd ed., Norton, 2010, pp. 1680–88.

Jameson, Fredric. *The Antinomies of Realism.* Verso, 2015

———. *Archaeologies of the Future: The Desire Called Utopia and Other Science Fictions.* Verso, 2005.

———. "The Historical Novel Today, or, Is It Still Possible." *The Antinomies of Realism,* Verso, 2015, pp. 259–313.

———. *Late Marxism: Adorno, or, The Persistence of the Dialectic.* Verso, 1990.

———. *Marxism and Form.* Princeton University Press, 1971.

———. *The Political Unconscious.* Cornell University Press, 1981.

———. *Postmodernism, or the Cultural Logic of Late Capitalism.* Duke University Press, 1992.

———. *Valences of the Dialectic.* Verso, 2010.

Johnson, Cedric. "The Triumph of Black Lives Matter and Neoliberal Redemption." *nonsite,* June 9, 2020.

Johnson, Samuel. *The Rambler,* vol. 60, October 13, 1750. *Selected Writings: Samuel Johnson,* Ed. Peter Martin, Harvard University Press, 2009, pp. 126–30.

Joselit, David. *After Art.* Princeton University Press, 2013.

Kant, Immanuel. *The Critique of Judgment.* Trans. Werner Pluhar. Hackett, 1987.

Kingston-Reese, Alexandra. *Contemporary Novelists and the Aesthetics of Twenty-First Century American Life.* University of Iowa Press, 2019.

Konstantinou, Lee. "Neorealist Fiction." *American Literature in Transition, 2000–2010,* ed. Rachel Greenwald Smith, Cambridge University Press, 2017, pp. 109–24.

Kornbluh, Anna. *The Order of Forms: Realism, Formalism, and Social Space.* University of Chicago Press, 2019.

Kramnick, Jonathan, and Anahid Nersessian. "*Critical Response V*: Forms and Explanations: A Reply to Our Critics." *Critical Inquiry,* vol. 44, Autumn 2017, pp. 164–74.

———. "Form and Explanation." *Critical Inquiry,* vol. 43, Spring 2017, pp. 650–69.

Kraus, Chris. *Aliens & Anorexia.* Semiotext(e), 2000.

———. *I Love Dick.* Semiotext(e), 2006.

———. Interview with Anna Poletti. *Contemporary Women's Writing,* vol. 10, no. 1, 2016, pp. 123–35.

———. *Summer of Hate.* Semiotext(e), 2012.

———. *Torpor.* Semiotext(e), 2006.

———. *Video Green: Los Angeles Art and the Triumph of Nothingness.* Semiotext(e), 2004.

———. *Where Art Belongs.* Semiotext(e), 2011.

Krauss, Rosalind. *Perpetual Inventory.* MIT Press, 2010.

Kristeva, Julia. "Gesture: Practice or Communication?" *The Body Reader: Social Aspects of the Human Body,* ed. Ted Polhemus, Pantheon, 1978, pp. 264–84.

Kushner, Rachel. *The Flamethrowers.* Scribner, 2013.

———. *Telex from Cuba.* Scribner, 2008.

Kuspit, Donald. *The End of Art.* Cambridge University Press, 2004.

Laclau, Ernesto. "Can Immanence Explain Social Struggles?" *Empire's New Clothes: Reading Hardt and Negri,* eds. Paul Passavant and Jodi Dean, Routledge, 2004, pp. 21–30.

———. *Emancipations.* Verso, 1996.

Lang, Berel, ed. *The Death of Art.* Haven, 1984.

Lash, Scott. *Another Modernity, a Different Rationality.* Blackwell Publishers, 1999.

Lejeune, Philippe. *On Autobiography.* Trans. Katherine Leary, University of Minnesota Press, 1989.

Lerner, Ben. *10:04.* Faber and Faber, Inc., 2014.

———. "Actual World." *Frieze,* June 16, 2013. https://www.frieze.com/article/actual-world.

Lethem, Jonathan. *Dissident Gardens.* Vintage, 2013.

Levine, Caroline. "*Critical Response I*: Still Polemicizing after All These Years." *Critical Inquiry,* vol. 44, Autumn 2017, pp. 129–35.

———. *Forms.* Princeton University Press, 2015.

———. "Forms, Literary and Social." *Dibur Literary Journal,* vol. 2, Spring 2016, pp. 75–79.

———. "Model Thinking: Generalization, Political Form, and the Common Good." *New Literary History,* vol. 48, no. 4, Autumn 2017, pp. 633–53.

Levine, George. *Aesthetics and Ideology.* Rutgers University Press, 1994.

Levinson, Marjorie. "Posthumous Critique." *In Near Ruins: Cultural Theory at the End of the Century,* ed. Nicholas Dirks, University of Minnesota Press, 1998, pp. 257–94.

———. "What Is New Formalism?" *PMLA,* vol. 122, no. 2, March 2007, pp. 558–69.

Lewis, Sarah. "African American Abstraction." *The Routledge Companion to African American Art History.* Routledge, 2019, pp. 159–73.

Leypoldt, Günter. "Recent Realist Fiction and the Idea of Writing 'After Postmodernism.'" *Amerikastudien/American Studies,* vol. 49, no. 1, 2004, pp. 19–34.

Lindsey, Ursula. "The Novel after the Arab Spring." *New Yorker,* May 8, 2014.

Linskey, Annie. "Inside the Trump Tweet Machine: Staff-written Posts, Bad Grammar (on Purpose), and Delight in the Chaos." *Boston Globe,* May 22, 2018.

Lodge, David. "The Novel Now." *Metafiction,* ed. Mark Currie. Longman, 1995, pp. 145–60.

Lukács, Georg. *The Historical Novel.* Trans. Hannah and Stanley Mitchell, University of Nebraska Press, 1983.

———. "In Search of Bourgeois Man." *Essays on Thomas Mann,* Grosset and Dunlap, 1965, pp. 13–46.

Malik, Suhail, and Andrea Phillips. "The Wrong of Contemporary Art: Aesthetics and Political Indeterminacy." *Reading Rancière: Critical Dissensus,* eds. Paul Bowman and Richard Stamp, Continuum, 2011, pp. 111–28.

Manning, Erin. *The Minor Gesture.* Duke University Press, 2016.

Marcus, Ben. *Notable American Women.* Vintage, 2002.

———. "Why Experimental Fiction Threatens to Destroy Publishing, Jonathan Franzen, and Life as We Know It: A Correction." *Harper's,* October 2005, pp. 39–52.

Marcus, Laura. *Auto/biographical Discourses: Theory, Criticism, Practice.* Manchester University Press, 1994.

———. *Autobiography: A Very Short Introduction.* Oxford University Press, 2018.

Martin, Theodore. *Contemporary Drift: Genre, Historicism, and the Problem of the Present.* Columbia University Press, 2017.

Massumi, Brian. "Perception Attack: The Force to Own Time." *Theory after "Theory,"* eds. Jane Elliott and Derek Attridge, Routledge, 2011, pp. 75–89.

May, Susan. "Call and Response: A Conversation with Mark Bradford." *Mark Bradford: Through Darkest America by Truck and Tank,* White Cube, 2013, pp. 73–84.

McCaffrey, Larry. "A Conversation with David Foster Wallace." *Review of Contemporary Fiction,* vol. 13, no. 2, 1993, pp. 127–50.

McHale, Brian. *Postmodern Fiction.* Routledge, 1987.

McLaughlin, Robert L. "Post-Postmodern Discontent: Contemporary Fiction and the Social World." *symplokē,* vol. 12, nos. 1 & 2, 2004, pp. 53–68.

McMeekin, Sean. *The Russian Revolution: A New History.* Basic Books, 2017.

McQuillan, Martin. *Post-Theory: New Directions in Criticism.* University of Edinburgh Press, 1999.

Medina, Cuauhtémoc. "Contemp(t)orary: Eleven Theses." *e-flux,* vol. 12, 2010. https://www.e-flux.com/journal/12/61335/contemp-t-orary-eleven-theses/.

Melgard, Holly. *The Making of the Americans.* Troll Thread, 2012.

Metcalf, Stephen. "The Death of Literary Theory." *Slate,* November 17, 2005. https://slate.com/news-and-politics/2005/11/in-defense-of-literary-theory.html.

Michaels, Walter Benn. *The Beauty of a Social Problem: Photography, Autonomy, Economy.* University of Chicago Press, 2015.

———. "Fifty Shades of Neoliberal Love." *Neoliberalism and Contemporary Literary Culture,* eds. Mitchum Huehls and Rachel Greenwald Smith, Johns Hopkins University Press, 2017, pp. 21–33.

———. "The Force of a Frame: Owen Kydd's Durational Photographs." *nonsite,* vol. 11, March 14, 2014, pp. 34–43.

———. "Going Boom." *Bookforum,* February/March 2009.

Michaels, Walter Benn, and Stephen Knapp. "Against Theory." *Critical Inquiry,* vol. 8, no. 4, 1982, pp. 723–42.

Miller, Nancy K. "The Entangled Self: Genre Bondage in the Age of the Memoir." *PMLA,* vol. 122, no. 2, March 2007, pp. 537–48.

———. *Getting Personal.* Routledge, 1991.

Mitchell, W. J. T. "Image, Space, Revolution: The Arts of Occupation." *Occupy: Three Inquiries in Disobedience,* University of Chicago Press, 2013, pp. 93–130.

Morrison, Yedda. *Darkness.* Make Now Press, 2012.

Mostern, Kenneth. *Autobiography and Black Identity Politics: Racialization in Twentieth Century America.* Cambridge University Press, 1999.

Muth, Katie. "Postmodern Fiction as Poststructuralist Theory: Kathy Acker's *Blood and Guts in High School.*" *Narrative,* vol. 19, no. 1, January 2011, pp. 86–110.

Myles, Eileen. "What about Chris?" *I Love Dick,* Semiotext(e), 2006, pp. 13–15.

Nail, Thomas. "Revolution." *Keywords for Radicals: The Contested Vocabulary of Late Capitalist Struggle,* eds. Kelly Fritsch, Clare O'Connor, and A. K. Thompson, AK Press, 2016, pp. 375–82.

Nealon, Jeffrey. *Post-Postmodernism, or, The Cultural Logic of Just-in-Time Capitalism.* Stanford University Press, 2012.

Nelson, Maggie. *The Art of Cruelty: A Reckoning.* W. W. Norton, 2011.

———. *Women, the New York School, and Other True Abstractions.* University of Iowa Press, 2007.

Ngai, Sianne. *Our Aesthetic Categories: Zany, Cute, Interesting.* Harvard University Press, 2012.

Nguyen, Viet. *The Sympathizer.* Grove Press, 2015.

Nietzsche, Friedrich. "On Truth and Lying in a Non-Moral Sense." *The Birth of Tragedy and Other Writings,* trans. Raymond Guess and Ronald Spiers, Cambridge University Press, 1999, pp. 139–53.

Noland, Carrie. *Agency and Embodiment: Performing Gestures/Producing Culture.* Harvard University Press, 2009.

———. "Introduction." *Migrations of Gesture,* eds. Carrie Noland and Sally Ann Ness, University of Minnesota Press, 2008, pp. ix–xxviii.

———. "On Caroline Levine's *Forms: Whole, Rhythm, Hierarchy, Network.*" *PMLA,* vol. 132, no. 5, October 2017, pp. 1181–238.

Parker, Ashley, and Nick Corasaniti. "Some Donald Trump Supporters Warn of Revolution if Hillary Clinton Wins." *New York Times,* October 27, 2016.

Parker, Ben. "The Moments of Realism." *Los Angeles Review of Books,* July 28, 2015.

Peirce, Charles. *Collected Papers of Charles Sanders Peirce, Volume V, Pragmatism and Pragmaticism,* eds. Charles Hartshorne and Paul Weiss, Harvard University Press, 1934.

Plascencia, Salvador. *The People of Paper.* McSweeney's, 2005.

Postmodern/Postwar—and After: Rethinking American Literature, eds. Jason Gladstone, Andrew Hoberek, and Daniel Worden, University of Iowa Press, 2016.

Potts, Jason, and Daniel Stout. *Theory Aside.* Duke University Press, 2014.

Povinelli, Elizabeth. "The Persistence of Hope: Critical Theory and Enduring in Late Liberalism." *Theory After "Theory,"* eds. Jane Elliott and Derek Attridge, Routledge, 2011, pp. 105–19.

Puchner, Martin. *Stage Fright: Modernism, Anti-Theatricality, and Drama.* Johns Hopkins University Press, 2002.

Quendler, Christian. *From Romantic Irony to Postmodernist Metafiction.* Peter Lang, 2001.

Rager, Matt. "[_]Tree[_] of C[__]od[_]es." *Post45,* May 24, 2012.

Rajan, Tilottama, and Michael O'Driscoll. *After Poststructuralism: Writing the Intellectual History of Theory.* University of Toronto Press, 2002.

Rak, Julie. *Boom! Manufacturing Memoir for the Popular Market.* Wilfrid Laurier Press, 2013.

Rancière, Jacques. *Dissensus: On Politics and Aesthetics.* Continuum, 2010.

———. *The Future of the Image.* Verso, 2007.

———. *The Politics of Aesthetics.* Trans. Gabriel Rockhill, Continuum, 2004.

Roberts, Alasdair. *The End of Protest.* Cornell University Press, 2013.

Robinson, Adam. "How Should a Person Be? Talking to Sheila Heti." *BOMB,* June 11, 2012, https://bombmagazine.org/articles/how-should-a-person-be-talking-to-sheila-heti/.

Rodriguez, Barbara. *Autobiographical Inscriptions: Form, Personhood, and the American Woman of Color.* Oxford University Press, 1999.

Rodriguez, Juana. *Sexual Futures, Queer Gestures, and Other Latina Longings.* New York University Press, 2014.

Rosen, Jeremy. *Minor Characters Have Their Day: Genre and the Contemporary Literary Marketplace.* Columbia University Press, 2016.

Ruprecht, Lucia. "Introduction: Towards an Ethics of Gesture." *Performance Philosophy,* vol. 3, no. 1, 2017, pp. 4–22.

Ryan, Judith. *The Novel after Theory.* Columbia University Press, 2012.

Sanders, Bernie. "The Political Revolution Continues." June 16, 2016. https://berniesanders.com/political-revolution-continues.

Schiller, Friedrich. *On the Aesthetic Educations of Man,* trans. Keith Tribe. Penguin, 2016.

Scholl, Christian. "Prefiguration." *Keywords for Radicals: The Contested Vocabulary of Late Capitalist Struggle,* eds. Kelly Fritsch, Clare O'Connor, and A. K. Thompson. AK Press, 2016, pp. 319–26.

Schulz, Bruno. *The Street of Crocodiles and Other Stories.* Penguin, 1979.

Schwartz, Madeleine. "Interview with Sheila Heti." *Harvard Advocate* (Commencement 2011). https://www.theharvardadvocate.com/content/interview-with-sheila-heti.

Shields, David. *Reality Hunger: A Manifesto.* Knopf, 2010.

Shiff, Richard. "Move with Chance." *Mark Bradford,* ed. Christopher Bedford, Wexner Center for the Arts, 2010, pp. 74–93.

Shonkwiler, Alison, and Leigh Claire La Berge, eds. *Reading Capitalist Realism.* University of Iowa Press, 2013.

Siegel, Katy. "Somebody and Nobody." *Mark Bradford,* ed. Christopher Bedford, Wexner Center for the Arts, 2010, pp. 103–19.

Siegle, Robert. *The Politics of Reflexivity: Narrative and the Constitutive Poetics of Culture.* Johns Hopkins University Press, 1986.

Sim, Stuart. *Derrida and the End of History.* Icon Books, 1999.

Sitrin, Marina, and Dario Azzellini. *They Can't Represent Us! Reinventing Democracy from Greece to Occupy.* Verso, 2014.

Smee, Sebastian. "Mark Bradford: Dance Again." *Mark Bradford,* Phaidon, 2018, pp. 43–101.

Smith, Rachel Greenwald. "The Contemporary Novel and Postdemocratic Form." *Novel: A Forum on Fiction,* vol. 51, no. 2, 2018, pp. 292–307.

———. *On Compromise: Art, Politics, and the Fate of an American Ideal.* Graywolf, 2021.

Smith, Sidonie. *Subjectivity, Identity, and the Body: Women's Autobiographical Practices in the Twentieth Century.* Indiana University Press, 1993.

Smith, Sidonie, and Julia Watson. *De/Colonizing the Subject: The Politics of Gender in Women's Autobiography.* University of Minnesota Press, 1992.

———. *Women, Autobiography, Theory: A Reader.* University of Wisconsin Press, 1998.

Snelson, Daniel. *Radios.* Make Now Press, 2016.

Spiotta, Dana. *Eat the Document.* Scribner, 2006.

Stake, Robert E. *The Art of Case Study Research.* SAGE Publications, 1995.

Stern, Lesley. "Ghosting: The Performance and Migration of Cinematic Gesture, Focusing on Hou Hsiao-Hsien's *Good Men, Good Women.*" *Migrations of Gesture,* eds. Carrie Noland and Sally Ann Ness, University of Minnesota Press, 2008, pp. 185–215.

Stimson, Blake. "Gesture and Abstraction." *Migrations of Gesture,* eds. Carrie Noland and Sally Ann Ness, University of Minnesota Press, 2008, pp. 69–83.

Storr, Robert. *"And what I assume you shall assume. . . ."* *Mark Bradford,* ed. Christopher Bedford, Wexner Center for the Arts, 2010, pp. 39–56.

Strombeck, Andrew. "The Post-Fordist Motorcycle: Rachel Kushner's *The Flamethrowers* and the 1970s Crisis in Fordist Capitalism." *Contemporary Literature,* vol. 56, no. 3, Fall 2015, pp. 450–75.

Swindells, Julia, ed. *The Uses of Autobiography.* Routledge, 1995.

Tanke, Joseph. "What Is the Aesthetic Regime?" *Parrhesia,* vol. 12, 2011, pp. 71–81.

Taussig, Michael. "I'm So Angry I Made a Sign." *Occupy: Three Inquiries in Disobedience.* University of Chicago Press, 2013, pp. 3–43.

Toth, Josh. *The Passing of Postmodernism.* State University of New York Press, 2010.

Townsend, Sarah. *The Unfinished Art of Theater: Avant-Garde Intellectuals in Mexico and Brazil.* Northwestern University Press, 2018.

Virno, Paolo. *A Grammar of the Multitude.* Semiotext(e), 2004.

Walker, Hamza. "We Might as Well Be Brave: Conversations with Mark Bradford." *Mark Bradford,* ed. Christopher Bedford, Wexner Center for the Arts, 2010, pp. 95–101.

Wallace, David Foster. "*E Unibus Pluram*: Television and U.S. Fiction." *A Supposedly Fun Thing I'll Never Do Again,* Little, Brown and Company, 1997, pp. 21–82.

———. "Westward the Course of Empire Takes Its Way." *Girl with Curious Hair,* Avon Books, 1989, pp. 231–373.

Waugh, Patricia. *Metafiction: The Theory and Practice of Self-Conscious Fiction.* Methuen, 1984.

White, Micah. *The End of Protest*. Knopf Canada, 2016.

White, Roger. *The Contemporaries: Travels in the 21st-Century Art World*. Bloomsbury, 2015.

Williams, Jeffrey. "The Death of Deconstruction, the End of Theory, and Other Ominous Rumors." *Narrative*, vol. 4, no. 1, 1996, pp. 17–35.

——. *Theory and the Novel: Narrative Reflexivity in the British Tradition*. Cambridge University Press, 1998.

Williams, Raymond. *Marxism and Literature*. Oxford University Press, 1977.

Wittgenstein, Ludwig. *The Blue and Brown Books*. Harper, 1958.

——. *Philosophical Investigations*. Trans. G. E. M. Anscombe. 3rd ed., MacMillan, 1958.

Wolfreys, Julian. *Literature, In Theory: Tropes, Subjectivities, Responses & Responsibilities*. Continuum, 2010.

Wolfson, Susan J. "Special Issue: Reading for Form." *Modern Language Quarterly*, vol. 61, no. 1, March 2000: 1–16.

Wolfson, Susan J., and Marshall Brown, eds. *Reading for Form*. University of Washington Press, 2006.

Wood, James. "Human, All Too Inhuman." *New Republic*, July 23, 2000.

Wong, Hertha. *Sending My Heart Back across the Years: Tradition and Innovation in Native American Autobiography*. Oxford University Press, 1992.

Worden, Daniel. "The Memoir in the Age of Neoliberal Individualism." *Neoliberalism and Literary Culture*, eds. Mitchum Huehls and Rachel Greenwald Smith, Johns Hopkins University Press, 2017, pp. 160–77.

Yagoda, Ben. *Memoir: A History*. Riverhead Books, 2009.

Zamora, Daniel. "Can We Criticize Foucault?" *Jacobin*, December 10, 2014.

Žižek, Slavoj. "The Ideology of the Empire and Its Traps." *Empire's New Clothes: Reading Hardt and Negri*, eds. Paul Passavant and Jodi Dean, Routledge, 2004, pp. 255–66.

——. *Trouble in Paradise*. Penguin, 2014.

INDEX

abstraction, 54n26, 70, 154–62

activist art, 48–49, 51. *See also* social justice

Adorno, Theodor, 14, 37–38, 51

aesthetic autonomy. *See* autonomy

aesthetic regime, 38–41, 44–47, 50–51, 155

Aesthetics and Ideology (Levine), 14n11

Aesthetic Theory (Adorno), 37

affective citizenship, 19

affective neorealism, 55n27

African Americans, 11, 18, 42–43, 154–60. *See also* race

After Theory (Eagleton), 73

Agamben, Giorgio, 140n38, 142–44, 159

Ahmed, Sara, 25

Aliens & Anorexia (Kraus), 39–40, 45, 63n40, 65–66, 69

allegory, 47, 85, 89, 91, 100, 124–25

analytic philosophy, 93–96

Anderson, Linda, 24, 42–44

Andrews, Bruce, 103n21

anticapitalism, 2–3, 5, 36, 45–46, 60. *See also* capitalism

antifoundationalist theory, 3, 79, 81, 83, 90n15, 105

Antinomies of Realism (Jameson), 127, 128n29

Arab Spring, 112n9

Arendt, Hannah, 123n26

Aristotle, 3, 26–27, 38–39

art. *See* autonomy; commodification; end of art, the; heteronomy; participatory art; performance; pluralism; *specific artists and works*

art history, 35

art-life relationship, 40–42, 52

Art of Cruelty, The (Nelson), 49

art-politics homology, 36–37, 40–41, 60–61. *See also* form-politics homology

Attridge, Derek, 78n7, 79

Auster, Paul, 76

Auto/biographical (Marcus), 42

autobiography, 17–18, 24, 41–45. *See also* life writing

Autobiography (Marcus), 41n10

"Autobiography as De-facement" (de Man), 43n14

autofiction, 41

autonomy, 2–3, 7–8, 10, 12–14, 31–32, 35–47, 49–53, 55–58, 62, 67, 158. *See also* heteronomy

autotheory, 41

avant garde, 37, 56, 58

Barth, John, 101

Barthes, Roland, 74–75, 77, 81–82, 88, 96, 105

Bedford, Christopher, 157–59

Benjamin, Walter, 14, 37n4, 38

Berardi, Franco, 115

Berlant, Lauren, 9n6, 12, 19, 25–26, 31, 67n47, 68n48, 141n39, 142n42, 143–44

Best, Stephen, 157, 159

Beyond the Brillo Box (Danto), 35

Bishop, Claire, 38, 48

Bourriaud, Nicholas, 38, 48

Bradford, Mark, 11, 33, 154–62

Brecht, Bertolt, 38

Brillo Boxes (Warhol), 34–35

Bronk, William, 70

Brown, Marshall, 14n11

Brown, Nicholas, 35–37, 45

Butler, Judith, 53n25, 59n35

Buurma, Rachel, 57n30

capitalism, 3–5, 24, 35–36, 60, 79–80, 109–20, 131–34. *See also* anticapitalism; commodification; neoliberalism

case study, 8–10, 16, 19, 31, 33, 40, 62, 67–72, 146

Chow, Rey, 78–79

cinema, 142–43, 144n47

Cinema 2 (Deleuze), 103

Clinton, Hillary, 109

Coleridge, Samuel Taylor, 37

commodification, 34–36, 50–51, 111, 132–34. *See also* capitalism; neoliberalism

communism, 118, 122n24, 124. *See also* Marxism

"Conditions and Limits of Autobiography" (Gusdorf), 42

constructivism, 9, 32–33, 76, 80, 87, 114, 158

"Contemporary Novel and Postdemocratic Form, The" (Smith), 137n36, 142n40

Contemporary Novelists (Kingston-Reese), 40n8

Contingency, Hegemony, Universality (Butler, Laclau, and Žižek), 59n35

Cornell, Joseph, 100

"Course on General Linguistics" (Saussure), 61n36

Critique of Judgment (Kant), 12

Crowds and Party (Dean), 120

Dames, Nicholas, 84–85, 104

Danto, Arthur, 34–37, 45, 49–50

Davis, Ben, 35

Dawson, Paul, 127n27

Dean, Jodi, 118n19, 120

"Death" (Barthes), 96

Deleuze, Gilles, 30n38, 103, 118, 142–43

de Man, Paul, 43n14, 73

democracy, 116–17

Democratic Party, 109

Derrida, Jacques, 74, 76, 88, 91

Dewey, John, 27–30, 155–56

dialectics, 15–16, 37, 51, 67, 114–16, 120–23, 130, 134–35, 158

Dissident Gardens (Lethem), 7, 23, 112n9, 113–14, 121–26

Doctorow, E. L., 22–23

Drucker, Johanna, 38n7

Eagleton, Terry, 73

Eat the Document (Spiotta), 7, 23, 113–14, 131–36

Elias, Amy, 10n7

Elliott, Jane, 78n7, 79

Emancipations (Laclau), 59n35

emotion, 65, 67, 69–70

Empire, Multitude, and *Commonwealth* (Hardt and Negri), 110–11, 115–16, 119, 120n21

end of art, the, 1, 4–5, 6n3, 8, 24, 34–35, 39, 50, 153

end of theory, the, 73–82, 153

"Entangled Self, The" (Miller), 17n16

Erasure (Everett), 83

Eugenides, Jeffrey, 6, 23n30, 84–87

"E Unibus Pluram" (Wallace), 77

Everett, Percival, 7–8, 11, 21–22, 31–32, 83, 87, 92–97, 103

"Experimental Fiction" (Marcus), 102

false, the, 103–7

Female Complaint, The, (Berlant), 25, 141n39

feminism, 7–8, 11, 18, 24–25, 40–57, 62–65, 68, 70, 72. *See also* subjectivity

fiction, 1, 3, 5–10, 16, 75, 82–83, 111–12. *See also* case study; historical fiction; language; metafiction; science fiction; *specific authors and works*

Fischer-Lichte, Erika, 56, 58

Fish, Stanley, 81, 90n15

Flamethrowers, The (Kushner), 7–8, 10, 23, 32, 113–14, 136–42, 143n44, 144–52

Flusser, Vilém, 146n48

Foer, Jonathan Safran, 7–8, 21–22, 31–32, 87, 104–7

formal autonomy. *See* autonomy

"Form and Explanation" (Kramnick and Nersessian), 16n15, 27n34

form-politics homology: and the end of art, 5, 39; and the end of theory, 75–76, 79–82, 153; and generality, 6, 29, 72; and gesture, 146, 152; introduction to, 1–9, 13–18; and literature, 6, 24–25, 32, 58, 82–83, 88, 90, 107, 114, 126–28, 132, 135, 153–54; and revolution, 112–13, 119–21, 123, 126–27, 135; and vacillations, 4–9, 14–16, 19, 25, 32, 39, 46. *See also* art-politics homology

Forms (Levine), 15–16

Foucault, Michel, 118n16

Fournier, Lauren, 41

Fowles, John, 77

Frames of War (Butler), 53n25

Franzen, Jonathan, 97n16

freedom, 79, 81–82, 87, 90, 99, 157

Frege, Gottlob, 93

French Lieutenant's Woman, The (Fowles), 77

Fried, Michael, 37, 56

Future of the Image (Rancière), 52

Gass, William, 83

generality: and abstraction, 154–58, 161; and feminism, 25, 31; and the generic, 28, 32, 46–47; and gesture, 32, 54, 136, 141–44, 146; introduction to, 6–9, 16; and literature, 25, 31–33, 39–41, 57–58, 66, 114, 145, 148–49, 153–54; and not caring, 53, 70–71; and politics, 33, 41, 59–61, 72; and theory, 26–31, 40, 60–62, 67–69, 104, 107–8. *See also* particularity; singularity; universality

genericness, 9, 19, 25–33, 40, 41n10, 47, 53–54, 62–63, 67, 70. *See also* impersonality

genre, 8–10, 31, 62–64, 66–67

gesture, 8–9, 16, 23–24, 32–33, 114, 136, 139–52, 159, 161

"Gesture and Abstraction" (Stimson), 153

"Ghosting" (Stern), 144n46

Gillick, Liam, 48n20

Gitlin, Todd, 111, 118n17

"Goblin Market" (Rossetti), 2, 30

Goldsmith, Kenneth, 103n21

Greenberg, Clement, 20, 37, 49, 50n21

Grundrisse (Marx), 60

Guest, Barbara, 70

Gusdorf, Georges, 42

Hardt, Michael, 30n38, 110–11, 115–16, 119, 120n21, 128, 133

Hayek, Friedrich von, 118n17

Heffernan, Laura, 57n30

heteronomy, 2–4, 7–8, 10–14, 31–32, 36–53, 55–58, 62, 67, 158. *See also* autonomy

Heti, Sheila, 6–10, 19, 25, 31, 39–41, 45–58, 61–62, 63n39

historical consciousness, 8, 22, 123–28, 130, 133–34, 149, 151

historical fiction, 7–8, 16, 22–24, 32, 113–14, 121–37, 146–47, 152. *See also* fiction; *specific authors and works*

Historical Novel, The (Lukács), 22, 113–14

"Historical Novel Today" (Jameson), 24

Hobsbawm, Eric, 122n25

homologies. *See* art-politics homology; form-politics homology

horizontal immanence. *See* immanence

Horkheimer, Max, 14
How Should a Person Be? (Heti), 7, 10, 39–40, 45–58, 61–62
"Human, All Too Inhuman" (Wood), 127n27
Hutcheon, Linda, 15, 20–23, 81

"Ideological Analysis" (Jameson), 4
"Ideology of the Empire and Its Traps, The" (Žižek), 118
I Love Dick (Kraus), 11, 39–40, 46, 63–69, 71–72
immanence, 2–4, 7–8, 10, 13, 24, 32, 112–21, 128–39, 145–46. *See also* revolution; transcendence
impersonality, 65–66, 154, 159. *See also* genericness
intersectionality, 44, 114
inverted millenarianism, 1, 4, 24
irony, 20–21, 23, 50
isomorphism, 2
Italian autonomists, 115

Jameson, Fredric, 2–4, 14n11, 15, 20–24, 39, 80, 112–14, 127–28, 147–52
Jane (Nelson), 45–46
John Ford on His Deathbed (Kitaj), 66n45
Johnson, Samuel, 17n18
juxtapolitical, 9n6

Kant, Immanuel, 12–13, 14n11, 37
Kingston-Reese, Alexandra, 10, 40n8, 55n27, 57n31
Kitaj, R. J., 66n45
Konstantinou, Lee, 55n27
Kornbluh, Anna, 30n37
Kramnick, Jonathan, 16n15, 27n34
Kraus, Chris, 6–8, 10–11, 19, 25, 31, 39–41, 45–46, 62–72, 146
Kristeva, Julia, 74–75, 140n38, 142
Kushner, Rachel, 7–8, 10, 23, 32, 113–14, 128–31, 136–42, 143n44, 144–52

Lacan, Jacques, 76
Laclau, Ernesto, 59n35, 120n23
language, 61–62, 66–67, 73–78, 82, 92–108, 140n38. *See also* textuality

leftism, 4, 13, 38, 44, 79n9, 81, 83, 112n9, 121–22. *See also* communism; Marxism; social justice
Lejeune, Philippe, 41
Lerner, Ben, 5, 10–11, 112n9
Lethem, Jonathan, 6–7, 23, 112n9, 113, 121–27
Levine, Caroline, 2, 15–16, 29–30
Levine, George, 14n11
Levinson, Marjorie, 14n11, 78
liberalism, 18
life writing, 7–8, 10, 16–19, 24, 32, 40–42, 44–46, 62. *See also* autobiography
Lind, Maria, 48n20
linguistics. *See* language
literary realism. *See* realism
literature. *See* case study; fiction; historical fiction; language; life writing; metafiction; realism; theoretical literalism
Lodge, David, 76
logic, 27–29
Logic (Dewey), 27–28
Lukács, Georg, 22, 38, 113–14, 123–24, 133, 147–48

Malik, Suhail, 59, 61
Manning, Erin, 143n45
Marcus, Ben, 7–8, 21–22, 31–32, 87, 97–103
Marcus, Laura, 41n10, 42
Marriage Plot, The (Eugenides), 84–87
Marx, Karl, 60
Marxism, 14n11, 22, 30n37, 110–11, 123, 125, 128. *See also* communism
Marxism and Form (Jameson), 14n11
Marxism and Literature (Williams), 44n18
Mayer, Bernadette, 70
McCarthy, Tom, 11
medium specificity, 49–51
memoir. *See* autobiography; life writing
metafiction, 7–8, 16, 19–22, 24, 31–32, 76–78, 82–86, 89, 91, 97–101. *See also* fiction; reflexivity; *specific authors and works*
metaphor, 94, 103
metaphysics, 81–82, 95, 115–16, 127
Michaels, Walter Benn, 2, 13, 37, 45–46, 51, 57n32

Miller, Nancy, 17n16
Minor Gesture (Manning), 143n45
Mitchell, Joan, 70
Mitchell, W. J. T., 117
"Modality" (Everett), 93
modernism, 20, 56–58
Muth, Katie, 76n5
Myles, Eileen, 63, 70–71

Nail, Thomas, 114
Narcissistic Narrative (Hutcheon), 20n25
narrative, 127–31, 137, 148–52
Nealon, Jeffrey, 4n2, 79–80, 103
Negri, Antonio, 30n38, 110–11, 115–16, 119, 120n21, 128, 133
Nelson, Maggie, 45–46, 49, 70–71
neoliberalism, 2–3, 13, 18, 38, 45–46, 57n32, 71, 79–82. *See also* capitalism; commodification
Nersessian, Anahid, 16n15, 27n34
New Formalism, 14n11
New Traditionalism, 63
New York School (poets), 70–71
New York Trilogy (Auster), 76
Ngai, Sianne, 35
Nietzsche, Friedrich, 94
Noland, Carrie, 12, 136n33, 140n38
Notable American Women (Marcus), 21–22, 87, 97–103, 107
"Notes on Gesture" (Agamben), 140n38, 142
Notley, Alice, 70
Novel after Theory, The (Ryan), 84
novelist-critics, 10–11
novels. *See* fiction

Occupy Nation (Gitlin), 118n17
Occupy Wall Street, 110, 112n9, 116–17, 118n17, 120n22, 122
O'Hara, Frank, 71
Olney, James, 42
"On Interpretation" (Aristotle), 26
"On the Case" (Berlant), 67n47
"On Truth and Lying" (Nietzsche), 94
overdetermination, 31, 35, 39–40, 62–64, 98, 119, 157

"Participation" (Gillick and Lind), 48n20
participatory art, 3, 48–49
particularity, 25–26, 29–30, 43–46, 59n35, 62, 68, 72. *See also* generality; singularity; universality
patriarchy, 11, 42–43, 65
Peirce, Charles, 26–27
People of Paper, The (Plascencia), 21–22, 87–92, 105–7
Percival Everett by Virgil Russell (Everett), 21–22, 87, 92–97, 107
performance, 36, 48n19, 56–58, 66, 91, 125–26
personal. *See* singularity
Philippoteaux, Paul, 159
Phillips, Andrea, 59, 61
Philosophical Investigations (Wittgenstein), 29n36
Pickett's Charge (Bradford), 33, 158–61
Plascencia, Salvador, 7–8, 21–22, 31–32, 87–92
Plato, 3, 38
pluralism, 35–36, 49–50
Poetics (Hutcheon), 20, 22, 81
poetry, 70, 112n9
Political Unconscious, The (Jameson), 14n11
politics. *See* art-politics homology; communism; form-politics homology; immanence; Marxism; revolution; transcendence
Politics of Aesthetics, The (Rancière), 52n24
"Posthumous Critique" (Levinson), 78
"Postmodern, Postwar, Contemporary" (Elias), 10n7
postmodernism, 1, 8–9, 18n21, 20–23, 32, 74–78, 83–84, 100, 103
Postmodernism (Jameson), 1, 20–21, 112
post-postmodernism, 103
Post-Postmodernism (Nealon), 4n2
poststructuralism, 12, 43n14, 59n35, 73–81, 84–88, 91, 94–98, 103, 106
pragmatism. *See also* Dewey, John; sensible, the
Puchner, Martin, 56, 58, 140n38
Pynchon, Thomas, 101

race, 156–60. *See also* African Americans
Ragtime (Doctorow), 22–23

Rak, Julie, 18–19

Rancière, Jacques, 38–39, 41, 52, 58–61, 69, 72

realism, 22–24, 77, 83–87, 91, 97–102, 113, 123–24, 127–28, 136, 147

"Reality Effect, The" (Buurma and Heffernan), 57n30

referential pact, 41–42

reflexivity: and literature, 7–8, 31–32, 76–78, 82–87, 90–93, 95, 97–101, 104–7, 154; and politics, 3, 21, 79–83, 90; and theory, 2–3, 10, 12–13, 20, 74–75, 77–78, 80–82, 84, 87–88, 91, 93, 97, 99–100, 103–4, 106. *See also* metafiction

relational aesthetics, 4–5, 47–49, 51, 61, 93

representation: and abstraction, 156–58, 160; and art, 34–35; and gesture, 136, 141, 143, 146–47, 152; and literature, 22, 40–45, 57, 65, 70, 72, 91, 102, 121, 123, 126, 135, 137, 139–40, 147, 153–54; and revolution, 113–14, 117–21; and singularity, 46–47, 53–54; symbolic, 124–25; textual, 55–56; and theory, 3, 38–39, 43–44, 59n33

revolution, 1, 3–4, 7–8, 13, 23, 32, 109–27, 131–36, 142, 145–48. *See also* immanence; transcendence

"Revolution and Sex" (Hobsbawm), 122n25

Robbe-Grillet, Alain, 77

Rodriguez, Juana, 12, 136, 146, 148n50

Rossetti, Christina, 2, 30

Ryan, Judith, 84

Sanders, Bernie, 109

Saussure, Ferdinand de, 61n36, 74n3

scholarship, 2, 4–5, 12–13, 17, 34, 37, 43, 78–81, 136n33

Schulz, Bruno, 104–7

science fiction, 2, 23, 102, 114

Scorched Earth (Bradford), 157–58

self-reflexivity. *See* reflexivity

sensible, the, 52–53, 58–61, 67, 72, 104

Sexual Futures (Rodriguez), 136, 148n50

Shiff, Richard, 155–56, 158–59

Siegle, Robert, 83

Sim, Stuart, 4

singularity: and case study, 67–68; and literature, 6, 32–33, 39–41, 53–55, 57, 75, 94, 97, 104, 107, 153–54; and meaning, 31, 54, 58, 62, 70, 72; and politics, 33, 39–41, 46, 61, 71; and theory, 6, 25–26, 28–31; and women, 40–41, 46, 57, 62–65. *See also* generality; particularity; universality

Smith, Jason, 115n10

Smith, Rachel Greenwald, 137n36, 142n40

social justice, 7–8, 19, 29, 42–43, 48–49

Spiotta, Dana, 6–7, 23, 113, 131–35

Stage Fright (Puchner), 140n38

Stern, Lesley, 144n46

Stimson, Blake, 144, 153, 161

Street of Crocodiles, The (Schulz), 104–7

structuralism, 74. *See also* poststructuralism

subjectivity, 18, 24–26, 31, 40, 71, 100, 116, 146. *See also* feminism

Summer of Hate (Kraus), 39–40, 63

surface of equivalence, 58–59, 67

Sweet Dreams (Drucker), 38n7

Swindells, Julia, 43

Taussig, Michael, 117

Telex from Cuba (Kushner), 7, 23, 113–14, 128–31, 136

temporality, 68–69, 128, 133–35, 142n42, 144, 151

10:04 (Lerner), 5, 112n9

textuality, 55–57, 86, 89–93, 140n38. *See also* language

theater, 55–58, 140n38

theoretical literalism, 8–9, 16, 33, 78, 87–101. *See also specific authors and works*

theory. *See* aesthetic regime; antifoundationalist theory; autonomy; end of theory, the; generality; genericness; gesture; heteronomy; immanence; modernism; particularity; reflexivity; scholarship; singularity; transcendence; universality

Theory after "Theory" (Attridge and Elliott), 78n7

Theory and the Novel (Williams), 84n11

"Theory and the Novel" (Dames), 84

Torpor (Kraus), 39–40, 63, 64n42, 69

Toth, Josh, 76n5, 83–84

Townsend, Sarah, 18n21, 56

transcendence, 3, 7–8, 10, 13, 32, 112, 118–21, 129n29, 136–39, 144–45. *See also* immanence; revolution

Tree of Codes (Foer), 21–22, 87, 104–7

Trouble in Paradise (Žižek), 110, 118

Trump, Donald, 101n18, 109

underdetermination, 98

universality, 11, 25–32, 42–44, 59n35, 65, 68, 104–8, 153–54. *See also* generality; particularity; singularity

utopia, 13, 15, 20, 37, 84, 107, 146

vacillations. *See* art-politics homology; form-politics homology

Valences of the Dialectic (Jameson), 15

Video Green (Kraus), 70

Virgin Suicides, The (Eugenides), 23n30

Virno, Paolo, 60–62

Wallace, David Foster, 21, 23–24, 77

Warhol, Andy, 34–37, 49–50, 101

"Westward the Course of Empire" (Wallace), 21

Where Art Belongs (Kraus), 65

White, Micah, 110, 117n15

White, Roger, 35

Williams, Jeffrey, 84n11

Williams, Raymond, 14n11, 44n18

Wittgenstein, Ludwig, 29n36

Wolfson, Susan, 14n11

Wood, James, 127n27

Worden, Daniel, 18, 46

"Work of Art in the Age of Mechanical Reproduction, The" (Benjamin), 37n4

Zapatistas, 13, 117

Žižek, Slavoj, 2, 59n35, 110, 111n7, 117–20